More Advance Praise for

The Joy of Retirement

"Once the mindless myths associated with aging are dispelled, people of traditional retirement age must learn to identify the purpose they can pursue with a passion. With the help of books like *The Joy of Retirement*, our rapidly aging population can renew their motivation to systematically envision where meaning lies in a capstone calling."
—Helen L. Harkness, author, *Best Jobs for the Future,*
The Career Chase, Don't Stop the Career Clock,
and *Capitalizing on Career Chaos*

"Borchard and Donohoe have put together a comprehensive yet readable and truly helpful planning guide for anyone considering retirement."
—John P. Springett, retired Department of Defense senior executive

"I've just retired after 45 years, so *The Joy of Retirement* could not be more perfectly timed. David Borchard and Patricia Donohoe offer expert counseling and spiritual advice (combined with a dose of common sense) to those of us finding our way in the sometimes frightening world of life after paid employment."
—Mike Bowler, retired education editor, *The Baltimore Sun*

"With a rare combination of scholarship, wit, and common sense, David Borchard has pierced through the misconceptions about this phase of life and reminded us that retirement is not an end, but rather a new beginning—an opportunity for growth, creativity, and the discovery of one's authentic self."
—George McHenry, ex-lawyer turned artist

"I have retired after a long career in international health consulting, and I am now both a faculty choral director and a student going for my bachelor's degree in music. *The Joy of Retirement* effectively leads prospective retirees through the process I went through myself. Borchard's tools present the kind of challenges one needs to face at this transition point and provide readers with actual data so they don't have to rely on unreliable hunches and intuition. His hundreds of personal stories provide wonderful role models for going in whatever direction a person wishes to go."
—Robert S. Northrup, M.D.

THE JOY OF RETIREMENT

FINDING HAPPINESS, FREEDOM,
AND THE LIFE YOU'VE ALWAYS WANTED

David C. Borchard
with Patricia A. Donohoe

ΛMACOM
American Management Association
New York • Atlanta • Brussels • Chicago • Mexico City • San Francisco
Shanghai • Tokyo • Toronto • Washington, D.C.

Special discounts on bulk quantities of AMACOM books are available to corporations, professional associations, and other organizations. For details, contact Special Sales Department, AMACOM, a division of American Management Association, 1601 Broadway, New York, NY 10019.
Tel.: 800-250-5308.   Fax: 518-891-2372.
E-mail: specialsls@amanet.org
Website: www.amacombooks.org
To view all AMACOM titles go to: www.amacombooks.org

This publication is designed to provide accurate and authoritative information in regard to the subject matter covered. It is sold with the understanding that the publisher is not engaged in rendering legal, accounting, or other professional service. If legal advice or other expert assistance is required, the services of a competent professional person should be sought.

Library of Congress Cataloging-in-Publication Data

Borchard, David C.
    The joy of retirement : finding happiness, freedom, and the life you've always wanted / David C. Borchard with Patricia A. Donohoe.
        p.   cm.
    Includes bibliographical references and index.
    ISBN 978-0-8144-8056-4 (pbk.)
    1. Retirement—United States.   2. Retirement—United States—Planning.
  3. Retirees—United States—Life skills guides.   I. Donohoe, Patricia A.
  II. Title.

HQ1063.2.U6B67   2008
646.7'90973—dc22

                                                                    2007052951

Printing number

10   9   8   7   6   5   4

CONTENTS

PREFACE

IF YOU'RE IN THE FIFTY-PLUS STAGE OF LIFE, what's your reaction to being referred to as a "senior"? Some of my clients shudder at the word and severely object to such a label. Personally, I like the idea of being a senior. Do you remember your high school and college days when you couldn't wait to achieve the lofty status of senior? When you became a senior, then you probably thought you'd arrived and that you were now mature, experienced, and wise. You might have even looked down on the underclassmen.

In corporate life, folks work hard to become a senior partner, senior advisor, or senior executive. In ministry, pastors differentiate their status as senior from those who are associates or assistants. Why is it that when we reach a senior status in life, say about fifty-five or so, that we then are reluctant to acknowledge our graduation into this new status, which once was so desirable? Could it be that at fifty-plus we associate the word *senior* with the pejorative label of being "old"?

Old, however, is an old concept when it comes to the new human lifespan. Age is not so much a matter of chronology as it is of health and mindset. Satchel Paige, a colorful character from the sports world and possibly the greatest baseball pitcher of all times, once said, "Aging is a matter of mind over matter. If you don't mind, it don't matter."

Today seniors are generally healthier, longer-lived, and more active than ever before. In this new world, I suggest we consider achieving fifty-plus status as enviable. In Asia, you'd be revered. So why not enjoy all the hard-won freedom and wisdom that comes with this time in our lives?

◆ What We Want in Senior Life

As a career management coach and counselor, I've had the opportunity to work with hundreds of clients over the past 30 years, mostly ranging in age from 20 to 50. In recent years, however, I've been seeing growing numbers of individuals in the fifty-plus stage of life. They want help with reinventing their lives. Some of these individuals want to continue working, but in some new capacity or another; some want to engage in full-time hobbies; some want to volunteer; and many just say they don't know what they want.

Yet I've found that there are two things almost all of them are seeking. First, they clearly want more freedom to manage their lives and to be more autonomous. More or less, many of them say, "I've spent my time in the trenches. Now I'm looking forward to doing what I want rather than what is wanted of me." One of my clients in the process of planning his retirement said, "I feel like an adolescent again—free and ready for new things."

A second, and not quite so obvious, aspiration my clients have is to become more fully who they are. It seems that so many of us in the first half of life have focused on being what others wanted of us, what our professions required, what our corporate identity demanded, what made our parents happy, or what we thought we needed to be in order to fit in and to make it in life and work.

As we age, however, a shift tends to occur. We stop being so concerned about how others see us and become much more interested in being and becoming our "natural selves." I call this the *self-realization inclination,* and it's pretty much a bug that most of us get in the fifty-plus years. I hear clients refer to this aspiration in a number of different ways. Some talk of their desire to "be and do what I want," some talk of the "freedom to be me," and some say things like, "I'm looking forward to switching from being Mr. Corporate Guy or Ms. Career Professional to figuring out and being who I really am." The process of letting go and rediscovering or uncovering who you are is one of the wonderful benefits of graduating to the status of full-fledged senior.

◆ How This Book Can Help

It's one thing to harbor the aspirations of self and life reinvention, but how do you actually achieve them? That's a question I hear often from my fifty-plus clients. For many years I was working with one adult at a time in this process, but as the demand grew I realized the need to serve a bigger audience. For that reason, I developed a course that I've been conducting at the World Bank in Washington, D.C., over the past several years. The course has become quite popular, and individuals outside of the organization often ask me if they can attend.

Unfortunately, it's a service available only for employees. Additionally, a number of executives would like the service but are unwilling to take the course out of concern that others would see them there and get a wrong impression. Senior executives don't want others to think they are jumping ship, but they do want and need to plan for a different kind of future—one minus an executive title. While I occasionally deliver the course in other settings, those settings also are geared to a limited audience. Not everyone who might like access to a course of this nature or to individual coaching can afford it. Others shy away from what they might consider as "needing help with their life."

It's for these reasons that I have developed this book. My hope is that it will serve as a self-guided process for individuals looking to find new meaning and purpose in their lives as seniors. I have spent years—decades, really—developing a process to help those who want to get a bigger bang out of their senior years in terms of personal freedom and self-realization. If you are thinking of senior life as retirement and a time just for hanging out, this book may not be for you. But, if you are one of the many who see the fifty-plus years as the "Gateway to Freedom" and are excited about making the second half of life the best yet, read on. This book was developed for you.

The Joy of Retirement presents mind- and vision-expanding perspectives for creating a lifestyle for your senior years that is meaningful, enjoyable, and rejuvenating. The book features process, content, and assessment tools that have helped hundreds of fifty-plussers reinvent themselves and create fulfilling retirement lifestyles. The book evolved from my 30 years of career coaching and counseling experiences with adults, and, I hope, contains a large measure of the expertise and wisdom I've gained from working with so many individuals from so many different backgrounds.

I've designed a structured approach for authoring a new chapter of your life because I've found that people who are in transition and in a quandary about their future appreciate having a step-by-step approach. They want to see a path through the woods. I therefore designed the book as an orderly process for helping you resolve six of the major life issues that confront most in our fifty-plus years:

1. What do I really want (vision)?

2. Who am I, and who am I becoming (identity)?

3. What is truly important to me (values)?

4. What might I want to do more of and less of (talent application)?

5. Who will be the key players in my future (relationship)?

6. What kind of environment is best suited to my/our unique needs and aspirations (location)?

◆ Opportunities vs. Barriers in Senior Life Redesign

The good news for fifty-plussers is that the potential for self-realization is greater in your senior years than at any other stage of life. By then, you have the three core ingredients essential for autonomy and self-realization: freedom, life perspective, and a fully evolved personality. Throughout our early and middle adult years, most of us are too preoccupied with managing the serious business of our careers, raising families, tending to chores, and paying the bills to be all that concerned about something as abstract as autonomy and self-realization. Consequently, the urge to self-realize doesn't fully impact most of us as a developmental priority until later in life.

There is one rather large barrier that stands in the way of resolving the "so, now what?" question and achieving self-realization, which is that this task can be exceedingly complex. That's because, by nature, it requires clarifying your deepest aspirations, your strongest interests, and your most energizing talents. That's a task involving a process of objectifying a subjective domain, which is difficult work for most of us. Furthermore, even with your attributes and aspirations clarified, identifying the best way of expressing them in a world of unknown possibilities can be perplexing. Because the task can seem so daunting, all too many of us avoid the self-introspection and exploration required. Or, even more likely, we narrow the issue to something overly simple, such as where to live. Although a new home in a new environment can be engaging, at least temporarily, taking on a too narrow a perspective in life restricts your potential for discovering and becoming the incredibly unique creation you really are meant to be.

The complexity of this challenge, combined with the need to redirect our lives toward an uncharted future, means that many of us forgo the opportunity for self-realization and settle for a more mundane life style. Achieving the good life, from the self-realization perspective, isn't likely to occur by accident. For most of us, this is a process that requires time, thoughtful introspection, and a willingness to make difficult choices. This book offers an affordable solution to this challenge in the form of a self-guided process—one that has been tried, tested, and proven through my work with hundreds of adults and professionals in the field. The book offers tools for assessment and self-understanding, resources, and a planning guide for achieving self-realization. The book presents numerous examples from the lives of real people as role models for inspiration, hope, and creative ideas.

It should be noted here that this is a book about recreating your life and your identity in the senior years, and not about the important business of financing a retirement. Bookstores are full of excellent resources for planning and managing that important aspect of your life. Do a Google search on "retirement planning" and you will get tens of thousands of hits on the subject, the great majority focusing on financial planning.

Much less has been written about re-inventing your "being." That tends to be especially challenging for those whose work lives have kept them so busy they have had little opportunity for addressing the equally important issue of who I am becoming or who I will be when I leave behind my corporate identity, my professional persona, or my impressive job title, along with my youthful adulthood. By all means, one needs to address the financial aspects of senior life in order to enjoy the freedom of more autonomous living that life in the fifty-plus years offers. For sure you will want to address, if you haven't already, your financial well being. That, however, is a matter outside the realm of this book, one for you and your financial advisor to give careful consideration.

Also, this is not a book about retiring to a life of leisure and self-indulging ways to pass the time away. Your time remaining is far too precious a commodity for trivial pursuits. In fact, nearly 60 percent of baby boomers, those of you born between 1946 and 1964, indicate an intention to work after retiring (according to a 2005 MetLife Foundation Survey). But a majority of the work-oriented folks want to do something that provides a sense of meaning and purpose in their lives rather than full-time income generating. Whether you are planning on continuing to work during your senior years or transition into a more traditional leisure-oriented lifestyle, this is a once-in-a-lifetime opportunity to achieve full-fledged *self-realization*. This is a book designed for those looking to take full advantage of the new freedoms, the self-liberation, and the joy of graduating into senior status that life in the fifty-plus years offers.

◆ **Bringing Forth Your True Self**

Graduating into senior life provides the best opportunity most of us are ever going to have to achieve what the Gospel of Thomas attributes as a message from Jesus: "If you bring forth what is within you, that what you have will save you. If you do not have that within you, what you do not have within you will kill you." Regardless of your spiritual orientation, this quotation can be an inspiration to self-realize and enjoy the full promise of your human potential. I hope you find the pages that follow an inspiration as well.

Acknowledgments

WHEN ONE HAS BEEN IN THE COUNSELING PROFESSION as long as I have, it becomes difficult to determine whom to acknowledge for the ideas, insights, and factual experiences that have combined to form the content of this book. In general terms, however, I would be remiss were I not to mention Dr. Daniel J. Levinson, author of *The Seasons of a Man's Life,* and until his death in 1994, professor of psychology at Yale University. I had the good fortune many years ago to attend a workshop that he conducted while he was in the process of putting the results of his years of research into the final product of his ground-breaking book on the stages of adult development. I was able to correspond personally with Dr. Levinson for his input in a paper I was preparing for an individualized graduate school course on the subject of adult development. Dr. Levinson's work was a key inspiration in my decision to concentrate on adult development as the focus for my work in counseling.

In that regard also, I want to acknowledge Dr. Nancy Schlossberg, Professor Emeritus at the University of Maryland, both for the many top-notch professional seminars she hosted with luminaries in the adult psychology field while she was at the University of Maryland and for her significant personal contributions in her many publications. I recall vividly a professional seminar when Dr. Schlossberg debated Dr. Levinson about his concepts of predictable stages in adult development. Like so many others in the counseling profession, I have benefited immensely from the vast contributions that Dr. Schlossberg has made and continues to make in the study of adult psychology and life transition management.

I must also acknowledge my friend and colleague Dr. Frederic Hudson, both for his publications that have made significant professional contributions to the field of adult development (see the reference section of the book) and for the contributions he provided to so many through his Life Launch course and coach training program at the Hudson Institute of Santa Barbara, California. I have personally experienced Dr. Hudson's courses, even going to one with my wife, Pat, some 18 years ago. In my mind, Dr. Hudson is a towering figure in the field of adult development and personal growth. I have learned much from him over the years of our professional friendship and consider him to be both a mentor and a role model for adult development.

Although I did not have the privilege of personally studying with Erik Erikson, his work in identity formation and the stages of psychosocial development are such a part of the knowledge base in adult development that it's hard to know for what specific content of this book to acknowledge him. Instead, I feel it important to recognize his work in general terms for breakthrough insights in understanding the psychology of adult behavior and development through the ages and stages of the lifespan.

In more specific terms, for their contributions in the development of this book, I want to thank my colleagues at the World Bank in Washington, D.C. The assistance they provided enabled me to develop the course that has served as a primary conceptual and experiential basis for this book. I want also to thank my many colleagues in the counseling field for their interest and their input, suggestions, ideas, feedback, and the knowledge they have shared with me in the development of this project. In that regard, I especially want to acknowledge Dr. Arthur LaSalle, Dr. Elizabeth Lopez Murgatroyd, and Dr. Stephanie Kaye for their professional expertise and support over the years in helping to make this project a reality.

I must also acknowledge the hundreds of individuals in the fifty-plus stage of life who have participated in the workshops I've conducted and been my clients in individual counseling sessions over the past decades. Working with these individuals has been and is an ongoing learning experience. Their stories fill the pages of this book and bring life experience, reality, and the unique personal touch to its content. I have, or course, not used the real names of individuals, except where noted, and in some cases altered some details in order to protect the confidentiality of my clients.

I most especially want to acknowledge my wife, Pat Donohoe, for her direct support and assistance in ways too numerous to determine. She has been a constant source of ideas, reality testing, and intellectual input in this project from its inception some seven years ago to final manuscript. She has sat in on presentations and workshops I've delivered on the subject and provided encouragement and insightful feedback, both positive and negative. She has also been the book's chief copy editor and my writing coach. In both of these capacities, her background and expertise as a former English teacher, magazine editor, and college public relations director, along with her own well-developed writing talents, have enriched and deepened the book, not to mention the process of writing it—a process, I might add, that also enriched and deepened our own relationship. As an ordained Presbyterian minister, Pat has also helped me to explore and emphasize the significance of the spiritual dimension to life in our senior years.

For all of these many gifts, I am truly thankful.

David C. Borchard

CHAPTER 1

REINVENTING YOUR LIFE AT FIFTY-PLUS

"I knew who I was during my career in this organization, but I have no idea of who I'm going to be when I leave here."

—A 55-YEAR-OLD MALE EXECUTIVE PREPARING FOR RETIREMENT

"I've worked hard for the past 27 years doing the company's work, and now I am desperate to discover what I really want to do in the next chapter of my life."

—A 53-YEAR-OLD FEMALE PROFESSIONAL PREPARING FOR RETIREMENT

"Retirement for me has been the gateway to freedom."

—A 65-YEAR-OLD RECENTLY RETIRED EXECUTIVE

◆ Rejuvenation

If you're in the fifty-plus years, retirement no doubt has been on your mind, unless you've already made the transition to life beyond full-time employment. As I write this, I am 70 years old—chronologically, that is. I'd put my functional age at fifty-something, and I dislike the word *retirement*.

Have you ever checked out the definition of *retirement*? My dictionary defines it as "to withdraw oneself from business, active service or public life; to disappear, to take out of circulation; withdrawn or secluded; difficult to be seen, known, or discovered." With that definition, why would anyone ever want to be *retired?*

I don't want or intend to work full-time for any one organization ever again. But I do want more balance and diversity in my life than was possible when I was fully employed. That sentiment is one I often hear echoed from the hundreds of retirement-bound clients I have worked with over the years. How about you? Where do you stand on the question of how you want to be spending your time in the next chapter of your life?

As a freelance professional counselor and career management coach, I work with individuals transitioning to pension-supported lifestyles. The great majority of these folks are far more interested in life and work change than traditional retirement. My clients seldom mention the topic of retirement. Instead, they think about how to rejuvenate their lives by recreating, reinventing or redesigning the way they live. *Retirement* has a passive connotation. It sounds like something that happens to you because you have gotten old—through no particular fault of your own. *Life recreation,* by contrast, suggests a self-initiated action—one that originates from free will and intentionality rather than from an imposed condition. Maybe it's time to retire the word *retirement* in favor of a more positive term. I invite you to coin a new term for your exciting new chapter in life!

Exciting? Yes! But not without some work. The big challenge facing most of us in our fifty-plus years is how to recreate a fulfilling and meaningful life appropriate to who we are now, taking advantage of the life, work, and learning possibilities now available. There are at least three compelling reasons to pay attention to your new challenge:

1. At this life juncture, you may now have the opportunity for greater freedom by way of a pension-supported lifestyle.

2. Never before have you been this old, which also means you have less time remaining in this earthbound experience. This sobering reality makes the time we do have a valuable commodity, a potentially rich but limited resource.

3. At this point in our lives, we have more life-enriched experience, along with deeper self-knowledge from which to make more fulfilling life choices than we did in our younger years. This hard-won wisdom provides a reference from which to discern what is going to make us richer or poorer in body, mind, and spirit.

The process of life reinventing often begins around fifty-plus, when we find ourselves mulling over questions about life meaning, personal identity, and our core values. Here are some of the kinds of questions that typically arise in this self-questioning process (check any of these that resonate with you):

- ❑ What will I do when I am no longer committed to the structure of full-time work?
- ❑ Who am I now, and who am I becoming?
- ❑ What is it time to leave behind?
- ❑ What do I call myself when I no longer have a job title or organizational affiliation?
- ❑ What do I care deeply about?
- ❑ Where would I/we want to live if I/we could live anywhere?
- ❑ How much time do I have remaining in this lifetime?
- ❑ Why am I here?
- ❑ Will I become an old couch potato when I don't have to go to work?
- ❑ How will I know if I'm being successful when I am no longer being evaluated by my performance at work?
- ❑ Are my best days behind me?
- ❑ So, what's next?

We shall address these issues in depth in later chapters. For now, let's just acknowledge the reality of our aging selves. At fifty-plus, we have entered the ranks of what traditionally has been thought of as *elderhood* or *seniordom*. As we enter a new life era, it's time to let go of that which no longer serves us well or that which we can no longer sustain for some reason. This includes youthful vigor, self-esteem based on career success, or beauty based on unlined faces. At fifty-plus, it's time to fit into the skin of fully matured adulthood and create new reasons for being and thinking about ourselves. It also may be time to develop underutilized talents and interests, and possibly even engage in some new kinds of work, paid or unpaid.

◆ Change, Rejuvenate, or Hang On

Are you in a quandary of whether the time has come for a change in life, a change in yourself, or an unchanging hold on what you have?

You may not want to jump prematurely into an uncertain path, but you also may not want to stay stuck in a current rut simply because you fear change. If you have reached a plateau in your current situation and are running on the low side of motivation, you are probably facing the choice of whether to get rejuvenated through a big life-changing leap or to undertake a few small adjustments here and there. Big life leaps might include choices such as retiring from work, getting a divorce, taking on an entrepreneurial venture, moving to a totally new culture, or undertaking a major career shift. Smaller, life-rejuvenating adjustments might include engaging in some new interests like joining a meditation group, volunteering as a Big Brother or Sister, leading a Boy or Girl Scout troop, joining a church choir, initiating a new project at work, starting a new assignment within your organization, or enrolling in courses of personal interest at the local community college.

Of course, no one ever knows for sure what outcome will result from a decision to go forward with a major life change, and only you can determine whether you are prepared to take that leap. The following Life Vitality Assessment can help you determine whether the time has come to undertake a major transition, to make some small alterations in your life, or to remain a while longer in your current situation.

Life Vitality Assessment

Use the following rating scale to assess your current attitude in response to each of the 20 statements below. Record the number that best describes your response to each statement in the left-hand spaces. When you have recorded your response to all 20 items, tally the sum of all responses in the box provided.

Your rating scores	Describes me perfectly		Occasionally I feel this way		I never feel this way
	10 9 8	7	6 5 4	3	2 1

_____ 1. I would be completely content if my life were to continue pretty much as is over the next 10 years or more.

_____ 2. I have a rewarding work life and enjoyable leisure activities.

_____ 3. I would continue with my work and life exactly as it is even if I suddenly came into great wealth.

_____ 4. I continue to have as much or more energy and enthusiasm for my work and/or life situation as I have always had.

_____ 5. I never experience boredom or self-doubts about what I'm doing in my daily activities.

_____ 6. I feel personally empowered and am a creative force in continuing to make my life and work rich and rewarding.

_____ 7. I seem to be running on a full tank of energy and vitality pretty much all the time.

_____ 8. I am definitely not ready for retirement because there is much I still want to do professionally.

_____ 9. My love life is at least as full, rich, and rewarding now and for the foreseeable future as it has ever been.

_____ 10. I have a clear sense of what my core values are and believe they are fully congruent with my current life situation.

_____ 11. If I lost my work situation tomorrow for any reason, I am confident I could move onto an excellent new situation in short order.

_____ 12. I feel great about who I am and am taking excellent care of myself physically, emotionally, intellectually, and spiritually.

_____ 13. I find my current life situation highly challenging and feel good about what I'm learning and how I'm growing.

_____ 14. Those individuals who know me beyond casual acquaintance hold me in high esteem.

_____ 15. I am optimistic that I can continue on pretty much as I am now and for the foreseeable future.

_____ 16. I have a great family life and enjoy rich relationships with good friends and associates.

_____ 17. I am happy where I/we live and have hobbies and interests outside of work that enrich my life.

_____ 18. I am clear about my criteria for personal success and am on the right track with my life and work.

_____ 19. I believe that my current life and/or work situation enables me to contribute and develop my full potential.

_____ 20. My current life and work situation fully uses my best talents and top interests.

Record your total score from all 20 responses: _____

Interpreting Your Assessment Results

If your score falls within this range:	It suggests that:
175 or above **Fully Vitalized**	Your high score suggests you are comfortable with who you are and energized by the life you are currently living. Whatever you are doing seems to be working well for you, so keep it up. If you need to make some changes for any reason, do so carefully. You will either want to

	make small adjustments or recreate a similar type of situation.
150–175 **Sustained Energy**	You seem to be sustaining a fairly positive attitude and energy level in the quality and meaning of your work and life. A question to consider is whether your energy level is generally on an upswing, a downswing, or at a fairly even keel. You will probably want to sustain most of the activities and associations that bring out your best. It may be time, however, for some new dimension in your life, work, learning, or leisure that could boost your energy score above the 175 mark.
100–150 **Half Empty**	Your score suggests that you have just enough vitality to see you through the week—but very little in reserve. Your life and work are lacking full-bodied vitality. It may be important to make changes in some aspect of your life, such as your work, physical condition, mindset, hobby, or relationships. Make an investment of some time and effort to refill your life-vitality tank.
Less than 100 **Taking Stock**	Your score suggests the need for change. The closer your score comes to the zero mark, the more urgent the need. Find ways to get your battery recharged. Determine what you need to do, what you want to change, what you need to let go of, and what you need to bring forth or revisit to get revitalized. This book should be a valuable resource in helping to determine your real potential, reenergize your outlook and refill your life-energy tank.

◆ Old Stereotypes and New Perspectives on Life as a Senior

At the onset of the twentieth century, if you achieved the age of 50, you were old. A hundred years ago, the life expectancy was fifty-something. But that was then. Today, it's a different story. In his book *The Power Years*, Ken Dychtwald reports, "If you've already made it to fifty, you can expect to live at least until your mid-eighties, and thanks to impending scientific breakthroughs, these numbers will keep increasing."[1] That means that, if you transition from full-time work in your fifties or sixties, you still have about a quarter of a century remaining to hang around. Not only that, but there is a strong statistical probability that your coming years are going to be lived in good health and financial well-being. What are you going to do with that much time, and with the options and resources available for enjoying these years?

---

1. Ken Dychtwald, *The Power Years* (Hoboken, NJ: John Wiley & Sons, 2005), p. 13.

How rich and fulfilling your remaining years are going to be has a lot to do with your mental outlook at this stage of life. In her book *Don't Stop the Career Clock*, Helen Harkness, a psychologist in her seventy-plus years, illuminates the difference between chronological and functional age. Chronological age is what the calendar records, while functional age is a more accurate measure of how old you are based on your physical health, your emotional state of mind, and your creative spirit.[2]

We grow old, Dr. Harkness observes, by buying into the prevailing negative social and cultural expectations about chronological age. One can easily buy into these expectations with the result that we are programmed to begin declining in our fifties and then accelerate the downward trend in our sixties and seventies. But it doesn't have to be that way! Who says that declining functionality is inevitable in the fifty-plus years? That may have been true for retirement in the Industrial Era. Back then, most people tended to be used-up physically when they retired at age 65, and they subsequently contributed to the stability of the Social Security system by dying soon after. But that is history. In the twenty-first century, we take better care of ourselves, have improved health care, are living longer, and think differently about the post-fifty years. We remain vibrant by being active in mind, body, and purpose.

Assessing Your True Age

How old are you chronologically? ———

How old do you feel yourself to be functionally? ———

(Be honest here. How old do you actually consider yourself to be, rather than what the calendar says, or you hope, or perhaps pretend, to be? Use your gut level instincts to see what age comes to mind rather than attempting to figure it out rationally. Some things to take into consideration include your energy level, optimism about your future, curiosity about life and your physical strength and agility.)

There is an alternative to buying into the negative stereotypes about life as a *senior*. On the one hand, if you buy into the myth that being fifty-plus means being "over the hill," then you are more inclined to let yourself go—to become an aimless, grouchy old couch potato! On the

---

2. Helen Harkness, *Don't Stop the Career Clock* (Palo Alto, CA: Davies-Black Pub., 1999), pp. 78–83.

other hand, if you realize the full potential available in the *golden years*, you are more likely to live, think, feel, and act from the perspective of well being and vibrancy. A quick Internet search brings up countless numbers of role models of fifty-plussers recreating full lives and looking good in the process. Here are just a few examples (for more, visit *The Senior Citizens Journal* at www.SeniorJournal.com):

- Art Stander, a retired chemical engineer, started playing the cello at age 70. Now, at age 73, he is an accomplished member of Sixty Plus/minus, a group of amateur classical musicians, mostly age sixty-plus, who meet every other week to play chamber music.

- Lucille Borgen amazed the crowd at the Sixty-Second Annual Water Ski National Championships by winning the women's slalom and tricks event on her ninety-first birthday. Lucille, a cancer and a polio survivor, was the lone competitor in her age group. She got to the national finals through exceptional performances at regional championships.

- At age 94, Doris "Granny D" Hoddock, grandmother of 16, became a candidate for the U.S. Senate from New Hampshire. Haddock achieved national acclaim when she walked across the country to promote campaign finance reform.

- At age 70, Gene Glasscock completed a horseback journey of over 20,000 miles to visit every state capital in the lower 48 states.

- At eighty-something, newscaster Daniel Shore is still reporting the news and bringing his years of experience to his analysis of the day's events.

- Now well into his seventies, Arnold Palmer cannot play golf like a twenty-something Tiger Woods. But he still enjoys the game and shoots in the seventies—not the low sixties of his prime golfing years, but he has fun being who he is now, and he still delights thousands of fans when he shows up on the links.

At fifty-plus, we can be more relaxed as we allow ourselves to be released into the experience of fully matured self. In early adulthood, most of us were highly concerned about our looks and the image we hoped to be projecting. We conformed in ways expected by our employment situation and the communities to which we belonged. But in our fifty-plus years, we can let go of our old personas and concerns about how we think we are being perceived. We can let go of youthful narcissism and the need to fit in. At fifty-plus, we've earned the right to let go of all that, to free ourselves from old roles. The time has come to explore who we are at a deeper level, to open the door to our unexplored self and our authentic natures. As a wise friend of mine says, "Getting old just means becoming more of who you are."

◆ Location and the Good Life at Fifty-Plus

What is the good life in our senior years? Commercials tell us the answer is simple—it's the "perfect" retirement community. Just move to the right location and you'll enjoy the good life. Of course, the perfect place just happens to be the one being promoted. Changing location may, in fact, actually be the right retirement prescription for those with a single-minded passion for a golfing and clubhouse lifestyle.

Changing location, however, is not the total answer to everything for those whose interests range beyond golf. Nevertheless, location, along with financial considerations, almost always seems to get top billing for retirement planning. Could this be so because dealing with a concrete choice like location is easier than struggling to define something as intangible as one's aspirations for a rich and fully engaged life? Location is important, but it's not the only—or primary—consideration for those seeking self-fulfillment in their senior years.

◆ Self-Realization

What is at the core of fulfillment when one moves on from full-time work? The answer is fairly simple—but not so obvious. In the senior stage of life, whether in conscious awareness or not, the desire for self-realization becomes a primary motivation. Many people, when asked about what they want to do in retirement, say things like travel, consulting, volunteer work, or spending time with family and friends. But there is another, less obvious aspect of fulfillment for the golden years—to realize one's full potential as a unique human being.

Achieving a fulfilling lifestyle involves clarifying your aspirations for what you want to do and, even more importantly, who you want to be. The good news for fifty- plussers is that the potential for self-realization is greater in the golden years than at any other stage of life. Leaving full-time employment offers three core ingredients essential to self-realization—freedom, resources, and life experience. Previously, most of us have been too preoccupied with managing our careers and/or raising families to reflect upon something as seemingly abstract as self-realization.

Self-realization is an instinctive desire to become all that we are capable of and to contribute our best talents in deeply meaningful ways. A good analogy for appreciating the self-realization instinct exists all around us in the world of nature. There are thousands of varieties of plants, with each individual plant bearing within it the make-up of some ultimate potential. An African violet, for example, can become an eye-catching beauty when conditions nurture and bring out its full potential. The violet, however, can never become a rose, nor the rose a camellia. In this regard, people are like flowers. Shakespeare, for instance, could not have become Beethoven, nor could Grandma Moses have become Madonna. Shakespeare, however, might well have become a second-rate knight, a mediocre gardener, or a disillusioned alchemist, had he not realized his potential as a playwright. Unlike flowers, humans must make conscious choices to achieve their highest state of being. That is probably why humans come equipped with big brains in proportion to their body mass, while flowers, lacking such development, must rely totally on good fortune to achieve full bloom.

Taking full advantage of your opportunity for self-realization requires self-knowledge, an energizing vision for your future, and awareness of your best options for applying your knowledge and vision. For Christina, the self-realization process involved taking an early retirement from her administrative position to express long-pent-up creative needs.

For Carl, self-realization involved retiring from a full-time medical practice to a life of variety that allowed him to engage the full range of his interests and talents. To express his musical talents, Carl sings in a men's chorale group that travels all over the country. Teaching a college math course enables him to stay abreast of the subject and enjoy the challenge of turning students onto mathematics. Hosting foreign exchange students keeps him involved in international interests, while helping young people feel welcomed in a strange setting. To sustain his community-building interests, Carl engages in local service activities, such as the Rotary Club and consulting with Project Hope.

The urge to become self-realized doesn't fully impact most of us as a developmental priority until later in life. My younger clients are more likely to seek counseling for career-development concerns, which usually means getting a better position, more money, a more congenial boss, or a job better suited to their interests. Seldom do my younger clients bring up the issue of self-realization. I have observed over many years in my counseling practice that it is usually the fifty-plussers, especially those preparing to retire, who are most concerned about self-realization, even though they may think of it in other terms. My older clients are apt to say that they have spent their younger adulthood doing the organization's work, but now it's their time. Moreover, they intend to make the most of it! When we discuss what *making the most of it* means, the conversation inevitably turns to deeper self-understanding as a basis for making new life choices.

◆ Barriers to the Good Life

There is one rather large barrier that stands in the way of resolving the "so, now what?" question: This task can be a complex challenge. Clarifying one's aspirations and talents is difficult work for most people. Furthermore, even when these have been clarified, identifying the best way of making them happen in a world of unexplored possibilities can be perplexing. Because the task can seem so daunting, all too many of us simply avoid the self-introspection and exploration of options required. Or, even more likely, we narrow the issue to something overly simple, such as where we want to live. Although a new home or new location can be engaging, at least temporarily, an overly narrowed focus or premature jump into something new seriously jeopardizes the potential for expanded new directions in life, work, and learning.

The complexity of this challenge, combined with the need to redirect our lives toward an uncharted future, means that many forgo the opportunity for self-realization and settle for something less fulfilling. Achieving the good life, from the self-realization perspective, doesn't just happen. It requires time, introspection, and a willingness to make life-changing choices.

◆ Undiscovered vs. Discovered Self

As the title of this section suggests, we are each a unique entity composed of both a discovered and an undiscovered self. For that reason—and this is important—we are always more than we think we are. Although the discovered self is our everyday consciousness, the undiscovered self represents a whole new source of untapped potential. The undiscovered self is a new realm available to be explored and exploited, especially in the fifty-plus years when we are freed from the obligations of full-time employment and the responsibilities of earlier life.

The *discovered self* is how you have come to know and understand yourself. You should be aware, however, that your self-understanding is unavoidably limited, if not, in fact, flawed. You are, in some ways, like a fish in a fishbowl. You have only been able to understand yourself from within the limited confines of a bowl-bound perspective. Your self-view is a mentally contrived understanding composed of decisions, assumptions, and insights derived from life experience. In other words, your reality of self is completely a perceptual creation. Its development began in youthful programming and was altered thereafter through mind-filtered interpretations of identity-shaping experiences. Such interpretations are prone to misinterpretation and to subjective error.

We all possess an amazing faculty for dramatizing significant events in our lives in overly positive or negative ways. That, in turn, often leads us to crystallize our reactions to them into self-beliefs. For example, I remember concluding as a young child that I was oversized, awkward, and socially inept—all from one skating incident with neighborhood kids. We were playing hockey on the local pond, and I, clumsy on my new skates, kept getting in the way of a smaller, more verbally advanced girl. About the fifth or sixth time that I lumbered into her way, thereby keeping her out of the play, she yelled at the top of her lungs, "You're just an eighty-pound baby!" With that, she stomped off the ice. I felt foolish, offish, and thoroughly embarrassed. This was not, as you might imagine, a confidence-building experience for shaping my youthful identity.

Even today, all these years later, there remains a small voice in my psyche occasionally reminding me in certain interactions with women that I'm awkward, inept, and fully capable of instantly embarrassing myself. That voice has, I'm sure, been an inhibitor for me in certain social activities (dancing, for instance).

I also acquired the message from my small-town Minnesotan culture and too many cowboy movies that it was unmanly to express feelings of love and affection, or to have aesthetic needs of a creative bent. The results of those foolish understandings have put a crimp in my ability to freely express feelings of tenderness or to explore any artistic talents I might possess.

Some of us come to positive conclusions about who we are early in life. Such was the case with Winston Churchill, who, according to William Manchester in *The Last Lion: William Spencer Churchill: Alone, 1932–1940*, concluded at a young age that he was a genius.[3]

---

3. William Manchester, *The Last Lion: Winston Spencer Churchill: Alone, 1932–1940* (Boston: Little, Brown, 1988).

He then proceeded to operate from that assumption. Although Churchill's conclusion seems to have been accurate, if a bit arrogant, Hitler's early conclusion that he was an artistic genius appears to have been woefully misguided.[4] One can't help but wonder what role Hitler's misperceptions about himself played in leading him to perpetrate the horrors of the Holocaust. For most of us, the outcomes of our choices are not so dramatic or catastrophic. But who knows how your self-knowledge—or lack of it—could change the world? What early life experiences (from about the age of 1 to 21) can you recall that have influenced your self-concept?

Assessing Your Identity-Shaping Experience

In a Positive Way	In a Negative Way

For the sake of life-satisfaction, reassessing what we think we know about ourselves in our fifty-plus years can be a valuable activity. In this regard, it's worth reminding yourself that you are no longer who you were, and beyond that, you were probably never actually who you

---

4. For more information on this, see Peter Schjeldahl, "Hitler As Artist: How Vienna Inspired the Fürer's Dreams," www.NewYorker.com/archive/2002/08/19/020819craw_artworld (accessed 11/10/07)

thought you were anyway. At fifty-plus, therefore, it is worthwhile to get your conceptual foundations right. It's essential in order to proceed on the path of self-realization.

◆ Tapping the Undiscovered Self

When my graduate school psychometrics professor led a discussion on the Weschler Adult Intelligence Scale (WAIS), he related a story about the highest I.Q. score he had ever recorded, out of the thousands of WAIS assessments he had administered over the years. The intelligence of a cleaning woman at the university had come to the attention of an observant faculty member, who persuaded the psychometrist to test her. Alexia, the cleaning woman, had been born in Greece, the only daughter of a family with several sons. In that family's culture, sons were expected to become educated and have lives and work that capitalized on and developed their potential. The daughters were expected to remain uneducated and learn how to clean, cook, and take care of her family. Naturally, Alexia's perception of her potential became what her family expected of her—at least, until she immigrated to the United States and encountered the psychometrics professor. Shocked by the extraordinarily high I.Q. score she achieved, the professor encouraged her to begin taking courses at the university. At first, she was reluctant to do so. After all, she saw herself only as a middle-aged cleaning lady. Eventually, however, she was persuaded to try taking just one course. She excelled in the course and began enrolling in additional courses. The process of intellectual self-discovery proceeded slowly with one successful course completion after another. Alexia finally earned a bachelor's degree and then went to graduate school. In time she also reconceptualized herself as a highly intelligent woman.

Alexia's story is similar to an ex-dockworker acquaintance of mine who, in walking by a community college one day, out of curiosity stopped in to see about enrolling in a course. He ended up registering in an English course and, much to his surprise, received an A. On the basis of that success, he decided to take another course, and once again received an A. To further test this amazing achievement, he took another course, and then another and another, until he earned an associate's degree, followed by a bachelor's, and then a master's. Now he is a successful Ph.D. psychologist in California with a large and flourishing practice. Had he not stepped outside the comfort zone of his self-perceptions, however, he might have remained a dockworker, using only a small part of his intellectual and creative abilities.

These two stories may be unusual, but I believe they illustrate a common reality: how unaware so many of us are of our unrealized capabilities and potentials. We may not all possess the extraordinarily high I.Q. of Alexia, but the limited views most of us have of our unrealized possibilities may have blinded us to our own genuinely remarkable interests and potentials. It is this unrealized self that gives us the intriguing dimension of self-discovery in our post-fifty years.

◆ Revealing the Undiscovered Self

For any individual, the fullest measure of life is probably going to remain unrealized as long as the undiscovered self remains a stranger. The challenge of becoming acquainted with this stranger can be exciting; however, it may not always be an entirely pleasant experience. If you have ever had the opportunity of receiving behavioral feedback from colleagues at work, you know what I mean. Some of the feedback may validate what you already know about yourself; some of it may come as a shock. Feedback that comes as a surprise is an indication that you are being introduced to an unrealized aspect of yourself. That is true whether the news seems positive or negative. Some of us have as much difficulty accepting unrealized capabilities as we do in accepting our unacknowledged faults and shortcomings. Your undiscovered self includes some sludge and some gold. Whether sludge or gold, though, it may be worth mining.

The more we know ourselves, including our potentials and limitations, the more we are able to manage or change our less desirable elements. All of us have our fair shares of negatives and positives. When we are unwilling or unable to own our negatives, however, we are more likely to harm ourselves and others. Those of us unable or unwilling to uncover our unique gifts also may be hurting ourselves or others by depriving us all of something useful, unique, or beautiful. The vibrant little college town in which we live is full of interesting restaurants and boutiques, music and theater festivals, training and retreat centers, and parklands and hiking trails. Each one started with someone's vision, someone willing to share a passion and take that first step toward making it a reality that everyone could enjoy.

The self-realization challenge is to acquaint yourself with the full measure of your limitations and potentialities, especially those that you have not acknowledged previously. How then, you might ask, do you discover your undiscovered self? There are many ways, ranging from expensive therapy on the one end, to inexpensive self-reflection work on the other. Whether expensive or not, the process takes an investment of work, intentionality, time, and, above all, a willingness to explore your inner self.

The right therapist for you can be a big help in this journey. As a professional counselor, I am, of course, inclined to recommend therapy for those of us who have issues from the past that may be impeding our moving forward with the freedom we would like to have. I know that therapy has helped me let go of old scripts that have limited my horizons. I also know how important it is to find—be able to afford—a good therapist. If you are in the position to do so, I recommend checking with people you trust who have had positive experiences with therapy to get references. Then interview two or three, or more, until you find the right fit for you.

If therapy is not for you, there are other resources that may be as helpful. Feedback from others can be a useful source for the self-discovery process, especially if you are a good listener who appreciates the gift of someone who takes the time and energy to be thoughtful and honest with you. Many people could serve in this role—family, friends, pastors, colleagues, and supervisors, to name a few. It is helpful to have feedback from several people, since no one person knows you in all your work, play, and relationship roles. But each one will, no doubt, see strengths and shortcomings that you haven't seen or haven't been willing to recognize. There are a couple of other caveats to keep in mind with free-ranging feedback.

Not all of us are great at giving unbiased and accurate feedback. And some of us do not excel in receiving it. I believe, for example, that I am pretty good at giving people positive feedback that helps to validate their strengths. However, I find it rather difficult to give people negative feedback, especially if it appears that they may have a difficult time accepting it.

Another problem with feedback is that we can only provide feedback on observable behavior. Although behavioral feedback can help you to eliminate or change things that undermine your effectiveness, you also should remember that there is far more to self-knowledge than your observable behavior. The realm of the unrealized, undiscovered, and untapped self may not be readily apparent in the *you* that you have thus far presented to the world. Only you can uncover and clarify your innermost values, your deep-seated interests, and your unrealized capabilities. But in that you may still need some assistance.

There are many excellent books to help you with the process of self-discovery. I've listed several in the reference section of this book, so I will point out only a few here. One is Dick Bolles's perennial best-selling book, *What Color Is My Parachute*, along with the Web site www.jobhuntersbible.com for additional resources. I also highly recommend books and resources developed by Helen Harkness, whose Web site is www.career-design.com/. There are also many excellent self-assessments that are useful tools for self-discovery. These include the popular Myers Briggs personality profile and the Strong Interest Inventories, both of which can be obtained from most counseling professionals. Another assessment that many individuals have found helpful is the Passion Revealer, which can be accessed at http://passion.career-nsite.com. I developed this process specifically for adults who want to find the optimal situation for expressing their unique interests, talents, and skills. Many clients I have counseled and coached have found this assessment to be especially beneficial in helping them discover and validate their passion. The best approach, however, is to use a combination of approaches and assessments in your search for self-discovery.

Some people find that life coaches are also an important checkpoint in their journey. Coaches can be especially helpful after you have dealt with any therapy issues, uncovered your passion, and are ready to proceed with some concrete goals. I definitely recommend coaching at this later point in the process. Most coaches, however, are not licensed professional counselors or therapists and, therefore, are not equipped to provide the kind of help you may need to get to the point of setting goals that coaches can help you achieve. As with choosing a therapist, it is important to choose a coach that is a good fit for your personality and situation. If your budget doesn't allow paying for a coach, you may be able to enlist a friend or colleague to serve in that role.

It is also helpful to simply write out your goals in clear, unequivocal terms. No fudging! If your goal is to be a famous artist, it's highly unlikely that you'll ever reach it if you write a goal that is less than what you actually want. We'll talk more about this later in the book, when you will have an opportunity for writing out your goals in terms that are achievable and fulfilling. For now, just remember that most things are doable if taken one step at a time.

◆ Never Too Old for Orgasms

Do you think that people in their fifties, sixties, or later are too old for orgasms or other activities that engage passion to the fullest? If so, you may be stuck in a mindset filled with once-held myths about the limitations of seniors. Everywhere I look, I see advertisements promoting the "blue pill," stories about amazing athletes in their eighties and nineties, and research documenting the expanded longevity and health of older people today. Fifty-plussers by the thousands are redefining our concepts of aging. One such a person is Julia, a minister whose joyful presence was infectious and inspiring. My then-to-be wife and I were delighted that she agreed to officiate at our wedding 18 years ago. She was in her eighties then. I won't report on her sex life, but I can tell you that she was passionate about her work. She didn't even become an ordained pastor until the age of 65. One of this vibrant little woman's favorite stories, the kind she loved to sprinkle her sermons with, was being stopped for speeding while cruising "out west." As she told it, a stern patrolman pulled her over for speeding through the high plains country and informed her that he had clocked the vehicle she was driving at 84 miles per hour.

"Lady, do you know what the speed limit is out here?" he asked in accusatory tones.

Julia was not intimidated. In her sweet and gracious manner, she said, "Well, officer, I was just going my age."

Her answer did not keep her from receiving an expensive ticket—one resembling her age. But it did illustrate the way she lived her life. Julia was a loving role model for many—including my wife, Pat. Seeing the way she conducted a vibrant ministry and lived her life with passion helped Pat to realize that exploring her own passion for ministry was not beyond reason, even though she was nearing the age of fifty. She is now a Presbyterian minister, ordained at the age of 55.

Some of us seem to have a knack for knowing exactly what we want and how to go about getting it. Ely Callaway, formerly of Callaway wines and now of Callaway golf, appears to be someone who did. Poet and writer Maya Angelou, astronaut and Senator John Glenn, movie star/President Ronald Reagan, TV journalist Barbara Walters, singer/painter Tony Bennett, and author James Mitchener are all individuals who appear to have fully engaged their passion in their senior years. But how about the rest of us? What if we are not as blessed with fame, fortune, or other resources to support our creative visions? What if we feel impoverished by a lack of imagination, confidence, or chutzpa? What can we do to clarify our vision and make it happen? The processes in this book are designed to help you with that. But it also may be important to get support. How and where to find that support is a topic we address more fully in Chapter 2.

Too many dreams end up dying on the vine for lack of confidence and/or skill in implementing them. Many of us live half-realized lives because we have failed to create a vision that would put our unique gifts to full and enjoyable use. We go though life with our life energy thermostats set to the moderate position rather than turning up the "heat."

What are we waiting for? Are we conserving our personal energy in case we need it for some big, unexpected event? Some of us may not be ready for a highly energized state. Maybe it sounds too much like being in state of perpetual orgasm—and who would want that? But wouldn't you rather enjoy a life with orgasms than one with none at all? Wouldn't you rather have a life with passion than without? Based on my thirty years of professional counseling experience, I am of the opinion that orgasmiclike living is available to almost everyone in the fifty-plus stages of life. We all have the potential for activities that *turn us on* in work, learning, and leisure.

◆ Recreating New Life Through Adversity

Recently, I took a financial planning seminar from a vibrant lady. Being a child of the late 1950s and early 1960s, I have never been terribly excited about a life focused on money. It wasn't that I was opposed to money—although I did grow up Lutheran in a small Scandinavian community in Minnesota. That means I grew up hearing some scary messages about money. They had to do with things like money being the source of all evil and leading to eternal damnation. You might say that my conditioning included a bit of an anti-money message. Then one day I sat in on Clarisse's workshop. A financial educator, she helped me view money differently. I began to see that in itself, money was not evil and that, in fact, it could be used for great good. When invested wisely, it could, for instance, provide new opportunities for those living in developing countries. Clarisse helped me understand that a poverty-bound mindset or apathetic attitude was actually much more detrimental to the individual and the planet than a savvy approach to finances ever could be. I became convinced that failure to make farsighted decisions about money would probably be a terrible disservice to me—and my family—in later years. I got serious about reprogramming the way I had thought about money, and soon I began to see it as a concept, a medium of value exchange, and a resource for abundant life. I began to see investing in my personal future and the collective future of humankind as an important component of financial well being. For me, this was also interwoven with another new awareness in my life—my spiritual journey.

We are always changing, whether we want to or not. The question is how much conscious choice we want to exercise over the directions we pursue in our development. When I was in my twenties, for instance, I never gave the slightest thought to my spiritual development. That has changed over time. My participation in a Buddhist meditation group, yoga classes, and the Presbyterian Church (U.S.A.) are important new dimensions in my spiritual journey. For those of us interested in this aspect of our post-fifty development, there is a chapter focusing on this later in the book.

Some of us may have no interest in anything even remotely connected to things of a spiritual nature. Others of us may just want to focus on the concrete elements of our retirement. That's okay, too. I have one client whose only goal after shedding his career identity is to play golf. Another simply wants to fish. Obviously, those activities give them great pleasure. But even though these particular individuals might not use such terminology to describe their love of golf and fishing, isn't it possible that there is also a spiritual dimension to being out on a golf course or in the middle of a tranquil pond on a beautiful spring day? Isn't it possible that they have chosen these activities because they know, on some level, whether they verbalize it this way or not, that these are the things that feed their souls? Clarisse, for example, never used the term *ministry* when she talked about her deliberate choice of vocation or the adverse circumstances that led her to reassess her life. But if you listen to her story, you can certainly hear how she came to embark upon a *mission*.

Clarisse's passion for educating people about wealth came through her sudden and unexpected encounter with poverty. She had been married to a man of means who took care of all their financial matters. But one day he left her and their young daughter for a younger woman. Suddenly, she had no money and no working experience. She went through a series of reactions—shock, anger, and panic. She felt utterly helpless. But being a woman of high intelligence and strong resolve, she elected to do something about her situation. Aware of her ignorance about finance, she decided to become an expert in it and to help educate others about financial management. She found a way to go to the London International School of Finance, where she earned a master's degree in finance. Then she created a career for herself as a financial consultant/educator. Now she is not only a woman of means, but also an educator of people around the world, helping them see the real value of money for opportunity building.

* * *

Although no one welcomes adversity, that is often the crucible that forces one to discover and draw upon inner reserves of which we were previously unaware. Adversity can be a life teacher, as it most certainly was in Clarisse's case. A positive response to adversity can be life changing. The annuls of psychology are full of stories of the heroic journeys of individuals who have lost a loved one and used an excruciatingly painful experience to create a meaningful new direction in life. Albert is one such example. Albert had just retired from a successful career as an engineer when his beloved wife, a nurse, died suddenly from a virulent form of cancer. Through his grief, Albert enrolled in a nursing program at the local community college. He confided with me that he was setting off on this new course in his life in honor and memory of his dear wife. He intended to specialize in cancer care in continuation of his wife's dedication to the work. Albert's grief "softened" him, giving him a new awareness and purpose. The way he talked made it clear to me that he had recreated a highly meaningful life and that he would be a nurturing presence to cancer patients.

Martha, an executive at a highly prestigious corporation, was about to accept a vice presidency when she discovered she had serious family problems. She had been so invested in her work that she had grown out of touch with her husband and teenage son. She could either accept the vice presidency and lose her husband or devote her time and energy to saving her marriage. She opted to save her marriage. In the process, she decided to take an early retirement and make a career change to follow her heart rather than corporate success. Currently, she is working toward a master's degree in social work as a prerequisite to her new calling, which is providing therapeutic service to the elderly. She had observed the difficulties that many elderly people were having in managing their lives and was struck by their need for professional assistance. She used the ordeal of discovering her husband's marital "digressions" not only to save her marriage and the family life she held dear, but also to create a new, more meaningful calling for her life.

I am not suggesting that you seek out adversity as the vehicle for finding your true self and recreating a new life. Adversity happens to us all at various times in life. When it occurs, our only choice is how to deal with it. Some give in to their grief and check out of life. Others have been opened by the pain and prompted to recreate more deeply meaningful lives. As I write this, I have just finished an executive coaching session with an amazing woman. She lost her beloved husband to cancer a year and a half ago. Prior to his death, she had been a successful career-oriented executive with the federal government. She still is, but now she is a different person. Prior to her husband's death, her commitment was only to the agency's mission and getting the job done. Now she is committed to helping her staff grow and develop and become their best, a newfound mission for her. Although she is now eligible for retirement, she has recommitted herself to her work with a newfound purpose. She intends to move into the senior-executive core to have an even broader impact in making the government a more humane and nurturing place for people to grow and develop.

My earnest hope for you is that you will find within yourself the strength to use adversity to discover new inner strength and recreate a deeply meaningful new life. Times of adversity call for finding ourselves anew. Weathering adversity—or great success, I might add—involves transition, the subject of the next chapter.

◆ **Conclusion**

Although retirement typically means shedding occupational identities, letting go of old familiar ways, and bidding fond farewell to our youthful selves, it also can be a highly exciting time for self-discovery, life reinvention, and discovery of the creative spirit. A life liberated from full-time employment provides unparalleled opportunity for discovering your true passion, bringing forth hidden strengths, and pursuing a freer, more joyful and deeply fulfilling lifestyle.

What are some of these joys of seniorhood? Well, first, we may be fortunate enough to not need to work so much and so hard at what the company wants from us. Second, we may have more time and energy to take advantage of our life experience and self-awareness. Third, we can take charge of our life, work, and leisure. And, fourth, we are now in control of our personal growth and professional development.

Perhaps you now have the resources and experience to create something new and fulfilling. Perhaps it's time to build your dream house. Or perhaps it's time to downsize the old dwelling to spend less time on maintenance and more in what really engages your interests. Maybe it's time to take up French cooking, to get your pilot's license, or start your own ballroom dance studio. Perhaps it is time now for some soul work, to participate in spiritual retreats, to read and meditate. Maybe you're being called to the ministry or life as a writer or artist.

At fifty-plus, it's time to discover and develop your hidden passion. It's never too late for passion—for the real you to stand up.

CHAPTER 2

LIFE TRANSITIONS:
ENDINGS AND BEGINNINGS

"The new thing carries the day, spring supplants winter, the new year sends the old year packing. But there is no antagonism in this. Just succession. As long as our transitions continue, we are successful."

—WILLIAM BRIDGES, *THE WAY OF TRANSITION*

"I didn't see it then, but it turned out that getting fired from Apple was the best thing that could have ever happened to me. The heaviness of being successful was replaced by the lightness of being a beginner again, less sure about everything. It freed me to enter one of the most creative periods of my life."

—STEVEN JOBS, FOUNDER OF APPLE INC.

◆ Life as Transition

Undertaking any major life change is both an exciting adventure and a stressful proposition, and depending on the circumstances, typically far more of one than the other. Just about everyone goes through several changes in life, some small and a few major. Our first major life change few of us remember. That was, of course, the shockingly sudden shift from the warm comfort of the womb into life in the outer world. If we were lucky, we arrived to parents who instantly loved us and welcomed us whole-heartedly into this startling new reality.

Of course, some of us were more fortunate on that score than others, so that life began with differing perspectives on just what kind of place this old world is. We adjusted as best we could to life in the early years, until confronted with the next major life change, which for many was the infamous adolescent identity crisis. This, you may recall, involved struggling with the issue of "who am I as a person" and "who am I becoming" (as well as "who am I not" and "who/what is it my intention to refrain from becoming"). Some of us also had to weather even more traumatic changes such as the death of a sibling or loss of a parent through death or divorce. Our adult years were then filled with a stream of life-changing transitions of various kinds, some splendid and others painful (new loves and lost loves, career successes and failures, hopes achieved and those abandoned).

Most of us weathered the mid-life crisis with varying degrees of stress and success, and just when we were about settled in from that, we got hit with still another change event—offers for senior citizen discounts! Transitioning from full-time employment to retirement is one of those major life changes filled with both expected and unexpected outcomes and consequences. Then, eventually, we all must confront the final transition, departing this life for what heaven only knows.

◆ Change Is Mother to Transition

At this point, we need to clarify the terms *change* and *transition*. As used here, change refers to an event and transition to a process. Although a major life change alters our outer world, it also sets off a chain of inner reactions. Transition involves the inner state of adjusting to a dramatically changed life situation. Although most people are aware of what a life change such as job loss, career change, or retirement brings to their physical reality, few are as knowledgeable about the psychological adjustments required in accommodating to a new way of being. It's the psychological adjustments to a major life change that causes stress. That is because transition not only forces you to accommodate to new and differing outer circumstances in your life but also requires that you adjust emotionally to a new view of who you are. The loss of a spouse, for example, is a dramatic change event, but it's accommodating to the loss that is the hard part. That involves experiencing grief, adjusting to feelings of aloneness, transitioning to life again as a single, and then recreating a new life. A big life change can be almost like leaving the womb again—only this time with consciousness. The more you know about the transition process, the better equipped you are to deal with the psychological adjustments to a major life change.

◆ Navigating in Uncertainty: A Map for Transition

Here is a rather simple but profound aspect of transitions: They begin with endings and end with beginnings. Transition implies that you are leaving behind a known past and heading into an unknown future. But a major life transition also involves a period in the middle, a kind of a gap between the structured past and a newly recreated future structure. The time in the gap can be discomforting, but it can serve as the incubation period for an exciting rebirth. Being fully in the gap involves hanging out in uncertainty for an indefinite period of time. It's that which makes the transition unnerving for those of us grown accustomed to being decisive in knowing who we are and what we are about.

The more fulfilling and satisfying one's past structure has been, the more difficult will be the time in the gap. It's hard to give up what has been enjoyable and has provided a strong sense of personal identity. Saying goodbye to a valued past in some ways can be like a mini-death. We can never again be what we were, and who we are to become remains a murky question. The emotional element in transitioning to retirement is further heightened by the pervasive awareness that we can never again be young, accompanied by the fear that our best days just might be behind us.

Not everyone, of course, finds the transition gap stressful. You can avoid the uncertainty by predetermining what you are going to do and be before you launch into retirement. That's what my good friend Steve did. He had a vision of what his retirement would be, long before departing from his 35 years of government service. Steve knew that work was in the past and the future was going to be an enjoyable mix between golf, tennis, chess, travel, mind-expanding reading and learning, along with elder parent tending. Steve is fully enjoying his new life, had little transition anxiety, and confesses that he was "born to retire." Bob, by contrast, prior to retiring, determined only that he was going to take his comfortable pension and retire to a home in Florida. That's about as far as his vision for new life went, and his life in retirement, as you might guess, has been far less than joyful. He simply did not provide himself the transition time to let go of his old life and provide for an incubation period to a meaningful new life.

The point here is, if it is important to recreate a new life featuring self-realization, you are going to need to take full advantage of the rich soil provided by the transition gap. That involves letting go of your past life and hanging out with the discomfort of uncertainty without jumping too quickly into new situations and providing time for self-reflection. Figure 2-1 is a graphic representation of a life cycle featuring an ongoing process of making a shift from a *life structure* (a stable and well-organized period) to *transition* (a chaotic time of change and uncertainty). This model, "The Cycle of Renewal," is featured in an excellent book by Frederic M. Hudson and Pamela D. McLean titled *Life Launch: A Passionate Guide to the Rest of Your Life* (The Hudson Institute Press of Santa Barbara, Ca, 1995) (pp. 45–53).

FIGURE 2-1. THE CYCLE OF RENEWAL.

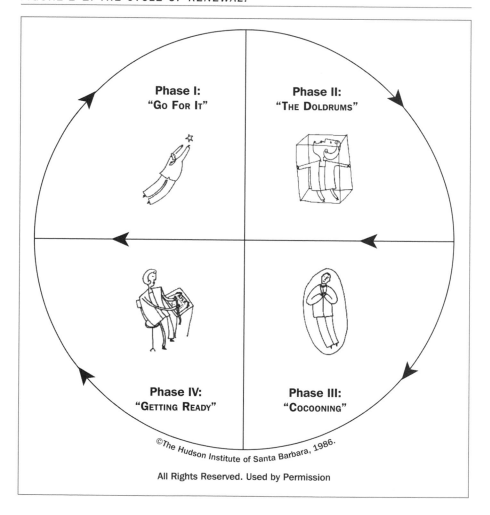

Phase I:
"GO FOR IT"

Phase II:
"THE DOLDRUMS"

Phase IV:
"GETTING READY"

Phase III:
"COCOONING"

©*The Hudson Institute of Santa Barbara, 1986.*

◆   ## A Life Story: Change, Challenge, and Transition

Hudson's model for understanding the life cycle progresses through alternating stages of order, reordering, disorder, and rejuvenation. That process, graphically depicted in Figure 2-1, in real life translates into a story such as the following. After graduating from college with a liberal arts degree, Nan applied for and was accepted into the Navy's Officer Candidate School. Becoming a naval officer seemed like an excellent way to acquire leadership experience, have some interesting new ventures, spread her wings, and see the world. She enjoyed the next four years, structured for her by the U.S. Navy. During this time she met Mr. Right, a Navy pilot, and they married. Shortly after that big life-changing event, she decided to leave the Navy and apply the educational training money acquired from her service to obtain an MBA degree. She saw this as a ticket into management, where she hoped to pursue a career in the private sector. Mr. Right, however, who loved flying and the military life, opted to pursue his career in the Navy.

After obtaining her MBA Nan landed a position with a large investment bank to launch her new career. Soon after, she found herself on the fast track of management, where she began making more money than she had ever dreamed of. There were, however, some pretty major downsides to this life. First, the job demanded a full commitment of time and energy, leaving very little of either for life outside of the firm. Second, she was now the mother of twin daughters, but because of her schedule she had to leave much of the mothering role to a nanny and to day care. Third, her marriage was unraveling, primarily because she had concentrated considerably more effort on her work than on her relationship, and also because Mr. Right's military duties engaged him on long stints away from home. Last, and not least, she had to admit to herself that while her success at work was gratifying and financially rewarding, it was not fulfilling. This work, she discovered, was not her passion.

Although all of these factors had been weighing heavily on her, the whole structure of her life came crashing down when she learned that her husband had been engaging in sexual liaisons in the numerous ports-of-call visited on his extended tours of naval duty. With that revelation, she decided the time for change had come. But what should she do? How could she change her life to be more fulfilling? For these questions, she obtained the services of a counselor, who helped her clarify her aspirations and what she wanted to do with the next chapter of her life.

What she decided was to leave both her high-pressure job and her phi-landering husband and go into teaching. She was able to parlay her management and leadership education and experience into a full-time teaching position at the local community college. But the transition as-sociated in making this change was emotionally draining. Letting go of both a marriage and the status of a high-performing corporate profes-sional was painful. On the positive side, she was excited about the idea of landing a job that seemed much closer to her heart, with the added benefit of having summers off to spend with her kids. She had been se-duced by the fast-paced lifestyle with the kinds of status and monetary rewards that the corporate world could provide. In her heart, she knew it was time to move on. But in her head she found it difficult to let go of the life structure in which she had invested so much of herself.

Time, as we know, is the great healer, and over the next few years, Nan grew into her teaching job. She took great pride in delivering mind-stimulating lectures and in helping her students, both young and mature, master the course content. She was generous with her time, spending hours individually with her students and taking an active role in college activities. This work, she found, was considerably closer to her passion than was her life as a banker. She appreciated having more time for her girls, and was enjoying a whole new circle of friends. Eventually, her sterling leadership skills became evident, and she was voted in as chair of her department. She did so well with these ad-ministrative responsibilities that she was eventually promoted to vice president for academic affairs.

In this new role, she was motivated to implement a number of educational initiatives, which included incorporating state-of-the-art information technology into the curriculum, implementing vastly ex-panded professional development programs for the faculty, providing computers for students at greatly reduced prices, and instituting edu-cational travel programs to fascinating places around the world. Her inspired leadership gained her visibility in academic circles, and she was persuaded to apply for a college presidency. She accepted the presidency of a rapidly growing community college, where she acquired a reputation for student-friendly activities, such as informal Friday af-ternoon gatherings with students around the college fountain, lunching with students in the college cafeteria, and invitations to the president's home for various campus groups.

TAKING TIME TO TRANSITION

After serving for many years in this position, Nan, then in her early sixties, began confronting inner and outer pressures to retire. Although she had become a much beloved president, the board of trustees encouraged her to retire in the interest of making way for a younger person. The board was uneasy about anyone being in the president's chair for more than a decade, and she'd been there for more than 16 years. In some ways, retirement was becoming an appealing idea. She wanted to visit more frequently with her adult children and grandchildren, to meet new people, and to travel more frequently. Retirement also offered the opportunity to do other things she had little time for, like take up tennis, assume a leadership role in a professional association and teach a leadership course. She did, however, harbor serious concerns about leaving a structured life full of meetings with important people and losing her position of power and authority. In facing the prospects of a freer but highly uncertain new life in retirement, she couldn't help but wonder if her best days might be in the past.

For help in looking at what interesting new options might be available in retirement she again elected to use the professional services of a career counselor, since that had proven so helpful in a previous transition. Her counselor discussed the transition process with her and suggested that she ease into retirement by taking some time off for self-reflection to attend to the emotional work required in letting go of her full-agenda life. Another purpose of the suggested sabbatical was to generate ideas for future possibilities and develop a vision of who and what she wanted next to do and to be. She liked this idea so much that she decided to devote a full year to self-reassessment before setting off in a new life course. Her counselor, therefore, was surprised when Nan returned after only a few weeks into her break for soul-searching, indicating that she needed immediately to decide what to do with her life and get on with it.

It turned out that the reason for Nan's suddenly felt need to quickly restructure her life came from pressures from her daughters. It seems her daughters were very uncomfortable with seeing their mom in an uncharacteristic state of indecisiveness and without a well-structured life. Also, Nan was getting several offers and feeling some pressure to take on various kinds of community, professional, and various other work activities. Although some of these sounded interesting, she was afraid of jumping too quickly into something new. On the one hand, she wanted clarity about what she wanted to do and who she

wanted to become. On the other hand, she was concerned about losing her marketability should she remain too long out of professional
circulation.

In helping Nan respond to these pressures, her counselor again re-
viewed the transition process with her and advised her to inform her
daughters that she was involved in meaningful work. It's just that this
particular kind of work was of a psychological nature, and for the time
being did not show up as structured activity in the outer world. For
support through this process, Nan established a transition team con-
sisting of a few friends and associates. This support proved extremely
helpful in a time that she was feeling disoriented, glum, and separated
from organization-based demands on her time.

Nan's days in transition were pretty emotional. At times, she was
excited about her possibilities for a new and freer lifestyle. At other
times she feared her best days were in the past and that she might
never again be in a position to make a difference and enjoy the lime-
light of leadership. In coping with the uncertainties of the transition
process, Nan found it helpful to take long walks down quiet country
lanes, both for exercise and to contemplate her interests and options.
She used her transition team to prod her with tough and thought-
provoking questions, provide her with feedback to the questions she
was confronting, and suggest options to explore and people with
whom to talk.

After several months of wandering in the gap stage of transition, an
appealing vision for her future began taking shape. Although she had seriously entertained the idea of establishing a consulting practice, she decided that it was time for something very different from her past life. She
had always been interested in art history, so she decided to enroll in some
courses at the local Academy of Arts. She also volunteered as a docent
at the municipal art gallery, where she could apply her newly acquired
knowledge. Additionally, she took up watercolor painting, and found she
had a real talent for this artistic endeavor. For fitness, she took up yoga
and joined a local tennis club, where she has become very competitive
with a mean serve and a slashing backhand. She enjoys time with her
daughters and grandchildren, though she has made it clear that she is
not a built-in baby sitter. She has established a new circle of friends with
whom she enjoys traveling and enjoying the many social and cultural activities of the community.

There were two areas, however, not being fulfilled in her new life.
The first was that Nan, a gifted leader, felt a yearning to again exercise

this aspect of her nature. After exploring a number of ways she might pursue this, including entertaining offers for board memberships of various organizations and a city council position, she eventually took on the role of spokesperson for the local chapter of Special Olympics. Second, she wanted to have some quality time with her grandchildren and to provide them with a legacy with which to remember her. For this, she elected to take each one on an extensive travel adventure as they become old enough to appreciate such a venture with grandma.

TRANSITIONS BIG AND SMALL

Nan's story is really a composite of a number of actual people with whom I am well acquainted. I have selected portions from these stories to highlight key aspect of transition management. Although few people become college presidents, Nan's story is typical of the life changes and transitions that most of us experience over the course of our life's journey. Some of us relish change and gravitate to it, some of us deal with it if we must, and some of us just dig our heels in and resist. Then there are those passive change avoiders who end up like leaves blowing in the shifting winds of time. There are those who look backward at life, idealizing the past, and those with a forward-looking vision for what is possible.

Nan experienced most of those stages at various times in her life's journey. In her early years, she tended to see change as an adventure, something to jump into like a youthful leap off the poolside highboard. Entering officer candidate training and being commissioned a naval officer is a case in point. Once established in a work situation, however, youthful spontaneity tends to give way to the structure imposed by the employing agency. Nan's life, after becoming a Naval officer, was structured for her by the U.S. Navy. Leaving the Navy involved life change but it was an easy transition, due in large measure because she initiated it with forethought, vision, and preparation. Knowing where you are heading makes leaving where you have been an easier proposition, though it does eliminate some of the adventure associated with journeying into uncertainty. Jumping too quickly from one structure to the next means missing the inner gold that many come to discover in transition. Had Nan taken more time for reflection and exploration, she might have realized that corporate life was not going to be a good fit. But, at that point she was young and full of preconceived notions of what the "good life" looked like.

Transitions and Mini-Deaths

In his book *The Way of Transition*, William Bridges discusses two kinds of transitions. The first, which he refers to as a reaction transition, involves dealing with a change over which we have no control, such as loss of a job or death of a loved one. The second type is a developmental transition, which involves gradually coming to the realization that one is no longer the person they were and that the luster has gone from what once had been engaging.

Nan was in the process of a developmental transition in her role as a corporate executive in coming to the realization that this work, although gratifying her desire for challenge and income, simply was not fulfilling her as a person. She might well have made a career shift over time in any circumstance, but the revelation of her husband's philandering changed the picture suddenly. Now she was dealing with a reaction transition on top of a developmental one—a double whammy. Her identity as a loving wife, a caring mother, and successful corporate executive were now called into question. She was suddenly thrust into a major life crisis. She needed to grieve her loss and then move on to recreate a new sense of purpose and identity. In these kinds of situations, time is the healer of a broken heart. But time alone may not necessarily provide a desirable transition outcome. Realizing this, Nan sought professional counseling for help in recreating a new, more satisfying professional life and rebuilding her self-esteem.

Reacting to any major change in what has been an important life structure can be emotionally consuming, all the more so if the change event occurs suddenly and surprisingly. Painful as the transition might be, however, it can provide a rich opportunity for self-realization and creative life-reinvention. For that to happen, however, one must be willing to first allow the *loss process* to fully sink in and grieve for what is gone. This stage of the transition can seem like a mini-death, for we are mourning a part of our life now gone forever. It is only through the grieving process that we can move psychologically to a place where, with an open mind and a willingness to address unknown possibilities, we can achieve self-realization and life rejuvenation. In Nan's case, she used this time to let go of her concepts about who she was, to wonder in uncertainty for a period of time, and then to decide what next to do with her life. From this dark period she went on to choose a new direction in her career, one that originated out of a deeper awareness of who she was and what was needed for a more fulfilling life. In the years following this transition, Nan felt continually grateful that she had used this painful experience to get to a better place in life and career. Why is it that it so often takes a painful episode to break us out of an unfulfilling life structure into one that is more satisfying?

CONFRONTING OUR AGING SELVES

In preparing for the big life event we have labeled retirement, one often has to deal with the combined weight of both a reaction and a developmental transition. At some point in the fifty-plus years we have to confront the reality that we are no longer the person we have been—we become senior citizens! A look in the mirror one day may provide the surprising reaction that your looks have changed—where did the gray hair and the wrinkles come from?

The age factor also may hit home in other ways when, after doing yard work all day, we realize aches and pains that we never before noticed. My wife, who at the time of this writing just turned 61, just came back with a new passport picture, which she was comparing to the one she had taken 10 years earlier. Her reaction was, "My god. Look at this: I've become an old lady!" Although these changes have been slow, gradual, and even predictable, they nonetheless can send us into a transitional tailspin as we confront the loss of youth and the onset of old age. Oh sure, we can attempt denying that, as most of us do, at least for a while. Eventually, however, our aging catches up to us and we come to realize that we are entering the final chapters of life. It is then that we have to confront the realization that death is a reality rather than an abstract concept, as most of us tend to have perceived it in our younger days. On top of this, we must now retire and recreate a new life and a new sense of purpose. Beyond that, we need to find a new identify, one that does not define us primarily by our work or our organizational title.

Nan, as she faced the retirement inevitability, had to confront both a reactionary and a developmental transition. The time had arrived for her to retire. For the most part, she felt ready for that, but with some reservations. Developmentally, she realized the time had come to create a new life chapter, but there was much about her professional life she found hard to leave. Once you have left such a position, you can't return. A leap off the diving board can't be reversed. Nan was hurt that the board of trustees was strongly encouraging her to retire. After all, she had worked hard for the college and established herself in a venerable light with students, faculty, and the community. But there is a time for all seasons, and autumn had arrived. She still had a lot to offer, much she wanted to do, and a new life she wanted to create. She was satisfied with the work she'd done and who she'd been. But time caught up with her, and that required self-reinventing.

It is important to assess, when one begins to feel stagnated, whether it's time for a mini-transition or a major life change. These decisions can be difficult during the course of one's career and become all the more so when one comes to the big life change called retirement. They are difficult because one must continually manage two worlds. The first is the inner world of self, where we dream, feel, perceive, and learn. The second is the outer world in which we live, work, and park our cars. For self-realization, we need to know who we are from the perspective of talent, personal values, and deep-seated interested. Finding the fit, the place to best apply this self-knowledge, means knowing what options are available. With the combination of self-knowledge and identifying those possibilities in life, work, learning, and leisure, we are in a position to set course on a satisfying and fulfilling journey of self-realization. That is the challenge that Nan faced—and that we all confront—in creating a meaningful retirement.

◆ Life Change and Transition Readiness

For whatever reason, some of us need change and seek it out, while others hate and avoid it. But love or hate it, change is inevitable: Even after ruling the planet for millions of years, the dinosaurs finally succumbed. Sometimes change comes quickly in big surprise packages, such as a debilitating accident. At other times it comes imperceptibly slow, such as with the aging process. For the slow, unavoidable changes in life, such as the transition of our children from infancy to autonomous adults, there is not much to do but watch the process in awe. When a big change happens suddenly, we must deal with it by grieving the loss, allowing ourselves adjustment time, and then moving actively to recreate a new life.

Retirement is one of those big, life-changing events. Most of the clients I have worked with over the years looked forward with anticipation to the new freedom retirement offers. However, many have unsettling feelings about entering this new territory, citing concerns about retirement being a prelude to early death. Such concerns certainly can generate a degree of caution about leaping into retirement—or even easing into it, for that matter.

The following survey can help you assess how ready you are for undertaking a major life change and how stressful the transition might be. The assessment consists of conditions and perspectives that can cause one to view change with anticipation or trepidation. Assess where you fall on the spectrum of change, from being averse at one end to change predisposed at the other.

Assessing Your Transition Readiness: Change Aversion vs. Attraction

Directions

1. In each of the following questions, determine which statement above the dotted line best fits you, and then circle the point number below the line that corresponds to your assessment. For example, in question 1, if you have been in a stable work situation for 16 years you would circle the number 5 below the line corresponding to the entry for 15–20 years.

2. When you have completed all 10 items, record your total for all the points you have circled in the box provided at the end of the survey.

---

1. Until the present, about how years have you been in a stable work situation?

>35	30–35	25–30	20–25	15–20	10–15	5–10	2–5	1–2	<1
Points: 1	2	3	4	5	6	7	8	9	10

2. How supportive of change is the primary relationship in your life?

Totally unsupportive			Moderately supportive				Totally supportive		
Points: 1	2	3	4	5	6	7	8	9	10

3. How kindly do you take to making big changes in your life?

Hate it		Not crazy about it		Can deal with it			No problem		Love it
Points: 1	2	3	4	5	6	7	8	9	10

4. How optimistic are you about your future?

Very pessimistic			Somewhat optimistic				Very optimistic		
Points: 1	2	3	4	5	6	7	8	9	10

5. How would you describe your memories of past changes in your life?

Dreadful		Pretty bad		OK			Pleasant		Joyful
Points: 1	2	3	4	5	6	7	8	9	10

6. How much choice do you have over the life change situation you are facing?

None		Little		Some		Considerable			Total
Points: 1	2	3	4	5	6	7	8	9	10

7. How much of your sense of self-worth and personal esteem are wrapped up in your professional identity and/or your organizational position?

All of it		A great deal		Significant portion			Little		None
Points: 1	2	3	4	5	6	7	8	9	10

8. How big do you consider the upcoming change in your life to be?

Complete life change			Moderate			Minimal life change			
Points: 1	2	3	4	5	6	7	8	9	10

9. How much thought, exploration, and planning have you or will you devote to preparing for all aspects (lifestyle as well as financial) of your new life?

None		Very Little		Some		Considerable		A great deal	
Points: 1	2	3	4	5	6	7	8	9	10

10. How much control over your future do you feel that you can realistically exercise?

None		Very Little		Some		Considerable		A great deal	
Points: 1	2	3	4	5	6	7	8	9	10

Total points for all 10 items: _____

Assessing Your Results

If your score totaled 75 to 100 points, you appear ready for and well positioned psychologically and supportively to effectively manage transition stress and capitalize on any life-change situations you may be facing.

If your score totaled 50 to 75 points, you appear to be moderately well positioned psychologically and supportively to manage any life-change situation you may now be facing. There may be some things you can do, however, to better manage transition stress and improve your chances for a successful outcome to any major life change situation you will be facing. Look over the following list of "Guidelines for Managing the Stresses Associated with Life Transitions" for clues of what you might do.

If your point total was under 50, you may be facing a difficult time emotionally in managing the stresses associated with any life-changing transition. If possible you may want to postpone the transition until you can get support and better prepare for the transition. Review the following guidelines for ideas on how you might improve you transition management skills.

Guidelines for Managing the Stresses Associated with Life Change and Transition

• *Use the life chapter concept.* Think of your life as a series of chapters in a book, with past chapters representing your personal history and future chapters as blank pages upon which your story will be recorded. You are more likely to achieve passion in your daily living and invent some exciting new themes to your book of life if you exercise creative authorship over your future chapters rather than being a passive observer of your life. Think of the next chapter of your life as a five-year story awaiting your narrative composition. Create that chapter from the perspective of in-depth self-knowledge, well-seasoned experience, expanded innovativeness, and fuller awareness than you ever before were capable of exercising. A cautionary note may be in order here: it's worth bearing in mind that perfection in the creation of your story is neither likely nor necessary. After all, you can edit and revise your story as it unfolds in everyday experience. In this, you want to author interesting narrative-theme development based on creativity steeped in self-knowledge, rather than to lay out an inflexible blueprint for your future.

• *Create an appealing vision for the next chapter of your life.* Vision provides energy-generating power. A compelling vision energizes the human system and provides a navigational map for achieving your full potential. When the times call for reinventing your future, the lack of a coherent vision handicaps the likelihood of becoming your best. And worse, the lack of an engaging vision for you future may keep you frozen in memories of the past and anxieties about your future. At the World Bank, people talk about the ghosts who walk the halls. These are actual people who retired years ago but continue attempting to relive the good old days with whomever they can capture to reminisce about the past. Chapter 3, on vision generating, is designed to help you achieve an energizing mental image for your future.

• *Maintain an active physical exercise program.* Physical exercise serves as a magic pill for health and vitality. Exercise is especially beneficial, however, when dealing with stress or anxiety accompanying a major life transition. The endorphin release that comes through exercise lasts longer and is far more beneficial than that obtained from devouring a box of chocolates or the alcoholic spirits of your choice. The problem is that when we are undergoing a period of stress and uncertainty we are more likely to reach for the chocolates or the chardonnay than to strap on the walking shoes or hit the treadmill. A good antidote to this transition languor is a well-structured exercise regime. Decide what you are going to do, set a schedule for doing it, and then do it—rain, shine, or ennui. If you already have a physical exercise regime, stick to it religiously in times of stress and uncertainty. If you are new to the exercise business, now is a good time to join a gym and get some coaching for establishing a regular workout program. Something as simple as a 30-minute brisk walk every other day can be a life-enhancing and stress-reducing tonic. So be well, and we shall look for you in the workout room.

  • *Create a support team.* There is a tendency with most of us, especially the self-contained types, to go it alone. When things get tough, the tough get going, right? Well, the "tough," the wussies, the nerds, the shy wallflowers, and even the genteel sophisticates would do well to bear in mind that going it alone in times of stress can be downright stupid; here's why. When people are operating under conditions of stress or anxiety, their intellectual systems are overpowered by emotion, and impulse tends to replace constructive thinking. It's common knowledge that two heads are better than one. This is especially true when stress associated with a major life change undermines one's thinking. In the interest of taking fuller advantage of the new freedoms and the opportunities for self-realization, consider creating your personal transition support team.

SUGGESTIONS FOR CREATING A TRANSITION SUPPORT TEAM

Who should be on this support team? First and foremost, you will want someone who is an excellent listener and thoughtful feedback provider. Stay away from advice givers, no matter how well intentioned they might be. The suggestions of advice givers are likely to be more appropriate to them than actually helpful to your unique situation. Furthermore, they are going to feel disappointed if you don't take their well-intentioned advice. Identify a main person for your transition team and make a point of having regular conversations with him or her. If you don't know someone who can fill this bill, hire yourself a good coach. For the best results, get three or four people in your support network to provide broad perspectives and to keep from overburdening any one person. A supportive spouse or partner can be helpful, but bear in mind that what you do and how you change is going to have an impact, probably major, on his or her life. For this reason, not all partners are going to be excited or highly supportive of your prospects of a major life change. So, even if your spouse is excited, supportive, and helpful, get some other good-thinking, nurturing souls on your transition team. Also, on your transition support team consider including a financial planner, a couple of joyfully retired folks, a supportively creative idea person, a career counselor and/or personal coach, and a humorist (levity is good anytime, especially when you want to energize your creative brain and need a diversion from stress-induced gravity).

• *Give yourself incubation time.* Clients often tell me they feel pressured to take the first thing that comes along, particularly if it involves a work-related opportunity, a new relationship, or a move to a new location. They are under the impression that they had better jump on this opportunity out of fear that this may be their best and/or last option. The problem with the first on-the-radar-screen option is that this is unlikely to be one's best opportunity. I encourage clients to take the time to define their criteria for success as the basis for knowing what to look for. It's difficult to achieve self-realization without having some basis for determining what it is that is going to provide you with a feeling of happiness. More about this later, but for now, please keep in mind that taking full advantage of the freedom offered by retirement requires both self-knowledge and a broad range of good choices. Investing in incubation time for deepening self-knowledge and expanding choice options increases your chances of achieving self-fulfillment from less that 50–50 to upwards of 100 percent.

• *Exercise your choice-making power.* It's in making choices, especially good choices, where we experience a sense of autonomy and personal power. The problem in major life transition situations is that many of us go through a necessary period of uncertainty, which renders decision-making difficult, possibly even unwise for reasons discussed later. So, how do you maintain a sense of empowerment, while in the transitional gap between the ending of one structure and the beginning of the next? First off, you don't want to make any big life choices before investing in some research, self-reflection, and option exploration. But this involves the big things in life, which still leaves hundreds of lesser choices to be made. We're talking about small everyday choices here, like what are my priorities today, and what do I elect to put on my daily activities list? If, for example, you need to get new tires on the car, decide when you are going to do that and then follow through. If it is time to call your sister in Connecticut, decide when you will do it and then do it. If it would be fun to spend a day with your granddaughter, decide—well, you get the picture. There are thousands of small decision situations available everyday, some that must be made, such as paying the water bill, some that might be fun (like taking a walk in the woods), and some that would be beneficial (like arranging to identify and explore work or volunteer possibilities with agencies of interest). Effectively and assertively managing the small things in your life can give you the sense of being in management control of at least some aspects of your life during a time of unsettling uncertainty. Exercising such control can help you feel a bit less adrift, powerless, and possibly even less disoriented.

• *Plan together if you are in a committed relationship.* Life choice decision making can be easier for those making their plans as an individual than it is for those in love relationships. It's pretty obvious that the life-changing choices you make now as an individual are going to determine the course of your future. It's also true that your choices will impact your spouse/partner, for good or not. For this reason, it is important to reflect, research, explore options, and make decisions jointly. The reason for team planning is pretty vivid in my memory, having to do with an example from my parents—my father, specifically—of how *not* to go about life-change planning. My father had created and managed a successful business throughout his adult life. The problem was that his work kept him so busy he had precious little time for fun, leisure, or family life. He was pretty much 24/7 work-preoccupied. That left my mother, a stay-at-home housewife, a kind of work-widow. When my father was in his mid-sixties, he sold the business, and my mother thought, finally—now we can do together the things we had dreamed. She was thinking of things like travel, visiting family, taking in an occasional movie, and even spending quiet times together at home, unencumbered by Dad's preoccupying worry about work. Her hopes for the future were not to be, however, as my father—without consulting her—transferred his work preoccupation into a professional association and a part-time business he started with his brother. It somehow didn't occur to Dad to engage his wife in retirement planning as an equal partner. The result was predictable. She felt disenfranchised and angry. So, if you are in a committed relationship—one that you want to be mutually happy and fulfilling—plan together. In doing so, be sure to take into consideration the values, hopes, and aspirations of you and your loved one.

• *Understand the transition process.* It can be reassuring to know what to expect psychologically in adjusting to a changed state of being that comes with making a major life change. Many of my clients have found the Transition Roadmap, described previously, to be a helpful reference in dealing with psychological adjustments associated with accommodating to any big change in life. You might want to bookmark that page as a reference when reacting to the discomfort of transition disorientation. Remember, the movement arrow in the "Cycle of Renewal" points from ending, through transition gap, to new beginning. You may have days filled with high energy that comes with thoughts of new freedoms and possibilities followed by days of doubts and uncertainty. That is a normal part of transition. It's all a part of the letting go, rediscovery, and reinvention process of life transition.

◆ Change, Transition, and Heaven

The fifty-plus years are a time filled with change and transitions for everyone, whether we are married and have kids, are single, or engage in alternative lifestyles. It's usually in our fifties that those of us who are parents lose our children to adulthood and become grandparents, a process both wonderful and nostalgic. When our kids abandon the nest in favor of adulthood, a significant life change ensues, whether welcomed or not. It is a predictable change and one for which we should have been preparing. But kids or not, married or not, few of us escape those life-changing events that require transition adjustments. We have all weathered life-changing events, such as lost loves, death of parents or a loved one, serious health challenges, losing your job, or paradigm shifts such as 9/11, Hurricane Katrina, or the technology revolution.

At some point most of us are faced with another adjustment—our parents becoming elderly and less self-reliant. And, we must adjust to the reality that they will not be with us forever. Their passing leaves us now as the clan elders—facing our own aging process and the unescapable eventuality of our own passing. Incidentally, I happen to like the word *passing* rather than death. It to me implies a transition to another realm. *Death,* by contrast, seems to speak of end and finality. This may be a mute point in the physical realm, but psychologically I feel it's important. Certainly the end is the final chapter to an embodied reality in this little life of mine. I prefer, however, to think that beyond this existence there is another dimension. Certainly most religions speak to an afterlife and unembodied existence, even if some "hard" scientist can't accept such an assertion. But then "hard" scientists have a difficult time accepting anything that can't be put under a microscope or observed through the orbiting Hubble space telescope, which at the time of this writing has not yet sighted Heaven.

I believe that it is important to come to terms with the ending of our lives in order to develop a philosophy for living our time remaining unencumbered by a debilitating anxiety of death, and "the end." In this regard, I often think of my dear friend, Dr. Faith Clark, a wonderfully vibrant woman, role model, and spiritual guide. Faith had Marfan's disease, a fatal and incurable softening of the artery walls. In confiding this heart-rending news to me one day, she related that because she never knew which day, or minute for that matter, was going to be her last, that she lived every day full-out, as if this were to be her last. Shortly after revealing this shocking news to me, Faith passed on. She spent her last day here delivering a seminar on a mind-expanding, whole-brain learning process that she had spent her short life researching and successfully applying to both children and adults. She passed on just as she was finishing the seminar for a business group extremely interested in her work. She had just enough time before passing on to advise her husband that she was going to be leaving.

Her husband, also a Ph.D. psychologist and a personal friend, shared with me a few days after her passing an amazing incident. He said that later in the evening that Faith had passed on, he was sitting on the edge of his bed grieving and thinking he didn't want to go on without his beloved, when a very strange thing happened. He was jolted off the bed with a sharp kick to the rear. Shocked, he looked to see who had kicked him. But, there was no one there, at least visibly. He realized then, he said, that this was a loving kick from his wife, who, communicating rather forcefully, was insisting that he get off his butt and to get on with his life. Painful as that seemed to him, that is what he decided to do. Prompted by that "kick," he has committed to living his life in joy, as Faith had always done, knowing that she remained with him in continuation of her gift of love.

Between the metamorphosis of our children into adults and our own passing on, however, there are many other changes and transitions to experience. Among these are changes both within and without. The outer changes include transitioning from the full-time occupations that have kept us so fully engaged and structured for all of our adult lives. As we retire, we are forced to confront and deal with multiple considerations and changing realities. Some find the shift from organizational life to be extraordinarily painful, while others have been looking forward to it with great anticipation. One of my clients, for example, was a 62-year-old economist who had spent his whole career at the World Bank and now was being forced into retirement. Money would be no problem for his post-organizational life. His pension would provide very amply for that. The major problem for him was what to do with his life now that his World Bank career was over. This was a change of both outer and inner consequence. It was an identity issue, and a major change in the routine of daily life to which he had long grown accustomed. He knew who he was as a senior economist at the World Bank, but not who he would become and what he would do in post-Bank life. He was going to have to create a whole new life for himself, but before he could do that, he was confronting the emotional aspects of a major life transition. Adjusting to retirement is most stressful for those of us who have been so totally committed to our work and to our work identifies that we stayed too busy to prepare for retirement.

◆ Changing Selves—Changing Identities

Another transition that we fifty-plussers have to deal with is one of a much subtler nature than creating post-organizational lives for ourselves. Because of the ingrained nature of the socialization process and the expectations of our culture we tend to overidentify and adapt to sex-role stereotypes throughout our adult life—that is, until sometime into our fifty-plus years. On the one hand, for men of my generation, being a "man" looked something like the personification of John Wayne. That meant valuing toughness (men don't cry), mincing few words, doing my job, and helping out the "little lady" (whether she wanted our big manly help or not). Women, on the other hand, were expected to be soft, gentle, kind, and loving (as well as pretty, sexy, devoted, and subservient). Women of my generation were supposed to be Barbara Billingsley's June Cleaver of *Leave it to Beaver*.

The sex roles we take on become a part of who we think we are, a part of our identity, and even unspoken agreements in how we relate to each other. This is especially so in marriage. What happens to our sense of self in the fifty-plus years when men begin to experience their softer sides and women their harder sides? How do we accommodate the changes in our own identity and how does one deal with a relationship in which their loved one is changing to become a different person? If we can't adjust to these changes in our selves and our partners there are consequences. One either has to give up on growth and development for the sake of the partner's ego, or perhaps leave a confining relationship that is inflexible to change. That may be why many fifty-plussers desperately resist change in the futile attempt to maintain a static existence.

THE GOOD NEWS IN SENIORHOOD

Change happens—like it or not, resist it or not. For those of us who are change anxious or change avoidant, we need to get creative in our thinking and expansive in our perspectives about aging (we have to age, we don't have to get "old"). Although there is no sense denying that aging comes with some downsides, it is validating to realize that there is also an upside. Forget the face lifts and the tummy tucks. Face it, you are going to age, and that means looking older. Too many facelifts and you are apt to take on the look of a beanbag that's pulled too tightly. Isn't it about time we begin seeing the beauty in the face and body of well-seasoned individuals who have acquired some experience in their features? Would you rather look like a department store mannequin or a uniquely evolved individual?

Why do we value aging in wine and disdain it in the wine drinker? A better option for addressing aging gracefully is to envision and capitalize on the growth opportunities in aging, while accommodating to what's in a natural state of decline. The following table highlights some of the potentials for growth in the fifty-plus years, in contrast to what is in decline.

Growth Potentials and Losses of the Senior Years

Growth Potentials for the Senior Years	Unavoidable Losses in the Senior Years
Spirituality	Youthful looks
Creativity	Throbbing loins
Self-fulfillment	Loss through death of family and friends
Transcendent love	Physical endurance
Love of learning	Naïvete
Wisdom	Dependency relationships with kids
Integrity	The values of youth and young adulthood
Humanity	Work-dependent relationships
Generativity (planting trees you won't see to mature growth)	A view of the future as an endless path ahead
Appreciation of beauty	Aspirations and dreams of our youth
Gratitude	Career ambitions

Humor	Life structured around necessities of a job
Expanded ability for forgiveness	Belief that we are invulnerable
Awe of creation	A semi-conscious perception that life goes on forever

One of the potential areas for growth in our later years is in the opportunity for becoming a soul mate and/or a nurturing presence to your loved ones, whether you are married, single, divorced, or widowed. We can change and grow, experiencing an expanding sense of self and providing nurturing support to our mates, partners, family, friends, and or fellow travelers. It is in the fifty-plus years that we have the greatest potential for achieving soul-expanding growth and to release and realize our full potential. But that requires leaving behind old expectations and old roles that have become too limiting.

In this regard, I recall a female client I was helping to find a new and more satisfying career direction. At that time, she was in her late forties and had been a very successful executive secretary. But, she had always thought that there was more that she wanted to do in her working life. Through the course of the counseling process, it became clear that she really wanted to finish her college degree and move into a management role. The problem was that her husband, a recently retired senior Air Force officer, had very different ideas for her—to quit her work to devote herself full time to him, their home, and traveling. She came to my office one day feeling pulled apart by her career desire on the one hand and her husband's pressure on the other. In responding to her dilemma, I asked her to envision her life several years out if she were to follow her passion versus her husband's wishes. It was clear to her that the path of growth was in career. But she did not want to lose her husband. I asked her what would be the likely consequences if she followed her husband's path for her, what that might mean for her, for him, and for their relationship. She realized that in going down that path, she was likely to end up an angry and unfilled woman, and that would not bode well for their relationship.

The outcome of this story is that she elected to follow her career ambition. She came by to visit me several years later to inform me that she had gotten her college degree and was now a manager in a health-care-oriented firm. She was thrilled about the change in her life and career, was feeling great about herself, and was fulfilled in doing good work. I asked her how her husband had dealt with this.

She said, "He is extremely proud of me and has become my biggest supporter."

What might becoming a soul mate and/or a nurturing presence look like for you? What will you be letting go of, and what might lie on the other side of your next life-changing, life-evolving transition?

IMAGINATION AND THE NEXT
SEASON OF YOUR LIFE

"I intend to create a studio for teaching ballroom dancing and hope to train dance teams to compete in the Olympics."

—A 54-YEAR-OLD WOMAN TAKING AN EARLY RETIREMENT
FROM A CORPORATE ADMINISTRATIVE POSITION

"After retiring I obtained a pilot license and purchased my own plane. Now I am a bush pilot having a ball flying in medical supplies to remote areas and flying people in need of medical assistance out to health care facilities."

—A 62-YEAR-OLD RETIRED CORPORATE EXECUTIVE

"I don't ever plan to retire. After all, I'm a seasoned professional operating at the top of my game. I'm just not going to work full time for any one organization ever again."

—A RECENTLY RETIRED SIXTY-PLUS MALE FINANCE ADVISOR

◆ Visions and Vineyards

As I write this, my wife and I are flying back to our Potomac River retreat in wild and wonderful West Virginia after visiting our daughter and her family in Southern California. They moved there, way across the country (without our permission, mind you) to enjoy year-round sun and warmth. While visiting with them, we toured the Callaway winery, where we learned that Mr. Callaway, back in the 1960s when he was CEO of Burlington Industries, also visited this area. While there, he had a vision. He pictured himself at this location as a vineyard owner at an age considered to be the retirement years. At the time of his visit, the area was little more than scrub-brush-covered sand hills. Mr. Callaway, however, was able to see in this forlorn spot not just what was, but what could be. Over the years, his vision evolved into a picturesque scene with rolling acres of grapes and a vineyard that converts those juicy orbs into enjoyable wines.

Few of us have the financial resources of a Callaway. You might be thinking—well, if I had that kind of money, I might also be inclined to buy a vineyard or pursue some other whim that only the rich can afford. Before dismissing this as a fanciful dream, consider this: Where does wealth really reside? Is it in the pocketbook, inheritance, or plain old good luck? If wealth was the key ingredient to achieving one's dreams, how does one account for the many stories of people who come into great wealth but whose happiness is not measurably enriched? Or, by contrast, how is it that so many with nothing more than a big idea have transformed their ideas into successful new ventures? Ideas capable of recreating a new and interesting new lifestyle are not restricted to the wealthy. Colonel Sanders, for example, had little money but big ideas for translating a tasty chicken recipe into a rather profitable business venture that became Kentucky Fried Chicken.

Within each of us resides a vast wellspring of imaginative power for generating ideas and vision. Mr. Callaway may have had deep pockets, but without the power of imagination he would have been poor in other ways. There is power in imagination. That is the source from which a creative vision for your future is likely to occur, rather than from the cookbook lifestyle options promised by the marketers of the "idyllic retirement community." Being freed up from the structure of full-time employment just might be your best chance ever to more fully realize the self you are capable of becoming and to create a life that will keep you young at heart into your nineties.

What do you want to do and who do you want to be at age 70, 80, or 90? Do you prefer to let your future happen by default or be dictated by the outmoded stereotypes about aging or the promises of retirement community promoters? Or might you rather initiate actions that would enable your unique talents and interests to flourish? The decisions of today determine who you will be and what you will be doing tomorrow. Not making a decision is, in essence, a choice to place your future in the hands of happenstance. Making a decision that fails to allow you to realize your full potential is a choice to play small in life.

An old bumper sticker says, "He who dies with the most toys wins." Although there may be humor in that adage, there is little veracity in it. I suggest, instead, this as a more fitting motto: Those who die self-realized in joy win. Admittedly, the latter lacks the wit of the former, but it is a motto promising greater likelihood of fulfillment, and most likely a longer and healthier life. You can decide whether you want your motto for life at fifty-plus to be humorous or revitalizing.

◆ Visions Realized and Unrealized

Jay had been a U.S. Naval officer achieving the senior rank of a full Navy captain who commanded ships of war. I met him at a creative problem-solving workshop about the time we were both turning 50. What immediately impressed me about Jay was his creativity and what he was doing/being with his life after leaving the Navy. His vision for this chapter of his life was multifaceted, one component of which was to develop his musical yearnings and another was to turn kids onto classical music. Jay brought his cello to the workshop and would lead us in a songfest over cocktails as we gathered on a deck with a mountain view of star-studded skies. On one of these evenings—spurred on, no doubt, by a couple of glasses of Chardonnay—Jay confided that he had come to realize a natural gift for the cello. He'd become accomplished with that instrument, even though he had only seriously taken it up after retiring. He also shared his recently discovered passion for music with others by leading a children's orchestra at the Kennedy Center in Washington, D.C.

Jay was clearly energized by what he was doing. It showed in the sparkle of his eyes, the sprightliness in his walk, and the vibrancy of his communications. Somehow he had been able to discover nuances of who he was and what kind of life he wanted. His willingness to be innovative in translating a passion for music into a new vision for his life enabled him to create a lifestyle radically different from his former life as a naval officer. I asked Jay how he had been able to operate so successfully in the Navy when he was clearly such a creative, musical, and self-expressive individual. These traits, as you might well imagine, were not highly valued by the military culture. With a wry grin, Jay shared that he'd been a closet creative during his naval career—but upon retiring, he knew the time had come to take the wraps off this aspect of his nature.

Has the time arrived for you to free up something stored away in the inner realm of your potential and interests? Maybe it's something that's been in a dark closet for so long that you have forgotten it was there. Or maybe there is something you haven't yet fully realized. Might this be the time to open the door on your closeted self to see what the light of retirement lifestyle might reveal?

In contrast to Jay, my old friend Terry had a dream that went un-realized. In exploring his options for an interesting post-military career as a Marine officer, Terry became intrigued with the idea of becoming a high-school guidance counselor. He was a charismatic leader with an incredible gift for relating to his men—inspiring them to perform at levels beyond anything they had previously experienced in life. As a Marine officer, he had generated such a sense of trust and affection in his men that they would do just about anything for him. In fact, he owes his life to his extraordinary ability to establish respect and rapport with others through his inspiring leadership. While serving as a field commander in Vietnam, his troops had come under heavy fire and Terry was seriously wounded and lying in an exposed area. Seeing his precarious situation, one of his troops unhesitatingly jumped on him, taking fire that killed him but saved Terry's life.

Following months of recuperation back in the States, Terry had an idea as to how his splendid gifts might contribute to the lives of kids. Unfortunately for him and the potential benefactors of his gifts, he failed to pursue his vision. Instead, he allowed his vision to languish in the misperception that he was too old to get a master's degree required to start a new career as a guidance counselor. He withdrew into a kind of semi-hibernation, making furniture for his home and family.

I don't mean to imply that there is anything wrong with that. In fact, he turned out to be a fine craftsman. The problem is that this was a secondary interest, as opposed to a primary passion. I have met in-dividuals whose primary passion was in woodworking and who thrived when they pursued this dream. It's just that Terry had an uncanny gift for inspiring others to perform at a level greater than anything they had previously experienced. When he was doing this, he was in his element. He could do many things well. But, in doing these other things, he was like a high-powered automobile operating in lower gear.

Terry's gift of charismatic leadership and his vision to become a counselor never happened. In retrospect, I wish I had taken a more as-sertive role in coaching Terry in the direction of his unique gifts. I would rather have seen him go for it and fail than not to even give it his best shot. I can't help but think that Terry let false assumptions prevent him from realizing his full potential. Even worse is the loss to the hundreds of kids who might have benefited from the gifts of his charisma and powerful leadership abilities.

Fears, unfounded assumptions, and outdated social and cultural stereotypes can be killers of dreams and inspired visions. These are bad germs that infect many, preventing their special gifts, both recognized and those unrecognized, from blossoming. There is an antidote, however, for these bad germs, and you don't even need a prescription. This is a case where self-medication is advisable. The prescription is to apply a liberal dose of self-realizing imagination to your aspirations for the future. If you need help in bringing out these ideas, talk with others about your dreams. Just be sure that you do so with creative and supportive people who are comfortable in out-of-the-box thinking and are unafraid to be imaginative.

◆ Ultimate Questions at Fifty-Plus

- *Why am I here?*
- *How much time do I have remaining?*
- *How fulfilling is my life currently, and will it be fulfilling in my advancing years?*
- *What's next?*
- *Is there something beyond this life?*
- *What happens to my loved ones when I'm gone?*
- *How might I recreate my life to be more meaningful?*

Have you found yourself pondering questions such as these? If so, welcome to life in the fifty-plus years. This is just a sample of the concerns typical of these years. If you have never experienced any of these kinds of troubling questions, you probably either have yet to enter the later half of life or have arrived but avoided confronting such apprehensions, at least so far. Or maybe it's not inner dialog but visual imagery that has awakened you to a new stage of life. Were you, for example, startled one day to see an older person in your mirror? Perhaps this reflection was followed by a realization that you are not the face you used to be but also not the person you once were. At some point for all but the most hardened avoiders, death becomes a personal reality rather than an interesting abstraction. No matter how realization strikes, creeping or crashing, we all sooner or later come to confront the certainty of death and what to do with the precious time we have remaining.

How do we effectively grapple with troubling questions about our mortality and quality of life issues? Do we dismiss them as too abstract or fearsome to confront and go foraging instead at the mall or grab a beer and watch another sports event on the tube? Or do we get a facelift and change the date on our birth certificate? Diversionary efforts may take our minds off from the reality of aging and its ultimate consequence, but only temporarily. We are far more likely to create a fulfilling new future through honest, soul-searching self-reflection than through denial or avoidance techniques.

There are good reasons for wrestling with the questions about life meaning in our senior years. One of these is that our aging is never going to reverse, fade away, or even slow down, for that matter. Like the river of no return, aging just rolls on relentlessly, even seeming to speed up in the currents of advancing years. A second reason for addressing questions about ultimate life meaning is that they are answerable. In fact, I have observed that renewal does occur to those willing to do the inner work involved in life review and clarifying one's personal aspirations. Finding meaningful answers to these "big" questions is, I believe, a key to reenergizing our human batteries. Acknowledging that our remaining days are numbered and that the number lessens by one full day every 24 hours has a way of bringing our attention to the here and now and to committing to self-realization.

Facing the fact that our time remaining is a constantly dwindling commodity can be distressing. If you address this sobering reality with open-minded frankness, however, you might find that you more fully appreciate the life you have and the life that could be. A key to living in appreciation involves being knowingly present and mindfully grateful of our experience in the current moment. Confirming this premise, a psychologist acquaintance of mine who works with patients in the terminal stages of cancer told me that many of these individuals come to see their cancer as a gift. The reason for that, he related, was that it brought them into grateful appreciation of every remaining moment. Before being diagnosed with cancer, these individuals, like so many of us, were so pre-occupied with their daily routines that they were missing the gifts available only in present time.

Personally, I have come to realize that mindfulness is the place to find spiritual comfort. This is confirmed by the teachings of multitudes of spiritual leaders who inform us that quiet meditation and conscious attentiveness are keys to experience a comforting cosmic consciousness.

In contrast, attempting to avoid fear of death in diversionary efforts to recapture youth or to numb one's unwanted feelings is ultimately futile. Rather than transcending fears of aging and of death, such efforts are actually more likely only to suppress them. When that happens, the suppressed fears then end up being carried around like lead weights in the mind. What we repress does not go away. Instead, it is simply shoved into the subconscious mind, where it is capable of producing undesirable side effects. In this regard, our repressed fears are likely to come back to haunt us in the form of free-floating anxieties. Avoidance means living a lie, while soul-searching reassessment promises authentic life renewal.

◆ Transcending Fear with Passion

In his influential book, *What Happy People Know*, Dan Baker reminds us of a psychological reality, which is that you cannot be fearful and appreciative at the same time. The human brain can hold only one of these strong emotions at any one time. Fear can consume us, making our minds an anxious prisoner. Clearly, this is not a great way to spend life in those "golden years." Fear can be a noxious bug, capable of stinging us where it hurts most, deep down at the gut level. On this matter, I know of what I speak, because I have been there. But I have also learned that while we can't avoid death, it is possible to move beyond being consumed by the fear of it. We can come to view death as nothing more than a doorway to whatever awaits us on the other side. I have chosen to adopt the view that what awaits us is good beyond words to describe. That has enabled me to make the reality of death less fearful by placing life appreciation more fully mindful on center stage.

We are here, I feel rather certain, to learn, to grow, to develop, to contribute, and to enjoy our unique gifts and potentials. I know that this process continues with many individuals into their last moments in this life. This realization can free us to transform fear of death into joy in life, a much happier state of mind. Our human minds even have the capacity to experience a passion for what we might do and who we are and can be. Developing an optimistic vision, a passion-based vision, for one's future leaves little room for the mind to entertain fear and anxiety. Self-realization, in this regard, just might be our ultimate life purpose. By self-realization I'm referring to our instinctive nature to become all that we are capable of and to contribute our best talents in deeply meaningful ways, as was discussed earlier in Chapter 1.

CORE-SELF CENTERED PASSION

Before proceeding further, however, I should also define what I mean by *passion*, as this word has multiple meanings and associations. First, I'm not alluding to the kind of impulse that motivates hormone-driven teenagers to parade about in jeans tighter than their own skins, nor in the irresistible urge of lemmings to do a mass exodus into the sea. Also, I'm not referring to the kind of egocentricity that caused Narcissus to waste away in self-fascinated obsession over his pond-reflected image, nor of the fever that drove the witch-hunters of seventeenth-century Salem, Massachusetts, to burn innocent young women at the stake.

Instead, I am referring to the kind of energy that caused Agatha Christie to write her mind-bending mysteries, Gary Larson to create his wild and wacky "The Far Side" cartoons, or Dizzy Gillespie to blow his horn like none other. I am referring to the energizing vision that motivated Walt Disney to create Disney Inc., Jacques Cousteau to explore the ocean depths, Steven Jobs to create Apple's Macintosh, and Clara Barton to create the American Red Cross. I am referring to the potential that resides within you and me, and most people to transcend a modestly satisfying existence into one that is much more engaging and vibrant.

The potential to experience passion is probably unique to humans. So far as we know, neither dogs, wallabies, nor canaries come equipped to experience passion, although they seem to be rather good at living in the here and now, with little apparent fear of death. Furthermore, as far as can be ascertained, no two people come hard-wired with the same kind of passion. Our passions may be as unique as our fingerprints and DNA codes. There is no other interest structure exactly like yours.

Why are your deep-seated interests unique to your being? There seems to be only two possible reasons: design or accident. It could, of course, be the latter. Like the distinctiveness of each individual snowflake, there may be no apparent reason for your uniqueness, other than perhaps Mother Nature amusing herself in multifaceted randomness. However, Mother Nature seems to have a generative and far-reaching intelligence for her creations, even if the rationale fails to register within the human brain during the few moments of geologic time it gets to experience. I like to think that the wonderful diversity in human interests, what turns us on, mind, body, and soul-wise, is not some kind of a cosmic accident. Perhaps, just perhaps, we are here to do something with our uniqueness. After all, if we all were inclined to be doing pretty much the same things, who would attend to all those other things that help make our collective human systems function? And who would create the future by exploring interests that transcend our current times and conventions?

RECHARGING YOUR BATTERIES

If it is true that you have been endowed with a unique capacity for life-energizing passion, wouldn't you want to capitalize on your gift? Of course, discovering and living our passion is neither easy nor obvious to most of us. In fact, some of us have mindsets that seriously reject such kind of thinking. Personally, I must confess that it has taken a long time for me to come to a passion-oriented mindset. It seems to go against the grain of my flatland Minnesotan-Lutheran-Scandinavian upbringing. I must admit to uneasy feelings that doing/being what I love is somewhat narcissistic, or possibly even sinful. Like many others, I suffer from programming that implies it is more proper to live selflessly in sacrifice to others than to own and pursue anything I might be passionate about. I'm not sure how messages of this kind come into being, but it probably has something to do with ingrained cultural messages we grew up with. On the one hand, some of us, myself included, were subtly indoctrinated with the idea that our most instinctual desires are most likely unrealistic or, even more likely, immoral and must therefore be resisted. On the other hand, conflicting messages about the importance of developing one's gifts versus the virtues of being humble and self-sacrificing keep some of us in a quandary about whether to let our "little lights shine" or to squelch personal aspirations in selfless sacrifice to others. With confounding messages such as these, is it any wonder that psychotherapy has become a growth profession?

Here is a theological question to contemplate: Would the Creator endow us with the potential for passion if it were not perfectly OK to do something with it? In fact, one might reasonably ponder the possibility that it could be a sin (mistake) to abandon the honest pursuit of one's true passion? Consider how different our world would be if well-known individuals failed to pursue their passion. Might the Creator have been pleased to see Einstein sacrifice his career aspiration to be a trolley driver, or opera star Kathleen Battle sacrifice hers to be an accountant, or Franklin Delano Roosevelt to pursue a vocation as marriage therapist?

Why was Mother Teresa impassioned to serve the neediest of the planet? Why was Martin Luther King energized to lead a nonviolent campaign for the full-fledged enfranchisement of African-Americans, rather than to take a safer course as a parish minister? Why did

Sigmund Freud and Carl Jung explore inner space and the Wright Brothers outer space? Were these just chance decisions made serendipitously or did they come from these individuals paying attention to their inner passions?

Is there something deep within you that might be calling you to some meaningful endeavor? The world is certainly better off for the passion-based orientations of well-known individuals like Beethoven, Shakespeare, Florence Nightingale, and Marie Curie. But it isn't just the famous who are imbued with this core of inner passion. We all have it! What is it that energizes you? Is there anything keeping you from being energized?

CONFRONTING OUR BARRIERS

Of course we all face impediments to knowing or pursuing our passion. What if, for example, you are a 42-year-old Roman Catholic woman who realizes a passion for the ministry; or a single parent who discovers a passion to be an archaeological explorer; or a 52-year-old upper-level executive who realizes a passion to be an international conflict-resolution mediator?

Few people find the process of manifesting a unique personal passion to be an easy undertaking. Many of us have made our early life choices out of concerns for making a living, getting by and getting ahead, or supporting our families. While these are worthwhile objectives, even important responsibilities—in themselves, they don't provide the kind of spark for living involved in fully pursuing a self-realizing and core-based passion.

Should you give up the pursuit of an aspiration if you find yourself in a life situation that seems to preclude realizing it? Fortunately, those individuals described in the preceding paragraphs did not. They went for it, and found ways and means for becoming who they wanted to be. The Roman Catholic woman became a Protestant minister, the 52-year-old executive is now an international mediator, and you will find out more about the woman harboring archeological aspirations later in the chapter.

Some of us, like Amadeus Mozart, Franklin Delano Roosevelt, and Madonna knew at an early age exactly what their passions were and how to pursue them in the world. For most of us, however, knowing what our passion is and how to pursue it is no easy matter. In fact, if we are to believe world-renowned Swiss psychiatrist Dr. Carl Gustav Jung (1875–1961), it would be improbable to really know what our passion is prior to the age of fifty. The reason for that is that one's passion lies partially submerged deep within the unconscious *self*. Full self-awareness is developmentally rare in the first half of life. It is somewhere around the age of fifty that we become more conscious of our inner self and feel the desire to undertake whatever adjustments are required to more fully evolve into that unique being. This phenomenon, which Jung refers to as *individuation*, becomes of heightened importance the second half of life.

Connecting with our unique individual passion is a goal worth seeking in our mid- and senior life years. By the age of fifty, self-realization becomes a critical issue for anyone seeking more than superficial existence from life.

◆ Pathway Dependency

Creative ideas have changed the world, and people in all ages and stages of life have made rejuvenating transformations through the power of imagination. Transitioning to retirement is a particularly good time to draw on your imagination as a basis for generating interesting new directions for your life. But perhaps you are one of those who believe that you lack imagination. If you are alive and functioning at fifty-plus, you have the basic mechanism essential for creative imagination. Dreaming is one form of imagination at work. Have you ever had an intuition about something? Possibly you were grappling with a problem of some kind when, all of a sudden in a flash of insight, an innovative solution popped into mind. That's your imagination in action.

Our brains, while not much bigger than an Idaho potato, are huge in their potential for imagination. For examples, think of what Thomas Edison's ideas have done for modern living, or what Helen Keller's breakthrough in creating the Braille language has done for the blind, or what the Wright Brothers' innovation produced for global travel. Unfortunately, many of us have let our imaginative powers atrophy from the time we were creative little kids. There are many reasons for that happening: an education system that taught us that there were right and wrong answers for pretty much everything, or organizational work settings where senior management did the thinking and left the doing to the worker bees, or social influences pressuring us to conform.

I recently conducted a workshop in which an economist indicated that there is a term in his profession that refers to the difficulty for human systems to change: *pathway dependency*. I think that is an apt characterization to describe the difficulty we have in changing a path we have grown comfortable with and to think and act outside of habit and convention. Most of us have been pressured, both by our own conventions and coercive outside inducements, to be inside-the-box performers. But retirement offers a wonderful opportunity to move outside the box and draw on our imaginative powers to invent new dimensions for our work, leisure, learning, relationships, and life in general.

◆ Tuning In on the Creative Mind

The good news is that your powers of imagination, even if they have been semidormant, can be reenergized. To release your imaginative abilities, you just need to exercise the creative side of your brain a bit. The value of doing so is that your imagination can set your life on an interesting new course and more fully engage your passion in daily living. Here are a few exercises to help awaken your imagination as a prelude for generating creative ideas for your future. See if you can come up with several out-of-the-box ideas for each. Don't worry if your ideas make sense or not, just have some fun (humor facilitates creativity) and massage your imagination:

- If whales could talk, in what languages might they communicate? If they could speak in English, what kind of a whale accent or dialect might they have? How would the whale voice sound differently at 50 fathoms than at the surface? How might female whales sound differently than males? What is the best compliment a male whale could make to a female whale, and visa versa? *(Starters: They might have a Welsh accent, compliment might be you have a whale of a body.)*

- What are nine unusual ways one could blow up a balloon? *(Starters: Stretch over tail pipe of car, or fill a balloon with baking soda, and attach it to a 2-liter bottle that is half-full of vinegar.)*

- Think of a dozen reasons why dogs have tails. *(Starters: They wag their approval of you, show what's up for them, chase them when things get boring.)*

- What are 15 things you can do with olives besides eat them? *(Starters: Use them for eyeballs for your snowmen or grind them up and use as deodorant powder.)*

- If you could go back in time for a moment and talk to a group of 18-year-olds in the year 1980, what suggestions might you offer them to take maximum advantage of your knowledge about the coming world in which they were going to be living? *(Starters: Learn Chinese, get a foundation in computers.)*

- If you could go back in time and coach the you of age 21, what five suggestions could the you of now provide your 21-year-old self to take fuller advantage of the world in which you were going to be living? *(Starters: Get conflict resolution training and learn how to effectively express and deal with your feelings; don't be afraid to think creatively and take some unconsidered small risks and well considered big ones.)*

- Had you won the $50 million lottery at age of 30, what seven things would you have done with that money to enhance your life? In what ways might your life today be different than it now is? In what ways would your life today be better, worse, or about the same had you won that lottery?

- If time, money, health, and resources were no obstacle at all, what six things would you most love to do before departing this world?

- What might you look like and be doing at 100 if you were to be in excellent health with all systems up and running? *(Starters: Consider facilitating a wisdom society of 100-plussers, recording stories of the changes in the art of being human observed during my 100 years, playing billiards with my grand- and great grand- children.)*

◆ Reinventing Your Life with Imagination

If you had a choice between winning the megabuck lottery and suddenly becoming exceedingly creative, which would you choose? If you're looking for a life of luxury and leisure, you're probably choosing the lottery; but if you find self-realization more exciting, you're probably going with creativity. The good news for those opting for self-realization is that creativity is a commodity you don't have to win; you already have it in large measure. Some of us, of course, are inherently more creative than others, and some have had the opportunity to develop our creativity to a fuller degree than others.

When you think of creative people, who come to mind? Are they individuals such as artists, marketing executives, fiction writers, or videogame developers? Although you might be inclined to think of individuals in these kinds of professions, it is encouraging to realize that you don't have to make your living as an artist to be creative in life. My sister Carol, for example, is an exceedingly creative person who is not an artist but is highly resourceful in life.

Carol has had to move around the country with her executive husband in one assignment after another. In each and every case, Carol has quickly created a whole new circle of friends, close friends I might add, and found work that is interesting, rewarding and which provides a useful service. Carol might not call herself creative; she would see herself instead as being flexible, resourceful, optimistic, and a bit of a free spirit. Those, however, happen to be important characteristics of creativity. Carol, in my mind, is a great role model of someone who has been able to continuously reinvent herself even when it means letting go of one good situation after another. She has had to be creative in managing a life of multiple changes. But she has no more resources than any of us when it comes to being creative in life. Here are some lessons that I have learned from Carol that could also be helpful to you:

- Stay optimistic: Your expectations are likely to become self-fulfilling prophecies.

- Make time for fun and take pleasure in what you are doing.

- Enjoy your family, friends, home, and a variety of good books.

- Good friends are everywhere; you just need to meet them.

- Don't get affixed to any particular image of who you are and are not professionally. Interesting possibilities abound when you are flexible, conversational, ask questions, smile, and have enthusiasm.

- When things get difficult, think things through, seek advice, and support from smart people, make well considered decisions, and have faith that things work out for the best—even if you don't know what is best at the time.

- Have a strong faith, but don't blame God when life doesn't unfold the way you think it should. We are here to observe, learn, and to grow.

- If you are no longer enjoying your work or what you are doing, let it go and find something more fulfilling.

- Perfection may not always be realistic, or even the most efficient use of your time and energy. Often, good enough is good enough.

- Don't be afraid to take on big projects of interest; you will grow into the situation and there are always people willing to help.

◆　Your Life/Work Reinventing Homework

Continue your imagination enhancing development by generating at least two additional options for situations you find yourself in over the next month. Naturally, not every life-choice situation warrants a great deal of creative thinking. I probably don't need to look too extensively at the options for how big a tip to leave for my lunch server (15 to 20 percent will work fine), whether to park the car on the left or right side of the street (first available spot will do), or whether to do my laundry on Monday or Tuesday. But life expansion can occur in small ways each and every day through exercising greater creativity in those choices. Think, for example, of your options in walking down the street: Do you meet people with a hollow stare, a grumpy look on your face, or not even see them because you are overly focused on personal priorities? Have you ever had your day brightened up by a stranger giving you a bright smile and cheery good morning? Small things can make a big difference.

For example, Jay felt he was a total loser as a young man. He came from a poor family, was doing badly in school. He was teased mercilessly, and was knocked around a lot by others. He was well on his way into a life as a perceived loser. But that all changed one day in what he refers to as a kind act rendered by a person he happened to encounter on the street. The "kind act" was simply a comment made by a teacher, who told Jay, "I see a lot of potential in you." Those words served to transform Jay's life. That simple message, delivered with sincerity, served as the basis for Jay to change his self-perceptions from pessimistic to optimistic. That single small event was also the spark that altered the direction of his life from that of a "loser" to "winner." Now a sixty-plusser, Jay has lived a highly creative, fun, and successful life. Words, and the way they are presented, have power, even life-changing power.

We are all creative beings, possessing great potential to expand our life and even contribute to the life expansion of others by the various ways we choose to present ourselves in the world and respond to others. Just for fun, remind yourself that for today only you are going to exercise creativity in the choices you make. How will you present yourself to others? What interesting alternatives will you see in the choices you make during the day? Try it a second day, then a third, and so on. In this small way, you just might reinvent yourself and have fun along the way.

Use this same kind of possibility thinking to move beyond pathway dependency to envision interesting possibilities for your next chapter of life. One of the nice things about creative imagination is that you can explore interesting ideas without having to do them. You can even use your imagination to evaluate how fulfilling an idea might be for you should you elect to pursue that in your life. This actually is a more efficient way of making life choices than leaping into something new. It is just possible that in creating an expanded list of ideas for the next phase of your life, you will discover one so appealing that you are compelled to pursue it. There is an exciting world available to you, but it may currently be residing in the realm of creative possibility in you mind.

The next chapter offers an assessment activity, the next step in this process of self-realization experience, for help in generating a general theme and a vision for the next season of your life. The chapter also provides some specific ideas for each of the themes revealed by the assessment and encourages creative thinking in expanding your list of options. Remember that the next season of your life will be only as interesting as you create it to be. Exercising your creative ability is your most valued resource for recreating a new life that takes full advantage of your assets of time, wealth, health, talent, and personal energy.

THE LIFE THEMES PROFILER: DEVELOPING THEMES FOR A NEW LIFE

"In seeing my Life Themes Profiler results I realized that I have been too security conscious in my career. It's clear to me now that I am a 'New Work Venturer' and that I want to take more risks and become more entrepreneurial in my future."

—A 50-YEAR-OLD PROFESSIONAL CONSIDERING THE
IMPLICATIONS OF HER ASSESSMENT RESULTS

"This has forced me to change my thinking about the future. I had planned to return to the company as a full-time consultant after retiring. But now I can see it's time for me to better balance my life with some new and interesting part-time work and an enjoyable hobby."

—A 62-YEAR-OLD MALE RETHINKING HIS RETIREMENT PLANS
AS A RESULT OF HIS LIFE THEMES PROFILER PROFILE

"The results of our Life Themes Profiler assessments brought home the realization that we needed to do some communicating and accommodating about our assumptions for retirement if our relationship was going to endure."

—A COUPLE REVIEWING THEIR ASSESSMENT RESULTS
RECEIVED IN A RETIREMENT PLANNING WORKSHOP

◆ **Developing the Core Themes for Your New Life**

The previous chapter emphasized reinventing your future through creating thinking. This chapter provides an assessment activity to help you envision the kind of a future suited to your needs and interests.

Recreating a new life involves four phases:

1. *Envisioning the nature of the kind of future you desire.* Beginning a new life journey starts with self-knowledge, which involves clarifying what it is that energizes you and generating a mental picture of what the ideal would look like.

2. *Articulating that picture into the written word.* It is difficult to achieve something you are unable to clearly articulate.

3. *Claiming your passion once you are clear about what it is.* That means both knowing and being able to say this is what I will do and/or who I will be.

4. *Developing a plan or a map for getting where you want to go and for achieving who you want to be.* The task of creating your own map can be challenging. It involves a process of life/work strategizing, creative problem solving, and planning. In that regard, you are more likely to develop such a life map intuitively through creative visioning than from careful analysis and detailed planning.

The fourth phase is discussed in greater detail in Chapter 9. For now, take the following assessment, the Life Themes Profiler, for help in addressing the first three phases of the life reinventing process. We shall further address the third phase in the following chapters.

Life Themes Profiler*: Finding a Theme for the Next Chapter of Your Life

Directions

Review each of the 20 items in the assessment and use the following rating scale to assess how true each statement is for you at this stage of your life.

Rating Scale

Completely Disagree	Somewhat Disagree	Partially Agree	Strongly Agree	Completely Agree

```
|   |   |   |   |   |   |   |   |   |   |
0   1   2   3   4   5   6   7   8   9   10
```

Write the number you have selected as your rating for each of the 20 items in the open boxes, as shown in the following example:

What are your intentions for the next chapter of your life?   A   B   C   D

1. I want to continue working but am looking to make a career switch or start my own business.   8

2. I intend to continue in my work full-time and to be fully productive for many more years.   1

When you have completed all 20 items, tally up your scores in each of the four columns (A, B, C, and D).

Rating Scale

Completely Disagree	Somewhat Disagree	Partially Agree	Strongly Agree	Completely Agree

```
|   |   |   |   |   |   |   |   |   |   |
0   1   2   3   4   5   6   7   8   9   10
```

What are your intentions for the next chapter of your life?   A   B   C   D

1. I want to continue working but am looking to make a career switch or start my own business.

2. I intend to continue in my work full time and to be fully productive for many more years.

3. I expect to quit working soon to enjoy a more stress-free, relaxing and leisure-filled life.

4. I'm ready for an employment-free lifestyle and intend to challenge myself in new ways.

5. There are still many things I want to do and achieve in work before retiring.

Rating Scale

Completely Disagree		Somewhat Disagree		Partially Agree		Strongly Agree		Completely Agree	
0	1	2	3	4	5	6	7	8	9	10

What are your intentions for the next chapter of your life?   A   B   C   D

6. I would enjoy undertaking an entirely new work-related venture at this stage of life.

7. I can't wait to retire and enjoy a freer life where I have the time to enjoy leisure activities.

8. I'm an adventurous sort who is ready for a new life of mind-expanding challenges.

9. Achievement in my work and career continues to be a primary motivator in my life.

10. I don't enjoy my work and want to move on to a more challenging work or career situation.

11. I'm tired of a life dominated by work and I'm ready to settle into a comfortable retirement.

12. I plan to retire and pursue my passion for adventure and expanding my frontiers.

13. Having absolutely no commitments and abundant free time greatly appeals to me.

14. I'm at the peak of productivity in my career and will remain working for many more years.

15. I look forward to the freedom to explore new avenues and pursue my passions in leisure life.

What are your intentions for the next chapter of your life?   A   B   C   D

16. I want to move on to a new work situation better suited to my talents and interests.

17. If money were no obstacle, I would have retired a long time ago to enjoy a life of leisure.

18. I feel a strong urge to stop working and move on to some engaging new life ventures.

19. I enjoy working and being productive and can't imagine life without a work-focused structure.

20. I'm sure to feel regret unless I find or create a more satisfying new work situation.

Total scores for Column A, B, C, and D   _____

Graphing Your Profile

Plot your total scores from columns A, B, C, and D along the corresponding axis of Figure 4-1. After plotting your scores, connect all four of your marked scores to obtain a visual representation of your preferences. Note in which quadrant(s) your scores are highest and lowest for insights as to what themes hold the most promise for the next chapter of your life.

FIGURE 4-1. PICTURING THE THEMES OF YOUR NEXT LIFE CHAPTER.

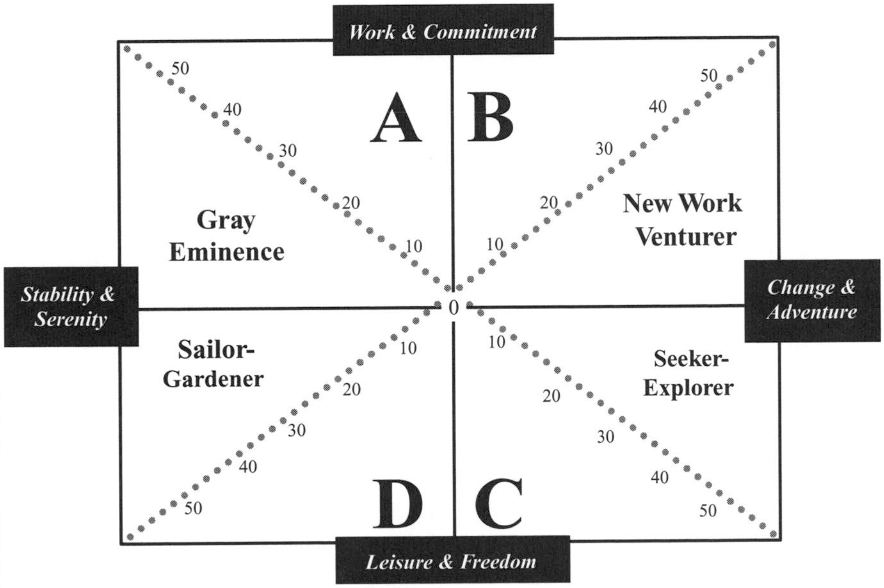

Assessing Your Scores

Very Low Score:	0–9
Low Score:	10–19
Moderate Score:	20–29
High Score:	30–39
Very High Scores:	40–50

◆ Visualizing Your Lifestyle Options

The Life Themes Profiler visually represents four basic considerations that retirement planners must address. One of these has to do with how much time, if any, will be devoted to continuing in work, versus how much leisure life one is ready and able to enjoy. There is, however, a less obvious decision to be made as we prepare to live longer, healthier, and more active lives than any previous generation in human history. This has to do with the choice of a stable and predictable lifestyle versus one of change and adventure. As you can see from Figure 4-2, these considerations have been placed at the opposite ends of two continuums. These continuums, in turn, form a four-quadrant model for help in designing your life in the senior years. The four quadrants developed in this model are designated with names characterizing important thematic lifestyle orientations.

It is important to note here that this model represents a dynamic process rather than a static situation. Over time, an individual's lifestyle preference may shift from one theme to another as motivations respond to changing circumstances. So, for example, having spent many years in a career that consumed a major portion of your enegies, you might feel inclined to relax and take life easy as a Sailor-Gardener. After some time enjoying this interlude, however, you may begin to grow a bit restless and look for some kind of activity to reengage your mind or respond to a new call to adventure. After doing some exploring and thinking about this, you might decide, as did a retired economist client of mine, to take some anthropology courses at a nearby university. While engaged in these courses, you might elect to accompany a professor on an archeological dig involved in researching the ruins of an ancient Anasazi civilization. This activity might engage you in a joint research project with the professor, which in turn leads to writing an

FIGURE 4-2. LIFE THEMES PROFILER.

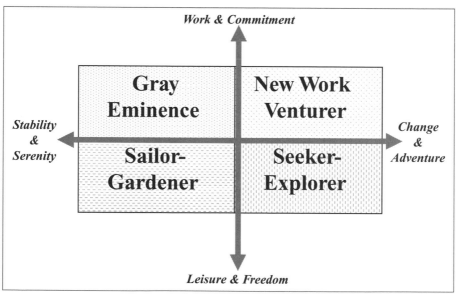

article together. Drawing on your professional knowledge of economics, your contribution in the article might be to flesh out the economics of the Anasazi civilization as it relates to the social, governing, and demographic picture of that once-great society. Such an experience might then lead to continued research and teaching a course at a university in your newly uncovered passion. The progression in this example, based on an actual case, would involve transitioning from Gray Eminence to a period of relaxing leisure as Sailor-Gardener, followed by a regenerated lifestyle as Seeker-Explorer. Later, you might add features of a New Work Venturer to the mix.

ACTIVITY: CLARIFYING YOUR LIFE PRIORITIES FOR THE FIFTY-PLUS YEARS

For ideas in clarifying your vision for the next chapter of your life, read the following descriptions for those areas in which you obtained the highest scores on your Life Themes Profiler assessment.

If you scored high in more than one theme, consider each of these areas to determine what aspects of those themes most appeal to you. Circle any of those you might want to include in your future plans. Also, you might want to use the suggestions offered by these examples to stimulate your own creative thoughts for additional ideas relevant to your high-scoring theme area.

GRAY EMINENCE

A high score in this style indicates that your career, or some aspect of it, remains a prime motivator, and you are not yet ready for retirement. You probably enjoy your work and may want to continue doing that, or something very similar, for the foreseeable future. People in the mature stages of their career who identify with the Gray Eminence theme are often motivated by a variety of factors. These may include a continuing need for power and status, leveraging their knowledge and experience, creating their legacy, mentoring younger staff, making a contribution to their professional field, serving their clients or organizations, finalizing long-sought career goals, or moving into senior positions or roles within their organization or profession where they can continue to contribute and exercise influence.

If the Gray Eminence category fits your aspirations, here are some options to consider for energizing the next chapter of your life:

- Take on a mentoring role with promising younger staff or associates.
- Determine what legacy you wish to establish and develop plans to create it.
- Transition into a senior advisory capacity with your current organization or as a consultant in your field of expertise.
- Assume a senior position or role within your organization or move to another organization where your knowledge and experience are valued and where you may have greater opportunity to capitalize on them.
- Develop a proposal for a needed initiative of interest to you and assume leadership of the project.
- Market yourself to assume a prominent role in a project or program of special interest to you or assume leadership of a project that needs revitalization.
- Take on a position of leadership within a professional association relevant to your profession or related field of interest.
- Take a retirement pension but continue to work with your organization or similar organization in a consulting capacity.
- Establish a consulting practice, either as a freelancer or in partnership with like-minded individuals or with an established consulting practice.
- Define and market yourself as an interim leader in your field of expertise for organizations in transition.
- Work with a temporary agency that provides executives and/or professional expertise to organizations with needs for such services. (Do a Google search for executive and professional agencies specializing in interim placements in organizations for your areas of specialty.)

GRAY EMINENCE EXAMPLES

Stephen Transitions to Consulting   Stephen enjoyed his work and was happy in his profession, but had grown weary of the routine and the stresses he was feeling about certain changes taking place within his organization. He yearned for a lifestyle in which he could operate more autonomously and have greater control over his own schedule. After mulling over his situation and discussing his options and their possible consequences with trusted friends and others, Stephen decided to retire. But he resolved to continue in his profession by serving as a consultant. This proved to be a good course of action for him, as his consulting business has prospered.

Looking back at the transition from full-time employment to consulting, Stephen recalled that it was strange walking out of the organization one day, after so many years of full-time employment, and returning the next as a consultant. He regrets now that he didn't work harder early on to extend his consulting business beyond his former employing agency, especially since changes in management have resulted in dramatically reducing his contracting days. He has been concentrating on extending his business connections recently and finds this to be interesting but challenging. He recommends that anyone planning to start a consulting practice establish a network of social and professional associates and schedule regular meetings with them. He learned through experience in setting up his practice that consulting can be isolating and lonely without such a network.

Retirement: Ready or Not   Michael had been with his organization long enough to be eligible for an early retirement with a pension that would enable him to live fairly comfortably, albeit carefully. Because he was feeling highly conflicted about whether or not to retire, he sought career coaching assistance. The nature of his conflict was that he enjoyed much of his work and was still a few years away from full retirement eligibility. But his work was causing him a great deal of stress. The source of his anxieties related to the nature of his work, which involved corporate-wide research projects. His responsibilities often engaged him in conflict with high-level executives who had big stakes in the outcomes of his work. The stress of this, sufficient enough for him to seek psychiatric help, was such that he was seriously considering jumping ship to escape the constant pressure. There was, however, one overriding barrier causing him to hesitate in this decision. He was having an exceedingly difficult time determining what he would do if he chose early retirement.

For help with this decision, he took a number of assessments, including the Life Themes Profiler. These results showed him equally distributed between Gray Eminence and Sailor-Gardener. This helped him appreciate that the kinds of work activities he was engaged with were challenging and meaningful, and well used his top strengths. With that realization, he discussed several possible options with his manager, from full retirement to consulting and part-time work.

Eventually, he decided to continue working full time for as long as he was enjoying his work and feeling that he was making worthwhile contributions. To manage the work-related stress he had been experiencing, he resolved to always take all of his vacation time to do fun things with his wife and family and also to better balance his life with enjoyable leisure activities. In opting for this course of action he discovered an added benefit. Knowing that he could retire whenever he chose, without worrying about his financial situation, provided a sense of stress-reducing comfort. As he put it with a sly grin, "After all, what's the worst they can do—fire me?"

NEW WORK VENTURER

Scoring high on this style means you are ready for change, but not for retirement! If this is you, you are highly motivated by a new work-related undertaking, such as creating your own business, initiating a new product or project, trying out an organizational reassignment, beginning a new career, or moving on to a new work situation.

If New Work Venturer is the right direction for the next chapter of your life, here are some things you might consider:

- Create your own business. A good reference is *Innovative Entrepreneurship* by Peter Drucker.

- Transition into a totally new and challenging career. For help in this you might want to engage the services of a career coach or counselor.

- Find a new work challenge that puts your talents and potential to the full test. A good reference for finding work to suit your talent is Career One Stop at www.careeronestop.org (click on "Explore Careers").

- Develop a proposal and seek funding for a project you care deeply about.

- Take on a challenging assignment, something you have never done.

- Seek an exchange assignment with a firm where you would engage in different kinds of work activities. For ideas on this topic, try a Google search for *secondment*.

- Work with or start your own nongovernmental agency. Do a Google search for *NGO*.

- Join the Peace Corps or similar types of organizations, such as AmeriCorps (www.americorps.org), Vista (www.friendsofvista.org),

Cross Cultural Solutions (www.crossculuralsolutions.org), or Earth Watch Institute (www.earthwatch.org).

- Return to college to obtain a degree or certificate to initiate a career in a new area such as nursing, architectural landscape, French pastry chef, bike mechanic, massage therapist, bar tender, vintner, or organic farmer.

- Find a niche to transfer a special knowledge, a natural talent or a unique personality asset into a new career direction such as a Web designer for small businesses in the area, tour guide for an attraction for which you have a special affinity, sportscaster for local baseball team, scoutmaster, or public official. An excellent reference for ideas and a process to translate deep personal interests into a resume-style marketing document is my book *Will the Real You Please Stand Up: Find Passion in Your Life and Work* (SterlingHouse Books, 2006).

NEW WORK VENTURER EXAMPLES

Project Leader Becomes Bed-and-Breakfast Network Manager

"I wanted to help establish a network of low-cost, family-run bed-and-breakfast (B & B) facilities in Peru," says Nada. "Poor countries often lack short-term lodging facilities for vacationers or local small-business travelers seeking low-cost accommodations." Nada believes the benefits for establishing such a network are helping the local economy at the grassroots level, enhancing the role of women (who will be the local B & B managers), and helping foster important cultural understanding between tourist visitors and Peruvian hosts.

Nada enjoyed her corporate career, but changes in the leadership structure and mission direction disturbed her greatly. In discussing her reactions to these changes with her manager, they came to a mutual agreement that the time had come for a parting of the ways. On that basis, Nada accepted a separation package that included a lump-sum payment for her many years of excellent service.

Nada, to attain the expertise necessary for her new endeavor, embarked on an ambitious training program. The first stage consisted of studying the applicable endeavors existing in Japan, France, and the Czech Republic. She stayed in B & B facilities in these countries to learn first-hand how networked systems were developed and operated, what kind of training and other assistance they received through their network affiliation, what kind of problems to anticipate, and how B & B services were marketed.

In the second phase of her self-directed training, she traveled into the Peruvian countryside to meet with families to identify areas where B & B facilities might be created and what kinds of help would be needed to develop these facilities. In the third phase of her training she attended short, formal executive training courses relevant to the task of creating and running a B & B network along with informal courses in NGO management.

With this training under her belt, Nada returned to Peru, the country of her birth after 26 years as a corporate executive in the United States. There she began dealing with endless problems and difficulties for establishing a Peruvian B & B chain. These included locating feasible sites with families interested in and capable of operating them, training new B & B owners in all aspects of managing these facilities, interacting with foreign tourists, and creating a supportive NGO structure in a country whose infrastructure had been devastated by years of internecine warfare. But her most difficult challenge was dealing with the many officials and the cumbersome state apparatus that creating this ambitious venture entailed.

Nada was motivated in this venture by the B & B networks that were established in Japan and France after WWII. But there were better infrastructures existing in those countries than those currently existing in Peru. Although the scale of this task has been daunting and the problems extremely frustrating, Nada remains hopeful that this venture will ultimately turn out as successful in Peru as earlier prototypes in postwar Japan and France became. But whether or not the outcome is fully successful, she is highly motivated in a meaningful endeavor and takes comfort in the knowledge that she has already taken important steps in making a difference in the lives of many individuals.

From Government Bureaucrat to Architectural Photographer   Jason retired after a career as an agronomist and was ready for something completely different. At the age of 61, he elected to pursue a newly discovered passion, which he affectionately referred to as "the photography bug." "I like things that sit still, giving me the ability to be careful and deliberate," says Jason about his decision to focus on architectural photography. His interest in photography developed through courses he had enrolled in at the Smithsonian Institute in Washington, D.C. It was there that he had become particularly intrigued with architectural photography. While still employed with his organization, he was able to further his growing interest in his new hobby by joining a local camera club. The photography bug became so pervasive, however, that he decided to make it his work rather than his hobby.

Jason decided to launch his new career by taking courses from masters in the profession. These consisted of a number of intensive educational development programs at places like the Corcoran School of Art, The Washington School of Photography, Anderson Ranch Art Center in Colorado, and the International Center of Photography. After completing this training, Jason was able to create a niche market—taking photographs of buildings for architects, real estate agents, and building contractors. His business soon developed through word of-mouth. "Someone sees a picture they like," says Jason, and they end up hiring you to take some for them, and then they tell someone else about you."

Apparently, enough people have liked Jason's work to enable him to be about as busy as he wants. Of course, he acknowledges, you have to keep pace with the changes going on within the field—referring to the digital technology revolutionizing photography. To stay competitive, he has to wisely invest time and money in professional development as an ongoing process.

Reflecting on his transition from bureaucrat to photographer, Jason found that there are up and down days. He reports that about six months after deciding to take an early retirement, "It hit me pretty hard. I woke up one morning wondering, what have I done, and will I ever make it as a photographer?" His advice to anyone going through such a transition is to create a good support group early on and use it for ideas, contacts, planning, and support in the down days, and to share the good news in the good ones.

From Administrative Assistant to Ballroom Dance Trainer   Lucile had been competing for years in the ballroom dance scene when she opted to take an early retirement from her administrative assistance position to do what, as she puts it, "lights up my mind and fills my heart with joy." She decided the time had come to take a shot at making a living in her passion for ballroom dancing. She would do that by training those with a bug for dancing in the ins and outs of ballroom dance. Her vision included not only training the growing legions of amateur ballroom dancers, but to train Olympic dancers for this new international sport.

Although this rather dramatic change in Lucile's career direction happened quickly, her vision for it had been evolving over several years. She loved to dance and would drag her husband off all over the country to dance competitions, where she and a dance partner were frequent winners. Her husband, incidentally, did not dance, but was supportive of her passion for dance and enjoyed watching her come alive with the tango, the rumba, and the cha-cha-cha. Lucy had been saving money for this venture for years, knowing that starting a dance studio would require a substantial stash. To acquire the additional training she thought would be needed for her new vocation, she enrolled in a ballroom dance program in London, which is apparently a hotbed for this sort of thing.

The last I heard from Lucile was that she was doing well in her new venture. Ballroom dancing has become vogue in recent years, and apparently there are scores of would-be dancers willing to pay well to have a ball on the dance-room floor, and in the process, stay trim, look great and feel young. Ballroom dancing, anyone?

SEEKER-EXPLORER

Scoring high in this theme suggests you are ready to stop working but not to retire in any traditional sense. You have, no doubt, been dreaming of doing something different, something challenging, and maybe even something associated with risk, adventure, and proving yourself in new ways and in new settings. Primary motivations for people in this category include things like testing themselves in nonwork situations, going all out in some demanding undertaking, learning something new and fascinating, achieving some new skill in a nonwork interest, exploring exotic places, pursuing a heart-felt passion or learning first-hand about unfamiliar cultures. Seeker-Explorer, as a metaphor, can assume a wide variety of forms—some highly competitive, others more exploratory in nature. The exploratory theme may involve both an inner- and outer-world focus. An inner focus could be something like achieving mastery in yoga, meditation, Tai Chi, or other type of spiritual practice. An outer-world focus might involve something like studying astronomy, tracing the family history, taking up competitive sailing, or joining walking expeditions through historical sites of Eurasia.

As a Seeker-Explorer, consider activities such as these:

- Play competitive chess, bridge, golf, billiards (pool), clay pigeon shooting, tennis, auto racing, or sailing. (Most sports of these kinds have league-sponsored activities, and local chapters such as The National Sporting Clays Association: www.mynsca.com and the Women's Professional Billiard Association: www.wpba.com.)

Note: The operative word here is *competitive*. Playing a game or participating in a sport just for the fun of it would not be enough for a Seeker-Explorer. For self-fulfillment, Seeker-Explorers need to engage their skills, knowledge, and wits against challenging competition.

- Try physical challenges such as mountain climbing, cross-country biking, or skiing, trekking in new and interesting places.

- Move to a new country to master the language, culture, and history.

- Engage in demanding volunteer work in a cause you feel passionate about, such as Habitat for Humanity, Red Cross Emergency work, hospice care, or school mediation work. (Doing a Google search for "Volunteer Opportunities" brings up thousands of organizations engaged in doing good work in the planet. You are bound to find several volunteer opportunities associated with a heart-felt cause.)

- Pursue advanced education in a subject area of great interest such as psychology, theology, mythology, metaphysics, history, art, geology, anthropology, dance, music, or historic preservation. Check the catalog of available courses at a conveniently located college or university near you for available offerings. The Internet is another source of rich educational offerings with programs available from leading institutions all over the world. Want to learn Chinese? How about taking an online course from Beijing University (www.educasian.com)?

- Assume a responsible, unpaid position with a professional association, spiritual, or religious institution or community service organization associated with a deeply felt personal passion. For a listing of thousands of professional associations, visit www.jobweb.com/Career_Development/prof_assoc.htm.

- Acquire a new skill or develop a latent talent and offer it as a free service to individuals and/or organizations that might benefit from your contribution. Try tutoring disadvantaged children, volunteering as a Big Brother or Sister, taking voice lessons and starring in local productions, acquiring a paralegal certificate and assisting older citizens with legal matters, or volunteering with the Small Business Association to provide guidance to individuals starting their own business.

- Venture forth and explore places you have never been, becoming acquainted with new people, cultures, and environmental wonders.

- Develop into a martial arts master, acquire schooling in a demanding spiritual discipline, master yoga and teach it, develop into a marathon walker and advocate the benefits of exercise, obtain credentials in speech communications and or coach with a local Toastmasters chapter.

• Master a craft such as furniture making, wood carving, doll making, home repair, glass blowing, violin crafting, cello playing, lapidary (jewelry making), quilting, stained glass, classic car restoration, water color, garden sculptures, piano, and so on.

SEEKER-EXPLORER EXAMPLES

Manager Becomes Bush Pilot   Luis retired after a long and rewarding career, but felt he was too young and energetic and restless for an idle lifestyle. However, he was clear that he relished his autonomy and never again wanted to be employed. The time had come to undertake something new and adventurous. But what, he wondered, could he do that would keep him active, engaging him in something fun and worthwhile?

In considering a number of possibilities, Luis decided to pursue something that had long intrigued him but he'd not previously been able to work into his schedule. He decided to obtain a pilot's license and purchase his own airplane. Today, or at least at the time of this writing, Luis is a bush pilot, flying needed medical supplies into remote areas of the developing world and flying out individuals needing medical attention from areas where such services are unavailable. He thoroughly enjoys his bush pilot/aviator lifestyle and relishes feeling helpful to others in need.

HR Manager Becomes Auto Racer   Peter, a long-time human resource manager with a large firm, was a Porsche owner and loved to cruise the open roads in his high-performing machine. When he discovered that there was a small group of similar-minded sport-car enthusiasts, Peter linked up with them for long weekend excursions whenever he was able. These occasional pleasure trips made him aware of a growing desire beyond occasional weekend jaunts. Eventually, the yearning became too compelling to resist. He became obsessed with auto racing. For years, he had been saving to purchase a racing Porsche. Now, he decided was time, while he is still young and healthy enough to take up racing. That led him to take an early retirement, buy the car of his dreams, and join a racing association.

When I last heard from him, he had yet to win a single race, although he had come close on more than one occasion. Those close calls were inspiring enough, he admitted, to generate a vision of frequently walking away with the big silver winner's cup. When he achieves that dream, his racing yearnings will have been fulfilled. At that point, too old any longer to take the racetrack turns at 160 miles per hour, he will always be able to take great pleasure in reliving the heart-throbbing, adrenaline-pumping, engine-roaring, dust-flying days of racing in the bucket seat of his beloved Porsche.

Mark Expands His Horizons   Many aspects of the Seeker-Explorer theme involve competition of one sort or another. There are also other motivators, however, that influence the choices and actions of individuals of the Seeker-Explorer persuasion. Mark is a case in point. Having taken one of the "What's Next" workshops I deliver for retirement planners, Mark told me that through this process he came to realize he was a Seeker-Explorer. But he wanted me to know that he would definitely not be climbing any mountains, nor engaging in any such type of physical or competitive endeavor. Instead, what motivated him was a highly active mind and relentless curiosity. This was an inner drive that manifested in a seemingly insatiable desire to explore as much of the world as his time and resources allowed. One way in which he intended to pursue his quest for expanded horizons was to move with his wife Maria, a highly spirited Latino, to a country he had never visited. Mark informed me he was anxious to begin this new adventure and that he intended to undertake this as a mind-expanding challenge by mastering the language, culture, and history of their new home.

About two years after Mark and Maria moved to their new country, I had the opportunity to talk with Maria. She informed me that in fact Mark was in all ways an avid Seeker-Explorer. He was a tireless explorer, she informed me, who was constantly traveling and on the go. His curiosity had been driving him relentlessly. Maria shared that when they take off on frequent excursions to places like Thailand or South Africa she, as a Sailor-Gardener, was perfectly content to relax, shop a little, take in some of the sites, enjoy the beach, or read a good book. With Mark, however, it is a different matter. He would employ a local fisherman to take him exploring to remote islands or engage a helicopter pilot to fly him around volcanoes. According to Maria, Mark never seemed to tire of his venturesome, explorative ways. His idea of relaxation would be something like going on safari in Kenya.

Sara Creates Hope for the Poor   Sara had worked long and hard all of her adult life in administrative support positions as a way of providing for herself and her family. During her working years she had dreamed of one day finding a way to provide opportunities for women and children living in poverty. Searching for ways that she might accomplish this objective, she often used her vacation time to travel in the developing world. On one of these occasions, while visiting a poverty-ridden area in Brazil, two things struck her. One was the beautiful craftwork that many women there produced as a way of generating some income and as a diversion from their oppressive living conditions. Another was the huge number of children idly sitting around watching TV in shacks so decrepit that could barely hold up a TV antenna. In reflecting upon these conditions, Sara developed a vision for how she wanted to implement her dream.

A few years after this moving experience, with the support of a retirement pension, she put her plan into action. The first step was to buy a farm in the country near the poverty-stricken city that inspired her vision. Her farm is located in an area that was once heavily forested but had been stripped bare for farmland in an environmentally damaging venture. For help in financing and supporting her project Sara created a nongovernmental organization (NGO).

She has gone on to renovate "lovely old buildings" in preparation for stage two of the project, which involves providing poor women of the city with a place where they can make and sell crafts through her NGO affiliations. The second phase of her project involves getting children from the city onto the farm to involve them in replanting the forest. Sara intends to infuse these children with a love of trees and nature. Her vision is that as the project evolves, the children will grow with the trees and learn effective forestry practices, along with skills for managing the farm. Sara's vision for this project vitalizes her in a way she has never before experienced. She is a vivid example of how pursuing a passionate dream can fully engage one's energy and enthusiasm for living.

SAILOR-GARDENER

Sailor-Gardeners are individuals who see retirement as a means for enjoying a quieter, more relaxed lifestyle. They believe it's time to slow down and take things easier, to "stop and smell the roses." Individuals scoring high in this theme often report that they have become stressed, burned-out, bored, or simply tired of their work and want to rejuvenate, have some fun, and take better care of themselves.

If Sailor-Gardener is the right direction for your next chapter of life, here are some actions to consider:

- Define your lifestyle needs and search for a location that meets your list of personal preferences. For this you may find Chapter 9 on finding your ideal location to be of special interest.
- Develop new acquaintances with others who share your values and interests.
- Reconnect with family and friends.
- Begin a healthy life-maintenance regime (exercise, diet, and spiritual life).
- Find or engage in hobbies and leisure interests that you enjoy.
- Become involved with a club (social, professional, health, etc.), community group, and/or a church/synagogue/mosque.
- Spend time with people you admire and wish to learn from and become better acquainted with them.
- Schedule fun/learning adventures to places that are romantic, historic, quaint, beautiful, remote, and so on.
- Plant a garden and watch it grow, landscape your backyard, and invite friends and casual acquaintances over to enjoy your koi-filled pond.
- Write poetry for your own enjoyment or that of your grandchildren.
- Take up walking on a regular basis with friends and neighbors.
- Take a culinary course in a particular cuisine and create splendid dinner parties.
- Study a subject that interests you, such as Jungian psychology, the Vikings, ornithology, Nobel Prize winners, Japanese culture, art history, the rise and fall of Sparta, and so on.
- Play Web-based games like pool, checkers, and chess live with grandkids and/or cyber-friends from around the world on Netscape games.

ACTIVITY: PRIORITIZING YOUR LEISURE ACTIVITIES

Make a list of all the things you wanted to do, be, or have but were too busy to do in the past. Your list might include places you wanted to visit, books you wanted to read, courses you wanted to take, sports you might like to try, musical instruments you wished to play, or clubs you wanted to join. Expand your list to 20 or more of such things and then prioritize the list based on those activities that will give you the greatest enjoyment. With prioritized list in hand, decide which two or three of these to undertake in your first year as a Sailor-Gardener and/or Seeker-Explorer, which in your second year, and so on.

SAILOR-GARDENER EXAMPLES

Maria Creates a Garden   Prior to retiring, Maria had spent her work years serving others. She didn't dislike this work, but it wasn't her passion, either. But now, supported by a retirement pension, she was excited about fully engaging in her passions—riding her motorcycle, tending her roses, and quilting.

Maria's life-long friend had landscaped a magnificent garden. For years, Mira had been admiring that garden, spending time enjoying it, dreaming about it, and envisioning creating a garden of her own. In planning for the next chapter of her life, she had been avidly reading landscaping books, visiting garden sites, and envisioning the kind of a garden she might wish to create. The process of creating and nurturing a garden answered a deep-seated need for Mira to work with her hands and create a beautiful setting in nature.

Johan Makes Furniture   Johan always loved working with wood. After retiring, he studied the fine art of furniture making. Now he can easily spend days on end in this labor of love. Although he has received offers to buy the fruits of his labors, he has resisted turning his hobby into a business because he doesn't want it to take on the pressure of work.

Clark Becomes a Sportsman   Clark is a crack marksman in the skeet shooter club. He is also a golfer and a fly fisherman. Although he doesn't hunt, he does enjoy shooting and is a member of a local club, where he bangs away during the week when most club members are at work. Although he is not an avid golfer, he enjoys playing a round with a congenial group of other retirees and frequently participates in tournaments at his club. You may also find him with his fly rod and home-made flies at a local trout stream, and he casts off a couple of times a year with a group of friends to the famous trout streams of Montana and the Delaware River in New Jersey. To fill out his days, he is an active member of Rotary and learns Spanish at the local college. He also meets once a week with a small group at the local bistro to practice Spanish and develop travel plans to Spanish-speaking countries.

◆ The Shape of Things to Come

Now that you have completed your Life Theme Profile, step back and take a look at it to see what this might suggest in devising a direction for the next chapter of your life. Does your profile show a strong presence in just one area, or are you double-, triple-, or quadruple-theme interested at this juncture of life?

Figure 4-3 shows a few of these multiple interest profiles.

FIGURE 4-3. SAMPLE PROFILES.

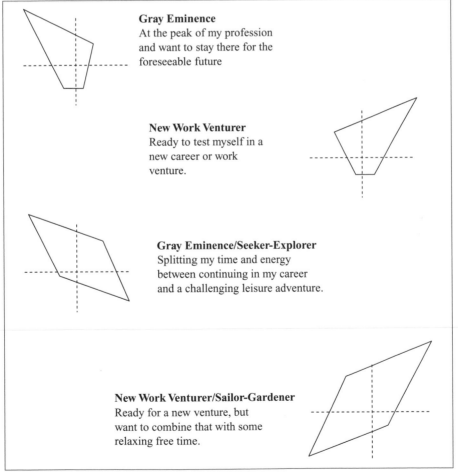

Gray Eminence
At the peak of my profession and want to stay there for the foreseeable future

New Work Venturer
Ready to test myself in a new career or work venture.

Gray Eminence/Seeker-Explorer
Splitting my time and energy between continuing in my career and a challenging leisure adventure.

New Work Venturer/Sailor-Gardener
Ready for a new venture, but want to combine that with some relaxing free time.

continues

FIGURE 4-3. (CONTINUED)

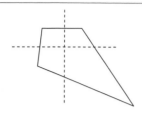

Seeker-Explorer
Ready to stop working and do
something adventurous and
challenging.

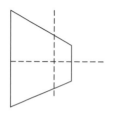

Gray Eminence/Sailor-Gardener
Seeking to balance career
achievement with a satisfying
leisure life.

New Work Venturer/Seeker-Explorer
Looking for new challenge in work
and adventure in life.

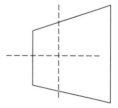

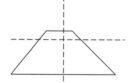

Sailor-Gardener/Seeker-Explorer
Retirement here I come.
Time for leisure and a bit of
adventure.

Gray Eminence/New Work Venturer
Not ready for retirement—
but do I stay with what I
have or launch a new work
venture.

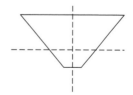

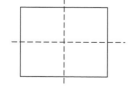

Four Quadrant Preference
Choices, choices,
choices. I want to do it
all—Stress!

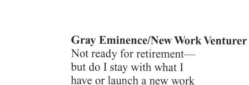

TRANSLATING YOUR PROFILE INTO A VISION

Developing a vision to guide your life course is a simpler matter for someone with a single dominant theme on the Life Themes Profiler than for those with multiple dominant themes. However, don't despair if you have interests running in different directions. The trick is to get all those diverse notes of interests playing together in two-, three-, or four-part harmony. How, for example, might you get it all together if your profile shows a preference for both Gray Eminence and New Work Venturer?

That was the case with Sue, who was a fifty-plus economist with the World Bank and also a fine artist (see Figure 4-4 for her profile). Sue was facing a mandatory retirement situation and had always planned to focus on her painting when she retired. She dreamed of setting up a studio to showcase and sell her artwork and also to feature the art of women she had come to know through her work in the developing world. Art had always taken second place to Sue's work, and now she relished the prospect of making it her primary activity.

As the date of her retirement approached, however, she began having second thoughts about her envisioned future. Although she

FIGURE 4-4. SUE'S LIFE THEME PROFILE.

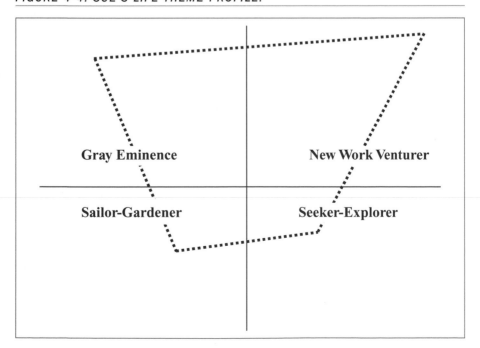

was eager to launch her new life chapter, she was conflicted by a pull from another direction. To put it in terms of the Life Themes model, she was feeling pulled by both the Gray Eminence and New Work Venturer themes. She was finding it difficult to let go of her professional activities for improving the economic conditions of impoverished women in Bangladesh. On the one hand, she could see that the efforts of the World Bank and other agencies were producing slow but hopeful results, and she was convinced there was more she could do professionally in support of this progress. On the other hand, if she were ever going to launch the New Work Venturer chapter of her life, at the age of 58, she needed to start moving in that direction. If she didn't soon launch her new endeavor, she feared becoming too old to make it happen.

She resolved this dilemma by proceeding with her retirement plans for transitioning into her new venture. But she also opted to continue with her professional work, at least for a couple more years on a part-time basis. Drawing on the professional network she had established over the years, she found a suitable consulting situation with the federal government in a project related to her interests. When I last spoke with Sue, she was busily engaged on both fronts of her new life as a Gray Eminence/New Work Venturer. She knew, however, that she was going to bring her consulting activities to final closure in two or three more years, when she would fully devote her time and energies to a New Work Venturer's life. Meanwhile, she was cutting out more time for painting, setting up her gallery, identifying women whose artwork she planned to feature, and doing satisfying work in the waning years of her life as an economist.

FUTURE PLANNING AS A COUPLE

In a committed relationship, planning together is essential if you want to be together harmoniously in the future. The Life Themes Profiler is one of the tools you might find helpful in this endeavor. Figure 4-5 illustrates why. This example is for a couple who retired at about the same time and attended my "What's Next" seminar to recreate a new life together. As Figure 4-5 shows, Donald's future interests profiled as a Gray Eminence/Seeker-Explorer, while Rita's was Sailor-Gardener and New Work Venturer. When they compared profiles, they were shocked and a bit dismayed to find how different their visions for the future were. Donald loved the work he was doing and intended to continue as a consultant indefinitely, or as he said, "to die in the saddle." He also loved to travel and explore new and exotic places all over the world. He was proceeding into retirement under the assumption that he would consult for 30 or so weeks a year and that he and Rita would spend the rest of the year traveling together. Rita had a different vision for retirement. She was looking forward to enjoying their beautiful new home, gardening, grandmothering, and taking advantage of free time to get into great physical condition. Her assumption was that she and Donald would be enjoying her vision of the ideal lifestyle together. She also harbored aspirations of making occasional appearances on the speaking tour as a motivational presenter in her professional area.

FIGURE 4-5. LIFE THEMES PROFILES FOR RITA AND DONALD.

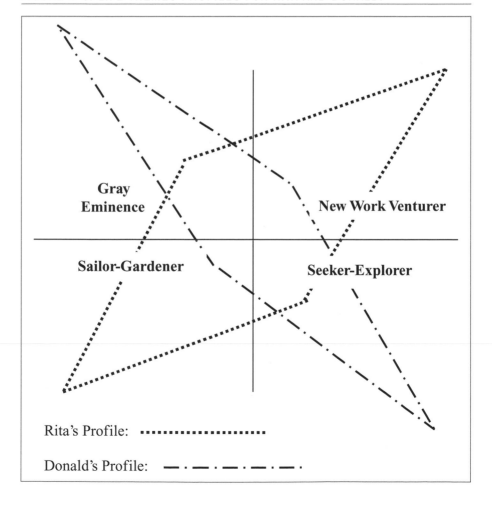

Gray
Eminence   New Work Venturer

Sailor-Gardener   Seeker-Explorer

Rita's Profile: ••••••••••••••••••••

Donald's Profile: — • — • — • — • — •

Bridging their differences took some negotiating, since they were both strongly committed to their visions. While their differing expectations for each other in their new life has continued to stimulate some conflict, they are working on a manageable agreement. For the time being, Donald continues to pursue a busy consulting agenda. Rita often stays at home doing her Sailor-Gardening when Donald travels as a consultant. Then she goes on the road herself, occasionally to deliver a talk here and there. Rita has had to adjust to the fact that Donald has no interest whatsoever in the Sailor-Gardening lifestyle, and he to the fact that Rita would rather remain at home than to accompany him on his many trips. Rita, however, does meet Donald occasionally as he finishes a consulting job, and they have fun traveling to places of interest to both. Donald, in turn, plans to limit his consulting travel to spend more time with Rita. While this lifestyle is not exactly what either of them would have preferred, it seems to be a workable compromise. They frankly admit, however, that their marriage was headed for trouble had they gone forward in unexamined assumptions that the ideal lifestyle for one also fit the other. Without serious discussions and willingness to compromise, they would probably not be together today; or if they were, one or the other would have had to accommodate submissively to the other's wishes.

As things have progressed they both have developed a positive new sense of identity in the portion of their lives in which they go their separate ways professionally and take pleasure in the aspect of their relationship that involves many little honeymoons when together. They both attribute the insights acquired from the Life Themes Profiler for bringing their attention to a potential problem and opening the door to working toward an agreeable compromise.

◆ Prioritizing Your Interests

Are you one of those individuals with so many interests that you have difficulty deciding where to begin? Maybe you start out with approximately twenty-some things you're interested in doing, but before you really get going on these enticing options, you come up with another dozen or more possibilities. Then, as you start into these, they, in turn, produce still other tantalizing ideas and possibilities. As you're probably aware, such a diffuse focus can lead to stress and become an energy drain. There is a remedy, however, for what might be called unbridled interest production. That remedy is prioritization. For many, this can be a bitter pill to swallow, as it means forsaking some activities in favor of others. But, let's face it: this is the only way to orchestrate multiple motifs into syncopated harmony.

Then there are others with a different kind of problem, which is difficulty in identifying just what exactly it is that really attracts their interests. This happens to many who have been so focused on their career that they really have not had time to explore a world outside of work. For those challenged by what we might refer to as *acute interest limititus,* the problem is identifying interesting things to prioritize.

This is a fairly common condition, and for it, too, there is a remedy. That remedy begins with moving away from the mindset of "I don't know what I want to do." We can become conditioned to that kind of thinking, which then turns into a self-fulfilling prophecy. To make a change in this condition, you may need to begin by changing the way you think. As a mature individual, you must know deep down that you are capable of generating ideas of all kinds, including what could make your new life more interesting. Then, as you start to think differently, you move on to identifying and exploring options and making choices. Sometimes you have to dabble and experiment in new areas to see what it is that taps the most interest.

Whether you have too many or two few ideas, here is a process for using your assessment results to develop a manageable list of priority possibilities:

1. Review the list of options related to your high theme areas from the Life Themes Profiler and circle any that interest you.

2. From the choices you have circled select the *10* of greatest interest and record them on the following worksheet. Be sure to add to your list your own creative ideas.
   - In vision generating, you want to capture those ideas that pop into mind in strange places and unexpected times, like in the shower or driving, for example. It's a good idea to carry a capture notebook with you when you're in a vision-generating stage to write down those ideas that come to mind quickly, before they escape.
   - Should you feel the need to expand your list of options, a good way to do that is to look through the index of the yellow pages of a city telephone directory and note any entries that connect with your interests. This, incidentally, is also a good way to explore interests by identifying people and organizations engaged in things about which you might want to learn more. College

catalogs also can provide a rich source of ideas for interesting options.

3. When you have a nice sample of ideas on your list for the next chapter of your life, identify those for which you have the most energy and establish your priorities.
   • Number your priorities from 1 through 10, with 1 being your strongest interest.
   • List your priorities in the right-hand column, as shown with the examples on the "Prioritizing Your Preference" worksheet. Use your intuition to prioritize your list on the basis of what seems to be the most intriguing to next most intriguing, and so on.

4. From your prioritized list, generate a vision as a thematic guide for creating a meaningful direction for the next chapter of your life.
   • Draw on your imagination. Think outside of the box here: after all, you are going to be living your life out of the full-time employment business that has kept you boxed in for so long. So get creative here. Be outlandish!
   • You might find it useful to write out and then revise the written version of your draft until you are satisfied that you have created the vision that captures your new purpose in life.

5. Discuss your vision with others as a way of further fleshing out and crystallizing your ideas. Write out your vision and post it somewhere where you will look at it frequently. To provide a few ideas of what a vision statement might look like, look over these samples.

INVENTING YOUR LIFE ANEW: SAMPLE VISION STATEMENTS

• Sailor-Gardener: Go fly-fishing, become a benevolent grandparent, and get season tickets to watch your favorite baseball team where you can hear the crack of the bat and smash peanut shells at your feet.

• Sailor-Gardener/Seeker-Explorer: Explore the wildlife inhabiting the Polynesian Islands and Boy/Girl Scout leader.

• Seeker-Explorer/Gray Eminence: Become an organizational development consultant and budding Aikido master.

• New Work Venturer/Sailor-Gardener: Own an exercise equipment shop for seniors and country trails biking enthusiast.

- New Work Venturer: Become credentialed as a counseling psychologist specializing in therapy for individuals in life's final stages.
- Gray Eminence/Sailor-Gardener: Mentor/coach future leaders in my field and social chairman of the community garden club.
- Seeker-Explorer/Sailor-Gardener: Become an Appalachian Trail explorer and student of the history of the Iriquois League.
- Sailor-Gardener/New Work Venturer: Lead the local walkers league and English language tutor for nonnative speakers.
- Gray Eminence/New Work Venturer: Become a part-time executive coach to corporate management and Elderhostel tour guide.
- New Work Venturer/Sailor-Gardener: Volunteer for the Women's International Coalition for Economic Justice, advisory board member for the Jack & Jill Toy Company for creating games that promote gender equality, and jubilant grandmother of my growing brood.

Prioritizing Your Preference

Life Theme	Interest Area	Priority
	Example	
Gray Eminence	• Do part-time consulting.	5
Sailor-Gardener	• Take up the piano to play a little Gershwin and Joplin.	3
Sailor-Gardener	• Practice yoga and meditation.	2
Sailor-Gardener	• Study Latin American history.	4
Seeker-Explorer	• Climb in the Andes Mountains exploring Inca civilization.	1

◆ Making Your Vision Happen

A good vision for reinventing your life is one that connects personal interests with a good fit in the real world and provides both motivation and a direction for the next chapter of your life. But to provide life-reenergizing impetus, it is not enough to have a vision. The vision also must be implemented. How many people do you know with grand visions that never go anywhere? What stops many people from going forward with their new life vision is knowing how to make it happen. That, no doubt, has something to do with the fact that it is difficult to see how to do and become something markedly different from what you have been and done. Probably the most important thing you can do in this regard is to use the content of this chapter to create a new vision for your future and then to translate that into a plan of action. From there, it's just a matter of implementing your envisioned new life one step at a time.

Recreating a new chapter in a step-by-step process may seem like slow going if you're one of those whose busy work life has conditioned you to be oriented to quick results. It's unlikely, however, that you can jump from an old structure into new life situation in a single giant leap. Implementing a new chapter of life that is markedly different from the old is likely to be an evolutionary process as opposed to a quick-change event. Perhaps the best advice in making a major life transition is to be future-oriented and to enjoy the process in the current moment. Take comfort in the knowledge that you will get to where you want to be and will become who you want to be. A couple of mixed metaphors are appropriate to this process: Rome wasn't built in a day, and haste makes waste. So be bold in recreating your future vision, remain optimistic, be persistent and patient, and enjoy the process. It's your life, and you don't either want to miss the moment with an overly obsessive focus on the future, nor forfeit the future you could have for lack of vision in the moment.

In transitioning from a full-time employed centered life into a retirement lifestyle you are not only leaving a core structure behind in the form of your career purpose, you are also saying goodbye to your work associations and to the "you" that was. Few of us are content with becoming a has-been. You may know of individuals who retired to lives without recreating either a vision for a new life or generating a revitalizing new personal identity.

At one of the organizations where I work, these has-beens are referred to as *ghosts in the halls*. This is in reference to those who retired from their jobs but continue hanging around their old workplace looking to engage the currently employed in reminiscing about the "good old days" and/or to provide their views, usually of a derogatory nature, of what they see happening to the place.

In this chapter, you have been engaged with what might fill your next life chapter with meaning and purpose. In that regard, The Life Themes Profiler has helped hundreds of individuals clarify their visions and reinvent interesting new lives. Hopefully, you too have found this a useful process. In the next chapter you will have the opportunity to invent a new "you" to replace the one you leave behind as you transition into your next life. Use that chapter to keep from becoming a has-been and to become instead a reinvigorated new you.

SELF-LIBERATION:
TRANSCENDING OLD ROLES

"I knew who I was as a finance specialist and a senior advisor but who will I be when I retire and leave my work and my job title behind?"

—AN ECONOMIST PREPARING TO RETIRE

"Today I'm important, I am somebody. My staff greets me in the morning, they bring me coffee and treat me with respect. The day I retire and walk out the door, however, all that stops. Then who will I be?"

—A CORPORATE EXECUTIVE DISCUSSING RETIREMENT CONCERNS

"I've worked hard all my life supporting others and doing the organization's bidding. I've always been in support roles to others both at home and work. I don't even know who I am outside of Mr. Executive's secretary or Dr. Wonderful's wife. Now it's my time. I want to be my own person and do the things I want to do."

—AN EXECUTIVE SECRETARY RETIRING FROM 30 YEARS OF SERVICE

◆ Changing Life Roles

"All the world's a stage, and all men and women merely players." Shakespeare reminds us that we are all actors on the stage of life. Once you were a daughter, then a mother, and finally a grandmother. Or maybe you were an executive, a finance specialist, a high-performing professional, an academic, a banker or administrative support staff. In the course of our lives, we have all assumed an assortment of roles— some we chose and others we just fell into. But over time, we essentially become our roles. Some of us love the roles we've been playing and some of us hate them, or at least some of them. Whether by choice or by chance, with love or hate, a major life change involves changes in those long-term roles that have scripted our acts in work, at home, and in play. Because it is so easy to unwittingly fall into roles, both positive and negative, it is better to carefully choose what new roles you want to assume and which to end.

To change roles, it is useful first to get clear about what specific roles are contributing to your current state of identity. With that awareness, you're in a better position to decide what roles it's time to leave behind, which to continue, and what new roles it is time to develop. This chapter provides the means for examining the basis of your current personal identity as a reference for recreating a new you for the next stage of your life. In this regard, you will want your new roles to be consistent with the vision of your future that you were conceptualizing in the previous chapter.

◆ Your Identity

What's your reaction to these questions: Who are you? How do you present yourself, or perhaps I should say your image of yourself, at work, at home, and in your professional and social interactions? Who do you perceive yourself to be deep down within the private domain of your core being? And, beyond that, who will you be when you leave your organizational connections behind and enter the senior stage of life?

Our personal identities provide us with a powerful sense of who we are, and who we're not. Identity for most of us is a complex matter. We might see ourselves a certain way in a work setting (assertive leader, strategic thinker, person of action, consensus builder, etc.), another at home (devoted spouse, doting grandparent, caregiver, Mr. Fix-it, Ms. homemaker), and still another in social interactions (attractive individual, community organizer, golfer, etc.) Identity functions like an internal script for behavior, the choices we make, the things we will try (and not), and the way in which we present ourselves in the world. Without a core sense of personal identity, we would have difficulty functioning effectively in the world. We would look and feel like an actor who had no idea what the theme, setting, or plot was in the play.

Some of us have developed positive identities, some negative— most of us are a mixed bag with a sense of assurance and optimism in some arenas of our lives but lacking self-confidence in others. Some individuals develop an identity through a realistic assessment of their talents (Picasso the artist) and others develop an unrealistic sense of self (Hitler the artist). The later example highlights the value of making accurate assessments about one's self (your talents, personal attributes, and your virtues). The world undoubtedly would have been far better off had Hitler, in fact, become an artist rather than a disgruntled fanatic believing himself a talented painter robbed of deserved artistic recognition because of racism. In contrast, the world is a better place for the likes of Nelson Mandela, who clearly possessed both a strong sense of self and a highly accurate assessment of his personal attributes.

◆ Changing Identity

The dictionary defines the term *identity* as "the sameness of a person at all times and in all circumstances." Does that definition, implying that one retains a consistent view of self throughout life, ring true for you? My own experience seems to contradict that premise, at least to a degree. Although a general sense of personal identity may remain with us through prolonged periods of time, we are never finished entities, neither on the inside nor the outside.

If a picture could be taken of one's self image over different intervals of time, we might be surprised to see an interesting progression of change. Our sense of self would be seen to change ever so slightly over some periods. At other times, however, one's identity may be altered rather quickly by dramatic changes happening either on the inside or outside. Externally, an extraordinary event such as death of a spouse or partner, debilitating injury, financial ruin, inheritance of wealth, or an unexpected job promotion to new levels of responsibilities can cause relatively quick changes in identity. A forced retirement from an identity-defining position can also severely alter one's self-view.

Identity-shifting changes go on internally as well. There are developmental, conditional, and reactionary aspects to identity evolution. (I was inclined to use the word *progress* here, but that implies that one's sense of self grows progressively better over time. Unfortunately, however, in that department one can regress as well as progress). Developmentally, I know my sense of self is not the same at age 70 as when I was 16, 21, or 43.

If you're a parent of adult children, you no doubt remember the consternation you experienced as your kids were in the midst of the infamous adolescent identity crisis. That is the period in life in which a youthful child begins actively separating him or herself from parents both physically and psychologically. Although this is a critically important step developmentally in the child's maturation process, it severely challenges our parenting abilities, possibly even to the point of endangering our sanity. Developmental psychology (e.g., Erik Erikson's stages of psychosocial development[1]) teaches us that those who fail to undergo that tryingly difficult period of adolescent identity crisis may either fail to establish a clear sense of who they are and remain identity confused (identity diffusion) or prematurely identify with someone they greatly admire and attempt to take-on their version of that individual (identity foreclosure).

In reflecting on that transition in my own case, I am still amazed by how I morphed from pudgy, awkward kid into a lean athlete (frog to prince transformation) and the hugely positive impact that it had on my youthful self-esteem. Additionally, I realized at a young age that my peers seemed to relate well to a kind of humor that involved not taking myself too seriously. From that awareness I developed a self-deprecating sense of humor, along with an orientation to seeing the funny side of things, which became an adapted part of my adult identity. I also remember my adolescent sister in orthodontic braces and horn-rimmed glasses crying inconsolably in my mother's arms. "I'm so ugly," she wailed. That stage for her soon passed, however, as she transformed into such a lovely young woman that it was all I could do to keep my lecherous friends from her. Through that developmental episode, she transformed from self-conscious shyness into a good-humored, gregarious extrovert.

One's identity alters over the years through physiological changes over which we have little control. Early in life, with hormones hopping, you might have viewed yourself as a sexy thing, a pimply outcast, a social star, or clumsy toad. Fortunately, our hormonal states change over time or we might end up overpopulating the planet with countless numbers of offspring in senior-life attempts to fulfill unabated sexual desires. We know that hormonal changes in the post-fifty stage of life induce women to become more assertive and goal oriented and men to become softer and more affectionate. Even Arnold Schwarzenegger,

---

1. Erik Erikson, *The Life Cycle Completed (Extended Version)* (New York: WW. Norton, 1997).

alias Terminator-turned-governor, showed a softer, more compassionate side in his efforts to provide health care for all Californians. The results of these developmental transformations have produced both joy and consternation in many a relationship. It's not unusual, in the post-menstrual stage of life, for a wife to become engaged in a new vocation or avocation while her husband focuses on winding down his career and looks forward to more "together time" and enjoyable leisure.

Can you recall the changes you experienced in your own transition from adolescence into young adulthood and the way in which those changes impacted your identity? That transition no doubt changed you in many ways, including the way you came to see yourself as timid or assertive, inept or competent, shy or flirtatious, insecure or confident, pessimistic or optimistic, reserved or outgoing, and cautious or risk-taking. In what ways did you learn to adapt your identity through the transitions into young adulthood and then through the later stages of adulthood?

◆ Identity and the School of Hard Knocks

While we, or at least most of us, crystallize an autonomous identity in our young adult years, it does not get crystallized in granite—although some aspects of who you perceive yourself to be may have become hardened, like granite. You might, for example, have become a "conservative or liberal" during your college years and remained so, but changed in other ways. Maybe you transformed from a flirtatious young vamp or math whiz into Professional Woman or Mr. Personality. Our youthful identities respond situationally to life's bumps and bruises as well as developmentally to inner psychological changes.

Situationally, you might be confident, assertive, competent, and humorous with a group of friends on the golf course. But you may have completely different feelings in a work setting where you perceive yourself left out of the inner, power circle. Functioning for a long time in a setting that is unkind to one's esteem has negative consequences on one's sense of identity.

In contrast, performing in an environment where you feel competent and appreciated can do wonders for self-esteem enhancement. I recall, for instance, an ex-client, a bright and assertive woman working as a consultant in an "old boy" agency. In that environment, even though she was a high performer, she felt neither accepted nor appreciated. Over the years, that situation undermined her sense of self-worth to such a degree that she came to question whether she had the right stuff for her chosen profession. All of that changed, however, with career counseling. That helped to reconfirm that she did, in fact possess the right stuff. She then proceeded to find a similar job with another organization. In this new setting, she was highly valued for who she was, acknowledged for what she did, and rewarded by becoming a high-flying executive. Her depleted sense of self-worth, confidence, and esteem disappeared, and she regenerated a positive self-image.

How much one's identity evolves and changes is determined by how strongly one has adopted a particular view of self. The combination of one's genes, personal endowments, early programming, and life circumstances have a lot to do with the strength of the personal identity one develops. Contrast, for example, the identity strength of a Teddy Roosevelt or an Amelia Earhart with that of someone like a Willy Lohman character in Arthur Miller's *Death of a Salesman* or the shy little woman who, with no self-direction, goes through life doing what she assumes is expected of her.

Favorable early beginnings, however, aren't everything when it comes to developing a strong, positive sense of identity, and they aren't required for someone to succeed. Think of someone like Walt Disney or J.K. Rowling, author of the mega-best-selling Harry Potter books. They both came from humble beginnings and evolved into strong personalities through a combination of talent well used in productive efforts.

The point of this is that if you are not entirely happy with all aspects of your current identity, you can, with attention and persistence, grow a new one. We didn't, after all, come equipped in life with identities as we did with potentials, fingerprints, and hair color. Identity is an outcome of personal choices we made in response to our interpretations of life experiences. You can't, of course, change your past life experiences, but you can change your interpretations of your past, your present, and the vision of your future.

Regarding the latter, think of the identity consequences of someone who thought of herself as old at 65 and envisioned the future as a downhill slide. Contrast that with another 65-year-old who perceived herself to be young-at-heart and the future as an exciting time to learn, contribute, and have interesting new experiences. In the world in which we live, it seems to be easier for many to take on a dim view of the future than to see the bright side of things. If you are not blessed with an optimistic view of things, you must work harder at adopting that as your worldview. Although this is no easy task for dyed-in-the-wool pessimists or "rational pragmatists," the proven psychological benefits of doing so are well worth the investment. For help in transforming any aspects of your self-image that could use some enhancements, read Dan Baker's book *What Happy People Know: How The New Science of Happiness Can Change Your Life for the Better*.

◆ Identity-Shaping Roles

In full-bloomed adulthood, the roles we play in life and work provide a core-basis for our sense of identity. Ask a typical 18-year-old the question, "Who are you?" and you're likely to get a response like, "I'm smart, sexy, a good athlete, attractive, popular or studious" (or some less positive variant of those kinds of attributes). Ask a 45-year-old that question and you're likely to get role-based responses such as, "I'm an executive, a civil rights lawyer, a management coach, an aeronautical engineer, or a financial analyst." The 45-year-old might then add other non-work-life roles such as, "I'm a father or mother, a handicap 15 golfer, a Rotarian, a Unitarian, a conservative Republican, or a birder." Transitioning from adolescence into work-centered adulthood involves an identity shift based primarily on perceived personal attributes, as opposed to the seminal roles we plan in work and life.

Of course, we engage in many different kinds of roles and activities in life, and not all of them connect to our sense of identity. It's only those roles that resonate at a level of personal meaning that provide a sense of "This is who I am." You might, for example, engage in work that involves a significant amount of writing and be an excellent writer but have absolutely no sense whatsoever of being a writer. On the other hand, you might consider yourself to be a writer regardless of whether you have more *aspirations* about writing than actually producing much of it. The nature of one's writing might also provide a special sense of identity: You might identify yourself as a journalist, a playwright, a novelist, a poet, a children's book writer, or a science writer. The same is true with the nonwork roles in which we have some ego investment. You might consider yourself a golfer no matter how big or small your handicap. But you could also play golf routinely and well, and feel no identity investment connected to golf.

Unless you happen to be a total narcissist, you are probably aware of both positive and negative aspects of your identity. John the bank manager, for example, considers himself an astute financial analyst and effective manager, but only marginally adept as a coach for his employees. In his home life, he sees himself to be a caring father, a good provider, and a devoted husband. He also believes himself to be overly authoritarian, emotionally detached, and lacking in ability to reveal feelings of intimacy, fear, or joy.

The point here is that one's sense of identity is not an actual entity. Instead it is a perceptual reality. When crystallized into personal belief, perception becomes a core reference from which we operate. So, in John's case, the fact that he believes himself lacking as a coach and a nurturer programs his actions in daily life. His perceptions became a self-fulfilling prophecy. The truth is, these aspects of himself—his perceived traits—are actually behaviors that he could improve. As long as he continues to believe that these are inherited traits, however, he is unlikely to invest time or energy into making such improvements. Until John realizes that he can change those negative aspects, he will continue in his self-programmed ways—unless something happens to change his perceptions.

On the negative side, that something could be an unwelcome event such as a serious health issue, loss of a loved one, or a drift into alcoholism as a chemical replacement for the deep-seated need for human intimacy. On the positive side, a change might be a serious confrontation with an employee or his wife that convinces him to seek coaching or counseling. That encounter might enable him to realize he can change negative perceptions by changing behavior and, with that, his self-image.

It is far better to recognize and improve our negative self-images from pro-active self-initiative than in reacting to external events. My father left me with this important message from his deathbed. He had been a highly successful businessman and good financial provider for his family, but had been locked up emotionally. He was only able to really show and to communicate his true feelings of love and caring after being diagnosed with cancer. One of the last things he shared with me before passing on was a caution about putting off fun things. He had waited too long to realize and to enjoy the fun-loving side of his nature. To do that, he would have had to overcome the conditioning of the identity-shaping difficult times he endured through childhood and his early adult years. The effort, he realized too late from hindsight, would have been well worth the investment. I can't help but wonder if he might have lived longer had he created more fun time in his life.

Retirement planning is a time to take stock of both the positive and negative aspects of our self-belief systems. Now is the time to assess the positive aspects of your identity to see how to capitalize on those in your future years and to clarify the negative aspects to see in what ways you might rescript them.

◆ **Identity, Retirement, and Senior Life**

Most of the significant roles that dominate our time and generate our life's meaning are bestowed upon us early in life by circumstances (son, mother, first-born/the oldest, beautiful woman, big-guy) or the organizations in which we work (accountant, vice president, account representative, minister, division chief). In the fifty-plus years, however, we are faced with losing and letting go of many of our old roles and needing to recreate new ones. After all, how long can someone go around referring to himself as a retired economist, an ex-airline pilot, a nonpracticing lawyer, or an old IBMer? Of course, the short and easy answer to the identity question of who am I is that I am or will be a senior citizen (or as some now refer to this stage of life, young-old, second adolescence, my time, or third stage of life). But what kind of senior person do I choose to be?

Discovering the answer to this question can be especially difficult to those of us who have taken on a professional or organizational identity in our years of service to "the company" or to the profession. I may know who I was as chief finance officer, senior vice president, executive assistant, or certified public accountant, but who am I as a person—who am I now, and who will I become? A new, senior identity can also be difficult to create for those of us who have taken on and been programmed with a behavior and attitude-shaping role such as mother knows best, dear, hard-nosed rationalist, Mr. Executive, Ms. Congeniality, The Boss, ditz, number–two man (as one of my clients referred to himself) or busy professional.

Coming of age at fifty-plus brings changes, both internal and external, that can dramatically alter one's sense of personal identity. Adjusting to senior-citizenship, becoming grandparents, and retiring, all combined with the ever-nearing specter of death, are just some of the unsettling new realities we are forced to come to grips with during this phase of life. Some of these changes may come about slowly and gently, such as adapting to the physical changes that inevitably occur in our bodies, entering the grandparent stage, and transitioning to post-work life. Other identity changes happen quickly and unexpectedly. Suffering a stroke, a heart attack, or a cancer diagnosis can dramatically undermine one's concept of being healthy.

A sixty-plusser friend of mine told me that needing to undergo a hysterectomy operation destroyed her prideful view of being so healthy that she "never got sick." The death of someone dear can dramatically alter one's identity as a mother, husband, daughter, or friend. One day, usually around fifty-something, our own finiteness hits us with the re-alization that we have entered a time referred to as the *bonus years*. Un-til we hit the senior-stage of life, we are inclined to view our own death more as a distant abstraction than as an eminently real event. Whether death-awareness comes gradually or suddenly, the impact of this new "self" awareness is real and it's palpable, as just about any sixty-plusser in a reflective moment is likely to admit. This sobering awareness tends to bring us to a deeper and soul-searching reflection regarding what one's life is about and who one is becoming.

A new, deeper self-awareness can inspire us to profound new un-derstandings and prompt us to make life-enriching changes. Many as-pects of the new self-awareness as a senior person can be exciting and open doors to whole new worlds. One of my clients, realizing her cre-ative inclinations, retired from her administrative position in the cor-porate world and moved to Italy, where she studies classical painting. Another acquaintance retired from the State Department to pursue his spiritual passion as a minister. But coming to grips with aging and our closer proximity to death can also be uncomfortable, leading some to take desperate measures in a futile attempt to deny this reality.

We are faced with three choices in accommodating to the "senior" stage of life. One is that we can reinvent ourselves, capitalizing on the freedom of what Abigail Trafford (author of *My Time*) refers to as a "second adolescence." The second is that we can attempt to deny our age and search for a young lover and a sports car. Third, we can give into the old and depressive stereotypes of aging as a downhill slide into infirmity and death. In the second instance, we probably have all seen people in denial and know that the only folks they are deluding is themselves. If getting a zippy new sports car, a new abode or a younger lover is a life freeing and a meaningful endeavor, then by all means do it! But if such actions are merely an attempt to escape real-ity, it will be a hollow effort.

Ultimately, that will succeed only in delaying the confrontation with the hard question of, "Who am I going to become, and what will I do in this next chapter of life?" Although we may attempt to avoid or deny the inner and outer changes associated with aging, we are ulti-mately forced to deal with them—unless, of course, we choose to take a big step off a high bridge or escape into the soothing haze of alcohol. Coming to grips with graduating into seniorhood is important, because unless I can admit to my age and a future of becoming still more vin-tage, I'll be unable to tap the joys and possibilities of a new stage of life available to be lived!

In today's world, people are living longer, healthier, more active lives than at any time in human history. We live in a world of health and longevity, when old myths about retirement being a short period of idle time followed by quick death presents a totally inaccurate picture of the opportunities available to a rapidly growing army of youthful fifty-plussers. A new model of aging is emerging. No longer are fifty-plussers restricted by outmoded myths associated with aging. In this new worldview of fifty-plus, we are free of many of the responsibilities that encumbered us in earlier life. It is this that enables us to reinvent ourselves, our mindsets about aging and to create exciting lives.

A changing sense of self encourages reassessment. To recreate meaning in our lives, it will be important to invent new roles and to choose them wisely with self-knowledge. But how do you do that when there are more roles than one can even imagine, and only a few of which we might be aware? The answer is that the roles, in order to be identity enhancing and personally meaningful, must align with our vision for the kind of future we dream up for ourselves. The following table may provide some ideas for vision-congruent roles you might consider. Review the roles listed there to see which, if any, speak to you as potential new identity shapers. Add your own ideas to the table.

Possible New Identity-Based Roles

Gray Eminence

- Mentor/coach for younger staff
- Senior advisor
- Consultant
- Corporate board member
- Professional association executive
- Freelancer
- Special projects leader
- Lobbyist
- Interim executive
- Think tank associate
- College professor/lecturer in your field of expertise
- Other _____

New Work Venturer

- Entrepreneur
- Business owner
- Peace corps/AmeriCorps worker
- Career changer
- Foreign exchange worker
- Bed-and-breakfast owner
- Tour guide
- Foreign language teacher
- Skilled craftsman, crafts artist
- Mr./Ms. Fixit
- Vintner
- Night club entertainer
- Politician
- Other _____

Sailor-Gardener

- Gardener
- Biker
- Social golfer
- Fly fisher
- Reader of fine books
- Actor in amateur theater
- Club member
- Family archivist/ historian
- Culinary cook
- Grandparent extraordinaire
- Bon vivant
- Raconteur
- Amateur poet
- Meals on Wheels volunteer
- Other _____

Seeker-Explorer

- Auto racer
- Billiards/chess amateur champion
- Marathon runner
- Sailor-Venturer
- Competitive ballroom dancer
- Mountain climber
- World traveler/ explorer
- Martial arts expert
- Volunteer in resettlement camps
- Advanced education Seeker-Explorer
- Cause-oriented activist
- Private plane pilot with a search and rescue team
- Other _____

◆ Identity-Based Roles Assessor: A Tool for Self-Discovery

For a more in-depth process, complete the "Identity-Based Roles Assessor" on the following pages. As you complete the following assessment, keep in mind that identity-based roles are not always obvious. You might derive a sense of identity from being a manager in your work setting, but if you reflect on that a bit more deeply, the identity might more specifically be an aggressive leader, a no-nonsense decision maker, or a nurturing people developer. Or, on the home front, being a mother might be important to you, but what kind? Are you a soccer mom, a single mom, a working mom, or a homemaker mom? The more specifically you can define the roles that contribute to your identity now and/or in the future, the clearer you can be in defining who you really want to be next.

Identity-Based Roles Assessor

The following pages list some of the more common roles in which people engage in their work and lives. The list does not contain every conceivable identity-based role in which one might engage—such a list would be encyclopedic in size. Blank spaces have been left at the end of the assessment for you to list any other roles in which you have been currently engaged, or think you might want to take on in the future.

Directions for Part I:

To complete the first part of the identity-based assessment, review the list of roles and determine which roles contribute to your sense of current identity to some degree and which roles could be important in your future. Use the following notations to mark your choices in the boxes to the left of each role:

- **M (for Major):** any role that plays a significant factor in your identity in your current work and life situation
- **S (for Some):** any role that plays a small but contributing factor in your current work and life situation
- **D (for Desired):** any new role that you want to assume as a significant aspect of "who you are" in your next life chapter
- **Leave blank:** any roles that contribute nothing to your current identity and will play no role in the next chapter of your life

Part I: Identity-Based Roles

Define the roles you have been playing and those you want to play in the future.

	Analyst: penetrating thinker		Crone: wise older woman
	Animal lover		Conservative
	Accommodator: adaptable		Conservationist
	Adventurer		Coach: mentor, supporter
	Authority in my field		Conformist: traditional
	Attractive person, handsome		Christian, Jew, Muslim, etc.
	Aesthetic: love art and beauty		Dabbler: variety seeker
	"A" Type: hard driver		Dancer: ballroom, folk, etc.
	Artist		Diplomatic
	Biker		Devil's Advocate: reactor
	Brother: sibling and/or friend		Designer: dreamer, envisioner
	Balanced: fair, well-rounded		Discriminate: shrewd, careful
	Charmer: debonair, suave		Dispassionate: unemotional
	Critic: sharp wit and tongue		Educator: enlightener
	Compassionate person		Emotional: excitable
	Competitor: challenger		Empower: encourager
	Consensus builder		Entrepreneur: venturesome
	Computer whiz: nerd		Ebullient person: effervescent
	Creator: original, inventive		Executive: business leader
	Connoisseur: person of taste		Extrovert: outgoing
	Catalyst: change agent		Factual: exact, accurate
	Club/Association member		Family Man/Woman

☐ Farsighted: future thinker	☐ Industrious: productive, diligent
☐ Fast: do things quickly	☐ Introvert: reflective, introspective
☐ Flamboyant: colorful, flashy	☐ Influencer: makes views known
☐ Facile: fluent, smooth	☐ Implementer: makes plans happen
☐ Firm: stand fast for beliefs	☐ Innovative, imaginative, ingenious
☐ Follower: adherent, supporter	☐ Instigator: gets things going
☐ Fun lover: bon vivant	☐ Inquiring mind
☐ Fickle: changeable, mercurial	☐ Inspirer: motivator, encourager
☐ Fastidious: particular, picky	☐ Inscrutable: mysterious, elusive
☐ Firebrand: agitator	☐ Insensitive: cold, indifferent
☐ Frank: candid, direct, plainspoken	☐ Intellect: brainy, thinker
☐ Grump: surly, testy, crusty	☐ Intense: forceful, concentrated
☐ Gardener: love to work in the yard	☐ Individualist: one of a kind
☐ Gentle spirit: benevolent	☐ Intimate: affectionate, loving
☐ Golfer	☐ Intimidator: imposing, tough
☐ Goal-minded/focused/determined	☐ Investor: financially planning
☐ Generous spirit	☐ Intractable: headstrong
☐ Grandparent	☐ Intuitive: instinctive, psychic
☐ Handyman/woman	☐ Irreverent: saucy, brazen
☐ Harmony seeker/Harmonizer	☐ Jocular: jesting, witty, roguish
☐ Helper/Helpmate, supporter	☐ Judgmental: opinionated
☐ Homebody, Homemaker,	☐ Judicious: levelheaded, wise
☐ Hiker	☐ Kindhearted: compassionate
☐ Historian: history enthusiast	☐ Knowledgeable: well-informed
☐ Hobbyist: defining leisure activity	☐ Leader: pacesetter, pathfinder
☐ Horse person: equestrian	☐ Liberal: open-minded, flexible
☐ Humanitarian: philanthropist	☐ Listener: attentive, focused
☐ Humorist: entertaining person	☐ Loving man/woman
☐ Husband/Wife: devoted mate	☐ Loquacious: talkative, verbose
☐ Iconoclast: nonconformist, rebel	☐ Magnanimous: generous,
☐ Idealist: romantic, dreamer	☐ Manager: implementer
☐ Impish: puckish, playful, roguish	☐ Masculine: manly, hardy, virile
☐ Incorruptible: honest, trustworthy	☐ Matriarch: female family head
	☐ Meticulous: methodical, neat
	☐ Moderate: judicious, measured
	☐ Matron: stately older woman

	Modest: humble, unassertive		Reserved: aloof, formal
	Musician/music lover		Reconciler: unifier, mediator
	Mysterious: enigmatic		Reflective: deep thinker
	Naive: guileless, unjaded		Reformer: improves things
	Negotiator: mediator		Researcher: inquiring mind
	Nihilist: skeptic, agnostic		Resilient: adaptable, flexible
	Objective: impartial, unbiased		Resourceful: ingenious, clever
	Observant: vigilant, mindful		Reticent: cautious, restrained
	Opportunist		Risk taker: enjoys taking chances
	Optimist: positive in outlook		
	Pacifist: antiwar, peace maker		Romantic: sentimental, idyllic
	Parent: father, mother		Robust: vigorous, active, hearty
	Partner: collaborator		Sailor: enjoy sailing, boating
	Party person: fun lover		Scholar: learned, intellectual
	Patient person: persevering		Sedate: calm, composed, cool
	Patriot: loyalist, nationalist		Self-assured: confident, cocky
	Passionate, inspired, zealous		Self-contained: self-reliant
	Pessimist: negative in outlook		Sister: sibling and female friend
	Philosophical: theoretical		Sensible: wise, prudent, discreet
	Poised: composed, calm, assured		Sensual: erotic, sexy, physical
			Sociable: affable, friendly
	Practical: down-to-earth		Shopper: loves to store explore
	Professional: career specialist		
	Provocateur: stir things up		Son/Daughter
	Public servant : loyal		Spiritualist: mystic, psychic
	Raconteur: skilled story teller		Sportsman/womanTactful: diplomatic, discreet
	Reader: read widely and avidly		Tolerant person
	Reasonable person		Traditional: conventional
	Rebel: dissenter, non-conformist		Visionary: farsighted, prophet
	Refined: genteel, polished, suave		World traveler
	Reclusive: withdrawn, private		Writer: poet, communicator

Directions for Part II

1. *Identify your 10 top identity-shapers:* From the list of roles that you have marked with an **M** and **S,** identify and circle the 10 that you feel have been the most significant in shaping your self-concept in the current chapter of your life.

   • Record these on the "Identity-Based Roles Profiler" in order of priority (importance in the contribution to your ego-identity). List them in the column headed "Current Life Chapter Roles."

2. *Assess what roles to continue and which to abandon*: From your prioritized list of identity shapers in your current life chapter, decide which of your current roles you will want to:
   - Continue in your next life chapter: Circle these.
   - Leave behind: park them (record them) in the "Roles to Be Abandoned" parking lot.
3. *Consider new role possibilities*: Record all roles from the assessment that you marked with a **D** (of possible interest to your future) in the "Desired Roles" section of the "Identity-Based Roles Profiler."
4. *Deciding on your Future "Top Ten:"* Decide which roles you wish to feature as most important to recreating a new identity for the next chapter of your life:
   - From those you have circled in the "Current Life Chapter Roles" and those you have listed in the "Desired Roles" box, choose the 10 you feel are the most important for the next chapter of your life.
   - Record those top 10, in priority order (most important in the #1 spot, next most important in the #2 spot, etc.) in the box headed "Next Life Chapter Roles."
5. *Importance versus priority*: In the parking lot for "Valued Roles—No Available Space," record any roles that you have identified as desired that didn't make it into your top 10. These should serve as a reminder to keep focused on your top priorities and not get sidetracked with lesser priorities.

The following Identity-Based Roles Profiler is an example of what a completed assessment might look like.

Part II: Identity-Based Roles Profiler

Sample

Current Life Chapter Roles	*Next Life Chapter Roles*
1. Authority in my professional field	1. Spiritual person
2. Leader/Manager	2. Husband
3. Problem Solver	3. Grandfather
4. Husband	4. Gardener
5. Industrious	5. Golfer
6. Implementer	6. Writer
7. Grandfather	7. Humanitarian
8. Intimidator	8. Reader
9. Investor	9. Observer
10. Negotiator	10. World traveler

Parking Lots

Desired New Roles	Roles to Be Abandoned	Valued Roles— No Available Space
Gardener	Authority in my professional field	College professor
Golfer	Leader/Manager	Historian
Writer	Industrious	Problem solver
Humanitarian	Implementer	Investor
Reader	Intimidator	
Observer	Negotiator	
World traveler		
Spiritual person		

Part II: Identity-Based Roles Profiler

Current Life Chapter Roles	Next Life Chapter Roles
1.	1.
2.	2.
3.	3.
4.	4.
5.	5.
6.	6.
7.	7.
8.	8.
9.	9.
10.	10.

Parking Lots

Desired New Roles	Roles to Be Abandoned	Valued Roles— No Available Space

◆ Growing into a New You

Growing into and becoming comfortable in a new identity usually results from a process rather than a quick event. Old habits and structures generate inertia. The bigger the change, the longer it may take to
make the psychological adjustments involved in accommodating to a
new way of being, to grow into a new you. By way of personal example, I recall making the transition from naval officer to professional
counselor. I was excited about making this transition and set out to obtain the necessary degree and experience. But the professions of naval
officer and counseling psychologist involve decidedly different ways of
being. Naval officers give orders, expect instant obedience, tolerate no
back talk, and have powerful authority to enforce their demands.
Counselors listen empathetically, ask nondirective questions, expect
and need to have back talk, and possess no authority to enforce their
suggestions. Naval officers walk, talk, think, operate, interact, and see
themselves completely differently than any counselors I know. You can
take off the crisp Naval officer's uniform, which is intended to command
respect, and don the softer appearing, and non-attention generating

garb of a counselor's attire, but it takes time to learn to walk the walk, talk the talk, and grow comfortable in a new role.

The challenge of doing something and being something quite different might conceivably prevent you from making a major change in roles. Even if it weren't difficult to change yourself, those around you might scoff at the idea of a naval officer becoming a counselor or, an economist becoming a social worker, as was the case with a recent client of mine. This client, after long and careful deliberation, was exploring the idea of taking an early retirement and obtaining a social work degree. With the degree, she intended to work in geriatrics, where she envisioned helping elderly individuals cope with the trials of daily living in their declining years. In exploring the idea of such a career change with university faculty members with whom she was well acquainted, however, she was shocked to find that they found it incredible that a Ph.D. economist would even consider such a change. In this regard, she found male professors to be the more incredulous of the idea.

Her female professors, by contrast, were a bit more inclined to understand her motives and be supportive of such a change. Although the reaction of her professorial friends was unsettling, she was clear enough about what she wanted to do that, at the time of this writing, she is in the final stages of obtaining her master's degree in social work and is interning in a geriatrics center. In another case, an ex-professional hockey player, who, through career counseling, had become excited about getting a degree in engineering technology, was laughed at by his wife and friends, who just couldn't fathom an old jock, at age 33, making such a change. Their reactions hurt him deeply and seriously undermined his enthusiasm for the envisioned new career. Fortunately, he had the good sense to stick with the counseling process and find more supportive friends in undertaking the change. In changing his image from professional hockey player to a techie, he eventually also found that he needed to change wives.

Of course, not all changes may involve the kind of psychological adjustments just described. But it is important to be aware that a transition from one identity-shaping role to another involves getting used to. For this reason it is important to have a clear vision of what it is you want to do and who you want to become to serve as your guiding force in making significant changes in your life. You might find it helpful to enlist support from family, friends, or business associates, or you might want to hire a professional coach or counselor. It's also a good idea to have in mind role models who have made significant changes in their lives and in themselves. Your role models for self-reinvention can serve as a vivid reminder that you, too, can change who you have been to become who and what you aspire to be.

Many individuals see ex-President Jimmy Carter to be such a role model. Carter, after losing the election in 1980, went through a demoralized period of dejection from the involuntary ending of his career and the prospects of an uncertain future. From that period, however, he recreated himself to become, among other things, a carpenter with and an advocate for Habitat for Humanity; founder of The Carter Center, with a commitment to advancing human rights and alleviating unnecessary suffering, and a Nobel Peace Prize–winning senior statesman.

One of my favorite role models for self-reinvention is Katharine Jefferts Schori. Schori is a wife, mother, and an ordained priest in the Episcopal Church. She is also an instrument-rated pilot, a skill that came in handy when she was traveling between the congregations of the statewide Diocese of Nevada, while serving as bishop of that district. But Schori started out as marine biologist after obtaining her doctorate in that field, with a specialization in squids and oysters. She worked with the National Marine Fisheries Service but decided to become a preacher when funding for her work dried up. She obtained a master's of divinity degree and was ordained in 1994 and has served since then in a number of capacities within the Episcopal Church. In 2006, at the age of 52, Dr. Schori became head of the U.S. Episcopal Church, the first woman head of an Anglican denomination anywhere in the world. In taking on her new role as head of the U.S. Episcopal Church, and as a liberal, she faces a church deeply divided over highly emotional issues about change and tradition in areas such as gay rights and the role of women in church leadership. Her response to the reactions by a number of conservative elements in the church against the appointment of a woman in this high position is that she will "bend over backward to build relationships with people who disagree with her."

And in that regard, she has had some previous experience. Recalling similar difficulties in her earlier marine biology days, she said the captain of a science research cruise she was on had initially pledged not to speak to her. But after 15 minutes on board, "He got over it."[2]

Although Carter and Schori are highly accomplished, talented, and unusual individuals, they are not alone. You, too, possess great talent— some developed, some not. In fact, there has never been another one anywhere at any time like you, and there never will be. In that regard

---

2. Kim Lawton's June 23, 2006, interview with Bishop Jefferts Schori, *Religion & Ethics Newsweekly*, available at http://www.pbs.org/wnet/religionandethics/week943/exclusive.html; and *BBC News*, "Profile: Katharine Jefferts Schori" (June 19, 2006).

also, you are not your job title, nor are you bound by any roles you are now playing or ever have played. You are a unique individual with multiple options. Now is your time to decide what and who you want to be and what roles you want to assume in reinventing the new you. Use your imagination to envision the new you, and then begin rehearsing the roles you aspire to play on the next stage of your life. Act III of your life story is about to commence. Who is coming on stage?

ESTABLISHING YOUR
CRITERIA FOR FULFILLMENT

"While being a college dean was gratifying, I realized that my heart was really in the classroom, helping educate students in the biology of life."

—A COLLEGE DEAN RESIGNING HIS POSITION TO RETURN TO CLASSROOM TEACHING

"Why is relationship a top value on my list and not among your top seven?"

—QUESTION ADDRESSED BY WIFE TO HUSBAND IN A VALUES ASSESSMENT PROCESS

"It's sobering to see how out of kilter my core values are with the way I've lived my life."

—AN EXECUTIVE REFLECTING UPON A VALUES CLARIFICATION
PROCESS IN A LEADERSHIP COURSE

RATING YOUR SUCCESS

How successful are you feeling in the current chapter of your life?

Completely
unsuccessful

Partially
successful

Fully
successful

◆   Matter of Life Success

How do you know if you're being successful in life? Answering that question is key to having a fulfilling life in your senior years. During your years in full-time work, success was probably determined largely by the imperatives of the workplace and the pressing responsibilities of home life. Success in the workplace, however, tends to leave precious little leeway for individuality. You either perform to the required standards or look for a new situation. Failing to adjust to minimally acceptable standards or acting out of character with company expectations earns condemnation via poor performance evaluations or even loss of a job. Business owners and senior executives in the private sector are clear about what success means. It's a bottom-line proposition. Failure in that arena means going out of business or being demoted into obscurity.

On the home front, you may have had kids to raise, family expectations to fulfill, or social obligations to meet. More than likely, success in your personal or home life has not been as easy to measure as it was at work. At home, there was no promotion or raise to earn for paying the bills on time or emptying the dishwasher or consoling a disappointed child. Yet at times, you may have felt that success at home was all that really mattered, even if it was intangible. At other times, you may have thought that there was no way you could ever feel successful at home—it was all you could do to keep hanging in day after day. Regardless of how you've evaluated your success at home and at work over the years, you will need to come up with some new criteria for feeling successful in senior life.

◆   The Changing Nature of Personal Success

Throughout our early and mature adult years, success is pretty much determined by exterior conditions such as the expectations of the times and the culture in which we live. Either we adapt to the imperatives of our external world or face the stigma and consequences of failure. But this all changes when we reach the senior stage of life and enter the realm of the "retirement years."

In senior life, our future no longer depends on performance evaluations at work, our dependent kids have become self-supporting adults, and we have achieved at least some degree of financial independence. Having newly acquired the freedom to choose the life we want, we now become confronted with determining what success in this new stage of life will look like.

Is it enough just to get out of bed and be here yet another day without any seriously debilitating ailments? Does success mean getting your golf game down to a low handicap? Or is success setting your own schedule without having to report to anyone else? Isn't just being alive, having a good cup of coffee and a newspaper (or a TV if you're more of a watcher than a reader), and a nice place to sit sufficient in itself? Is everything else just frosting on the cake? Why not simply settle for being grateful that your name doesn't appear in the obituaries on this particular day?

Prior to reaching the senior stage of life, most of us have not spent a lot of time deeply pondering the issue of what constitutes a successful life. Sure, we had some societal expectations guiding our choices about things like career development, marriage, children, a good home, and where to go on vacation. In senior life, however, we are no longer bound by the many standards, expectations, and needs that ruled our earlier years. At some point, probably around fifty-something, we graduate from a life dominated by obligations to a life with more freedom to do as we please and become the person we've always wanted to be. But this new freedom also opens us up to the old existential quandary: What is the good life? To answer that, we have to know what we want.

◆ Life Drift Preventative

As seniors, we need an internal reference for knowing what leads to a sense of fulfillment and what will enable us to reach the end of our lives with the fewest possible regrets. Having clearly defined criteria for success enables us to live each remaining chapter in our life with the self-reassuring knowledge that we are fulfilling our ultimate purpose in life—achieving self-realization.

It is important to remember here that in this context achieving self-realization does not mean living as a self-centered ingrate. To the contrary, true self-realization means living in full-out awareness of and gratitude for the gifts that we have to share and enjoy. Awareness and gratitude go hand in hand. It's hard to be thankful for gifts that we are not aware of having received. So as we leave our former obligations behind, we need to develop a new kind of awareness—one that grows out of an internal sense of who we've come to be and why we're here. Otherwise, we could find ourselves in a state of drift, reduced to the brittleness of dried leaves blown about by the cold winds of meaningless existence.

◆ Gratification vs. Fulfillment

For many years I served as the director of a career assessment and planning center at a large, urban community college that served both traditional college students and adults in career and life transitions. We also provided counseling services to members of the college community, including professors, administrators, and support staff who were feeling plateaued in their work and were looking for new directions in their careers and lives. To better serve these individuals, I created and delivered a series of life/career-planning seminars. These courses provided students with opportunities for reassessing their aspirations and career directions through various self-assessments, options exploration, and goal-planning activities.

Following one of these courses, the college community was shocked when a dean announced he was resigning from his position to return to classroom teaching. Why, asked his many colleagues, would anyone give up the perks that went with his position—better pay, more prestige, a bigger office, and a designated parking spot? The reason, he told us, was that while being a dean was gratifying, it was not fulfilling. As a result of the career/life-planning seminar, he realized that his heart was in the classroom, not behind an administrative desk guarded by an executive secretary. First and foremost, he said, he was an educator who wanted to turn students on to biology, a subject matter about which he was passionate.

Another example of life-changing awareness grew out of a coaching situation I had with a corporate executive. He had come to see me about a problem that was knotting him into a tangle of indecisiveness. His dilemma was over which of two altogether different courses of action to pursue in his career. On the one hand, he was being pressured to move into senior leadership within the organization. But for that to happen, he would have to diversify his managerial experience, requiring him to take on jobs that had only a modicum of interest for him. On the other hand, he'd been working professionally in a position for which he felt a great deal of passion. The nature of this work involved providing direct assistance to a clientele in critical need of his services. There was also a problem with this path, however. He had been in the same position for too long, according to senior management. The crux of the situation was that he wanted to be an executive but not quit what he loved doing in his current position.

I couldn't tell him what to do, of course, but I did ask him how long he expected to live. He immediately reacted by saying he didn't know, and, furthermore, why would I ask such a question? So then I asked him to intuitively give me his best guess as to his age at death and told him that the reason for my question would soon be clear. Okay, he said, he thought he would live until about the age of 87. Next I asked him to envision himself on his last day on earth, at the age of 87. With that as his perspective, I asked him to imagine that he had done what was needed to achieve his promotion to senior executive status and to play that out, like a movie of the mind, through the years right up to his last day on earth. Next, I asked him to mentally play out a second scenario, this one staying with the work he loved. What, I asked, did that feel like over time? Finally, I asked him to check out any other images that might come to mind and again mentally follow such a scenario through to his last day.

When he'd done all that, I asked him to compare all of these scenarios to see which possessed a greater sense of personal fulfillment. After mulling that over a few minutes, he looked me intently in the eye and informed me that he was clear about what he must do. As it turned out, achieving that promotion for him was not the path of ultimate satisfaction. His work was what mattered to him most. But to his surprise, he'd come to realize something else important. Through this process he'd gotten in touch with a strong need for autonomy. He would end up with serious regrets, he feared, if he didn't resign from his organization to create his own consulting practice. His consulting, however, would focus on the type of work he loved and had been doing.

These two vignettes reveal an important message about what's involved in living a fully successful life—namely, not to confuse gratification with fulfillment. *Gratification* is a reaction associated with achieving a need for some fancy that may have been prompted by media advertising. The job of advertising, after all, is to create within us a desire for something we don't truly need, like a car that will make the neighbors envious or facial cream guarantied to make us appear forever young.

Fulfillment, in contrast, is enduring. It's associated with a successful experience that leaves us with a rich memory. Gratification and fulfillment both feel good, but they resonate at different levels of the inner world. It's gratifying to win the lottery, get a promotion, have a great dinner at a fancy restaurant, receive a nice bonus at the year's end, or hit a lucky shot onto the last green. But our sense of satisfaction from such things usually tends to vanish rather quickly. How long does our excitement about a new car or sofa or golf club last? A week? A month or two? Sooner or later, the novelty wears off and we're on to something else that has seduced us. Not so with something that is truly fulfilling.

We feel fulfillment when we experience something that connects with our core values. To live a fulfilling life, therefore, we need to listen to the heart—a heart enriched with a good measure of experience, a little bit of wisdom, and a lot of self-knowledge. Fulfillment occurs in the moment and also remains in long-term memory. We know that what we're doing feels good, deep down in real time, and we remember it with fondness.

For Ginger Rogers, fulfillment must have come from a well-executed step that connected with her need to dance and dance well. For my friend Mary Kaye, fulfillment came when she discovered her core value of creativity and found the right expression for it in making "Indian" jewelry. Now she has another type of fulfillment to deal with—meeting the rapidly increasing demands for her lovely products. Gloria, a counseling psychologist, feels a sense of fulfillment by connecting her core value to meaningful work. She feels energized when she helps individuals resolve issues causing emotional pain and then helps them move on to exciting new directions in their lives.

What do you recall as being life-enriching experiences from the past? What might create fond memories in your future?

◆ Who Determines Your Success?

Who has determined your success in the past? Has it been your boss, your financial planner, or your friends? From the grand vantage of hindsight, I've come to realize that it was my father who I was desperately attempting to please throughout my young adult years. As I've mentioned previously, Dad was sole owner of a successful business that kept him preoccupied with business concerns until shortly before he died from prostate cancer at the age of 69. Physically he was a large man who I, and many others, found to be an intimidating presence. This was made all the more pronounced by his generally sullen, detached manner. He was also work-driven—off to his business early in the morning, home late at night, seven-days a week, with little time for involvement in family matters. Family was my mother's domain. The way I processed all of this left me with a subconscious obsession to please my dad. I wanted him to notice me and give me some attention. So I tried to earn his attention through stellar achievement. How else could I make him proud of me? What else would prove that he loved me?

It took a major failure in my life, which induced me to undergo counseling, for me to become conscious of my obsession and recognize the sheer folly of it. Finally, at the age of 33, I was able to let go of this obsession in favor of a more authentic, inner reference for defining my success. As an interesting side benefit of freeing myself from my old obsession, I realized that it was actually the image of my father that I had in my head that I had been trying to please—not my real father. In reality, my father had loved me all along; he just didn't show it in a way that I was able to recognize at the time.

It's not unusual for younger males to think that they must please, exceed, or rebel against their father in order to succeed. The image a person has of his or her mother also may be a benchmark for determining whether one is successful. A mother issue, in fact, was at the source of a problem for a client I counseled a few years back. His presenting, or "surface" issue, was that he wanted help for getting into the CEO track. But, in discussing his aptitude and motivations for that, it became rather obvious, to me at least, that this was a hollow objective. He lacked the fire-in-the-gut motivation that such a goal requires. In exploring that with him, it turns out that he'd somehow come to the conclusion, for whatever reason, that the way to make his mother proud was to become a chief executive officer. The essence of his real aspirations, however, was something extremely different. Having understood it was a fantasy mother in his head who he'd been endeavoring to please, he made a rather dramatic shift in his career plan. Instead of trying to become a CEO, he embarked upon a plan to become a disk jockey. I don't know if he ever realized his new dream, and if so, if that made his mother happy. What I do know is that he left my office unburdened from an unrealistic expectation. He walked out happy with a new, more realistic dream that was more in line with his personality and talents.

Mothers, fathers, and grandparents—they often have strong aspirations for their progeny. Spouses also frequently want their mates to succeed in the dreams that they have for them. How many spouses have urged a mate to do what is necessary to ascend the corporate ladder? How many parents have slaved away at unfulfilling work or extra jobs in order to be able to send their children to expensive colleges or universities? How many, for that matter, have stood in long lines to get their children enrolled in the "right" preschool? Who wants their children left behind in the race for the keys to success in our materialist culture?

A good friend of mine, an ex-Catholic priest, left the church to marry a woman he loved and to pursue a career in a suit rather than a robe. My friend, whom I'll call J. P., confided in me that he knew his actions would be the death of his mother. J. P.'s life as a Catholic priest fulfilled the lifetime dream his mother had held for him. She simply could not find it in her heart to forgive him for what she considered to be his unpardonable sin in abandoning the priesthood and smashing her pride in his prominent status in the community. His mother was so bitter, in fact, that she refused to attend his wedding. She died shortly after that, perhaps of a broken heart. It took courage for J. P. to break through the pain and disillusionment he felt at his mother's refusal to grant him the right to his own life. But he knew that he had to live his own life in a way that was fulfilling for him, rather than for his mother and her unfulfilled dreams.

I myself confess to wanting my oldest daughter to become a child psychologist. Fortunately for her, she has had the good sense to follow her own guidance in another direction, one that heeds her own calling rather than her father's wishes for her. Undertaking a major life transition is the time to reassess who has unduly influenced your quest for success in the past. Once you've figured that out, you are ready to decide who it will be in the future.

Use the following checklist for help in getting a clear picture of who has had excessive influence on your quest for success. You might begin by first checking anyone who has served as a defining agent of your success efforts in the past. Next, circle anyone who will serve as a significant inspiration for or judge of your success in the years ahead.

- ❑ Mother, father or other parental authorities
- ❑ Spouse or significant other
- ❑ Role model(s)
- ❑ The boss
- ❑ Colleagues at work
- ❑ Professional peers
- ❑ Former teachers/professors/mentors
- ❑ Religious community
- ❑ Contemplative community
- ❑ Civic community
- ❑ Children
- ❑ Grandchildren
- ❑ Friends and acquaintances
- ❑ Physician
- ❑ Work group
- ❑ Cultural and/or family heritage

- ❑ Country club associates
- ❑ Sports/recreation buddies
- ❑ Pub or tavern buddies
- ❑ Bridge club or other such group
- ❑ Historical or legendary heroes
- ❑ A dream idol or famous person
- ❑ Neighbors
- ❑ A spiritual guru
- ❑ Therapist
- ❑ Paramour
- ❑ Ego, sense of personal pride
- ❑ Authentic self
- ❑ Other _____

◆ Core Values and Ultimate Success

Now that you have focused on those you have chosen or allowed to inspire or judge your efforts at success, let's explore what's needed for you to experience fulfillment. I'm not referring to small successes here and there, although they are important and can add up over time to a substantial degree of success. What I'm referring to here is the kind of ultimate success that you want to be thinking about at this stage of life. This kind of success not only entails knowing that you're living a fulfilling life in the current moment—it provides fulfillment from the perspective of our final life review. Ultimate success is a profoundly personal experience: It can only be distilled from the you that flows directly from your core values.

Could you experience true self-fulfillment if the manner in which you were investing your life's resources (including energy, time, knowledge, wisdom, money, and personal/profession development) failed to connect with what you value most dearly? Imagine, if you will, someone who abandons a core value of autonomy for the sake of convenient employment in an organization where she reports to others in a role of hierarchical dependency. Certainly the basic need for employment would be met, but it would come at a high cost to well-being.

No matter how well we think we have succeeded in a given situation, success is doubtful when self-motivation is lacking. Self-motivation leads to that critical sense of congruency, of being true to yourself. If autonomy is a high-order priority, you owe it to yourself to find a way of becoming your own boss. My friends Sarah, Dan, and Thad are good examples of people who found ways of doing just that. All three had tried working for others but simply couldn't deal with being at the beck and call of someone else. They had to do their own thing. For Sara, that involved becoming an independent consultant. For Dan, it was creating a unique, one-man business. And for Thad, it was buying commercial real estate, fixing it up, and selling it at a nice profit.

RIGHT VALUES VS. ULTIMATELY SATISFYING VALUES

Have you ever made a remark about someone having no values? The truth is that we all have values; we just don't share the same set. As individuals, we may be inclined to think of our values as the "right" ones and the different values of someone else as "wrong." When people with one set of values vie for dominance over people with a different set, we often end up with conflict in families, communities, and the world. But values conflicts also occur within an individual.

If you've ever found yourself paralyzed by a choice you needed to make, the likely cause was that two deeply held values were in conflict. The previous story I shared of the executive in a quandary over which course to pursue is an example of an interpersonal values conflict. He was stuck between a desire for promotion and the need for work that was a heartfelt service. He resolved his conflict only when he realized which value outranked the other.

Values form the basic structures of our personal beliefs, determine organizational policies, and define national priorities. Some folks and some factions of like-minded individuals feel so convinced that their values are so supremely "right" that they feel duty-bound to impose them on the world, or at least their world. As we see everyday, there are people who have few qualms about killing those whose values they can't tolerate. Consequently, we have witnessed all too many examples of ethnic cleansing, religious wars, and deadly family feuds. We also have seen what happens when values issues become so highly charged and propagandized that a Right to Life advocate murders a Right to Choice activist, or when so-called peace demonstrators riot and ransack an urban district.

On a more positive note, we also have seen individuals with shared values coming together to promote good causes. The green movement, Doctors without Borders, and Save the Whales are just a few of the thousands of values-driven associations doing good things on our planet. We can only hope that we will see more individuals, groups, organizations, and countries adopt value systems that are based on compassion, tolerance, and serving the common good.

We all are subject to intensive values programming throughout our early years. In fact, by about the age of 20, our values are pretty much cut, dried, and applied. By then we are convinced that we know what's good and bad, right and wrong, acceptable and not. We've been fed the values for making these determinations by our family, culture, particular environment, education, and religious/spiritual affiliation—not to mention the constant bombardment we receive from the media. Much of our values programming has occurred at the subterranean level, so that we are usually not conscious of the huge amount of indoctrination we've absorbed from all these sources.

After the age of 20 our values may change, but not easily. It takes a psychological knock on the head or a significant emotional event to cause us to examine our early programming and values system. Life does, of course, present us with any number of such events, but even then we may resist taking a close look at the values that shape the choices we've made. We might be afraid that examining our values system will lead to changes that result in changing our whole life structure.

Let's say, for example, that we were values-programmed with admonitions to "always work hard, do what you are told, obey proper authority, don't trust minorities or folks over 50, go about your own business, and stick to your guns." No matter how much we attempt to live by these values, there is little likelihood of their providing richly satisfying outcomes. Some of us have been fortunate to receive values programming that supports life satisfaction; we may have grown up with revered role models for values like "It's better to give than to receive," or "Abide by the golden rule," or "Follow your dreams." Virtually none of us, however, has been value programmed so wisely and well that we couldn't benefit from an examination of what's at the core of our motivations and feelings and make some adjustments.

VALUES AND BEHAVIOR

Core values serve as operational guidelines for behavior, influence our views of others, and become the basis for our judgments and moral principles. Although values are not the sole impetus for behavior (personality style, habits, and attitudes about life are some other influencing factors), they are a primary determinant in matters both large and small.

Values play a key role in how big a tip you leave, how you treat others, what career path you've chosen, and who your heroes are, both in politics and legend. Values influence your judgments about others and become the basis for your self-judgments. The little voice that natters away incessantly in your head may be an indication of how well your actions conform to your values priorities.

For example, I have a little voice in my head right now, as I write this, nattering away about violating my vow to let go of 20 pounds. After I consumed a chunk of dark chocolate and washed it down with a double latte, a little voice piped up and said, "Don't you have any willpower? You should be ashamed! Unless you can control your eating habits, you're going to end up pudgy." If I had snacked on some fruits and nuts instead, no doubt I would have heard a little voice with a self-congratulatory message like, "Good choice! You bypassed instant gratification for long-term satisfaction." It may be important to listen to that little voice in your head for clues as to the values it speaks to.

Values influence and drive our behaviors in any number of ways, both consciously and unconsciously. I recall a rather humorous example of that. I was standing at a busy intersection in downtown Chicago a few years back while attending a national convention of the American Counseling Association. This was a huge convention attended by several thousand professionals, and scores of presentations were taking place in a number of hotels. In a rush to get from one hotel to another, I was impatiently waiting for a traffic light to switch from red to green so I could cross the street and get to a presentation I really wanted to hear. A quick glance up the street informed me that traffic was conveniently backed up enough to give me enough time to cross the street against the red light. As I began to cross the street, a woman standing next to me saw what I was doing and also began to cross the street. She took only a few steps into the street, however, and then I heard her say out loud, "But it's red." With that, she retraced her steps to the curb to wait for the green light she needed to sanction her crossing.

What strikes me most about this little episode is how our values influenced our behaviors. For me in this situation, a value involving intellectual stimulation took precedence over strictures for regulating pedestrian street crossings. I want to be clear here that I consider myself to be a law-abiding citizen. In this situation, however, one of my other values topped the one admonishing me about the risky business of crossing at an intersection against a red light in the downtown traffic of a major city. The woman on the curb also appeared to be attending the conference and may well have been heading to the same presentation. But for her, a personal value of obeying the law took precedence over getting to a presentation in time to hear a leading psychologist whose life work had done much to contribute to a more humane world.

At times we need others to help make us aware of what's really important. I was reminded of this in a recent coaching situation with a work-obsessed executive who is also a devoted husband and father of two young boys. Our discussion focused on his agenda-driven proclivities that carried over from work into his home life—with some significant benefits and some severe costs. One benefit was that he used a to-do list to help him be handy around the house. He was constantly fixing or improving something. The bad news also dealt with his to-do list. He was so obsessed with getting things done that he found it exceedingly difficult to relax and have fun. Somewhat chagrined with himself, he confided that he had recently been "too busy" to take time out to accommodate his wife's request to go for a little ride for a few moments of unstructured time together.

Around the same time, his wife intercepted him as he was about to head out the door to purchase some additional materials needed to complete his current project. When she heard that he was off to the hardware store, she blocked his way and insisted he take one of the boys along, to which he consented. Reflecting on that episode, he realized that the short time he spent with his son turned out to be a significant bonding moment. In retrospect, he learned that time with his sons was far more valuable than any satisfaction he would ever get for finishing a project on his to-do list. Thanks to his wife's timely interventions, he became more aware of his values priorities. He let go of his old programming to be constantly productive and began to be proactive in seeking other opportunities to enjoy his family.

How might your values be influencing your behavior? Does the programming you got about being productive frequently overrule how you respond to situations involving relationship or being in service to others? Has a value for career advancement ever caused you to violate a personal ethics value? Have you ever stood up for your value of a "committed relationship" by taking some action that has jeopardized a friendship or career advancement? Have you had a tendency to let daily routine and the tasks at hand preoccupy your attention to the exclusion of an alternative that might ultimately be more satisfying? If any of these situations fit you, it might be time to reexamine and reorder your core values. Are you ready to act on your deepest values in your daily action?

CHANGING VALUES AND SENIOR LIFE

Entering life as a senior citizen is definitely one of those "significant emotional events" calling for values reassessment. As I enter my seventh decade, I realize that my values priorities are no longer exactly what they were in adolescence—or even in my twenties and thirties, for that matter. Over time, spirituality, generativity, and health have all migrated out of my psychic backwoods to premier spots in my values landscape.

In our earlier days value priorities tended to focus more commonly on concerns around relationship, career, child-rearing and/or home-building, and identity clarification. Significant events may have altered our values priorities over time—maybe without our even being aware of such changes. But the most typical scenario I've found in my counseling practice is that when it comes to career and life choices based on our values, most of us have unconsciously cruised along the same roads that we did 20, 30, or even 40 years ago. Moreover, if we haven't been actively repairing and improving those roads over the years, they are probably in pretty bad shape by now. Over the years, we may have changed jobs, residences, cars, friends, wardrobes, entertainment venues, diets, and, yes, even mates, a number of times. But when, in all that time, have we even given a thought to updating our values?

When, for example, did you first decide to marry, and what were you seeking? Were you looking for companionship, a generous provider, a good-looking mate, someone with compatible religious beliefs? What would you look for today? When did you decide initially to pursue your career, and what was the basis for your decision? Was your choice based on money, fame, power, or the desire to change the world or affiliate with an organization you greatly admired? What would guide your choices today? The values priorities of your youth may have little relevance to the kind of fulfillment you want in senior life.

Over the years I've counseled scores of individuals in their senior years who have, in effect, remained prisoners to decisions made early in life, even when it later became apparent that these were poor decisions to begin with. Some remained with an unsuitable partner, career choice, or organization, even in the face of a significant gap between their values priorities and their current life choices.

One such individual was a medical doctor in his late forties who had been encouraged by colleagues to come see me. As a part of the counseling process that followed, he completed an assessment that showed strong proclivities to creativity. In reacting to his assessment results, he confided that in his early years he'd really wanted to pursue a career in the arts. His father, however, put the kibosh on that aspiration. His father refused to pay for an education that was only going to "relegate his son to the ignominy of becoming a starving artist." Honoring his father's wishes, he'd gone on to develop a successful medical practice. That, it turned out, was a choice that made him occupationally successful but emotionally unfulfilled. No matter how hard he tried, he simply could not get his heart fully into his work. Unfortunately for him, he felt it was too late in his life to make a change to pursue his passion in the arts. He would have to postpone such aspirations until retirement, he concluded, as he was just too much invested in a successful practice.

This story ends with an interesting twist. A few days after our last session and his decision to let the momentum of his past continue to dictate his future, he came back to see me. But, this time, not for himself. He asked if I could provide him with a couple of the assessments he'd taken to give to his adult kids, who were about to enter graduate school. Handing him the assessments, it occurred to me to ask if, by any chance, his kids were headed into the medical profession. With an ironic grin, he said, "Yes, and guess who was behind their decisions?" His reflections on his own personal experience led him to reprioritize his values about directing his kids' career choices. He had come to appreciate that personal satisfaction was a higher-order criterion for personal success than a father's values about security or vanity.

◆ Your Criteria for Personal Success

Ultimate success depends on making decisions that enable you to live congruently with your most precious values. That, of course, requires clearly knowing what your core values are and getting your values priorities straight. "Assessing Your Criteria for Personal Success" is designed to help you clarify and prioritize those values that are core to determining how successful and fulfilled your life will become in your next chapter of life. It is divided into three parts:

> Part I: Assessing What Success Means to You
>
> Part II: Prioritizing Your Personal Success Criteria
>
> Part III: Applying Your Criteria for Personal Success

IDENTIFYING WHAT SUCCESS MEANS TO YOU

In Part I, you will assess what defines your success in your current life by assigning a rating to each of the items in a list of Success Criteria. Then you will rate each item for how important you want it to be in the next chapter of your life.

PRIORITIZING YOUR VALUES

As you work through the process in Part I, you may discover that values priorities for your future do not match perfectly with those from your past. Seeing and understanding such differences will enable you to see where there is compatibility and where there's incongruity. Where there is compatibility between old and new values priorities, you can expect smooth sailing into a new life. It's where the gaps exist that you will want to pay special attention. It's there that you will need to make adjustments if you are to accommodate to a new way of being and doing. Part II will help you do this.

For instance, what if "Living a well-balanced life" came out as a top priority for your future but has not been so in the past? You might yearn for better balance but find yourself working against the currents of past obsessions, habits, and programming. Your early life scripting can make a desired lifestyle change so uncomfortable that you simply give up trying to change things and give in to old habits.

I find that rescripting my values programming involves a lot more than my good intentions. This became even more readily apparent to me the other day when I was talking with a friend who retired a few years ago after being a college English professor for 35 years. He was telling me how hard it had been to change his own deeply ingrained programming. In the process, he told me about a recent epiphany he had had.

"You know, David," he said, "for the first time since retiring, I am no longer feeling driven by the need to be productive."

Still experiencing the self-generating pressures to be productive, I couldn't help but be envious of his newfound freedom. How, I asked, did he get to this more relaxed, less obsessive state? His answer: Knowing what he wanted, how he wanted to be different, and acting on that agenda. There is, he added after a moment's reflection, something else—to be patient with yourself. That seems to be excellent advice, and I'm "working" on it.

APPLYING YOUR VALUES PRIORITIES

Before moving on to Part III, stop and evaluate where you are. What differences do you note in your values priorities from your current life versus those in the next chapter of your life? Note where there are congruencies and differences on your two lists. Comparing the two lists can reveal what's going to be easy and what might be tough in making the transition to your new life.

Perhaps you see that working for a cause you care deeply about has been and will continue to be a high priority. Or maybe you discovered a mission for which you've had a passion, but until now, had little time to devote to it. Such was the case with a client of mine who loved to work at a shelter for injured animals (hawks with broken wings, foxes missing a leg, wounded deer, and such). Before retiring she was able to find only a few hours here and there for this passion, but she was eager to devote a great deal more time to it in retirement when she could align her passion with the way she spent her time.

Where are the differences on your two lists? Is "being creative" a top priority for your future but not to be found on your current list? If that is the case, you may need to decide in what ways you want to be creative. There are many avenues for expressing your creativity, such as creative writing, quilting, watercolor painting, or creating games for Alzheimer patients—all of which were new life directions taken by retirees with whom I'm familiar.

Once you have identified your values for the next chapter of life, you will want to prioritize the core values for your future. A helpful process for achieving this objective is to evaluate aspects of your current life for insights to the future. Part III, "Applying Your Criteria for Personal Success," will help you with this objective.

As you take the following assessment, and especially as you work through prioritizing your values, you will probably find some comfort zones and some unexplored territory for your senior years. Whatever the results, just remember to be patient with yourself.

Assessing Your Criteria for Personal Success

The following assessment is designed to help you clarify and prioritize those values that are core to determining how successful and fulfilled your life will become in your next chapter of life. Follow the directions to complete each of the three parts and use your results as a basis for discussion, where appropriate, with your partner or significant others.

Directions for Part I

Step 1: Assess what defines your success in the current era of your life by assigning a rating to each of the items in the list of Success Criteria.

- Use the following rating scale to record your choices in the left-hand column headed "Current Life Chapter."
- Use the blank spaces at the end of the assessment to add any additional items that should be on your list.

Assessment Rating Scale for Success Criteria

4 = completely true for me
3 = significant degree of relevance for me
2 = some relevance for me
1 = little relevance for me
0 = absolutely no relevance for me

Step 2: Review the list of Success Criteria again and rate each item for how important you want it to be in the next chapter of your life.

- List your ratings in the right-hand column headed "Next Life Chapter."
- List any additional criteria you deem important to your future in the blank spaces at the end of the chart.

Part I: Assessing What Success Means to You

Current Life Chapter	Success Criteria: The Bedrock Values of Personal Fulfillment	Next Life Chapter
	Receiving promotions in work	
	Having financial well-being	
	Living a well-balanced life	
	Being respected for who I am	
	Receiving recognition as a top performer in my professional field	
	Having autonomy (reporting to no one but myself)	
	Engaging in work I enjoy	
	Having a nine-to-five job	
	Enjoying a hobby/leisure activity	
	Knowing that what I do makes a difference	

	Using and developing my talent	
	Traveling and exploring the world	
	Being entrepreneurial	
	Being in a committed love relationship	
	Learning and growing as a person	
	Being physically fit and healthy	
	Presenting an attractively appealing appearance	
	Enjoying quality time with my family life	
	Enjoying solitude, quality time to myself	
	Owning a pleasingly comfortable home	
	Being creative	
	Engaging in interesting challenges	
	Contributing to future generations	
	Gaining recognition for my achievements	
	Feeling at ease and comfortable about myself	
	Enjoying status—prominence by position or achievement	
	Being in a position of power and influence	
	Working for a cause I care deeply about	
	Affiliating with a prestigious organization	
	Excelling in a sport or athletic activity	
	Living true to my religious or spiritual beliefs	
	Having access to a wide array of cultural activities	
	Being actively involved in community life	
	Applying my knowledge and wisdom	
	Socializing with friends	
	Having great toys (car, boat, motorcycle, etc.	
	Other:	

Directions for Part II

From your assessment results, complete the following chart to determine your values priorities from your current life chapter and those that you intend to establish as your priorities for your next life chapter. As much as possible, identify and list your values in priority order. Which single value do you hold most deeply? Which is next? What's after that?

This may not be an easy task. You may find many values competing for top billing on the current and futures stages of your life. Should you find that narrowing your list down to the top 10 might be too challenging, you might wonder why you should bother. Don't give up!

Here are some ways that having clearly defined and prioritized values can benefit your quality of life:

- Making choices and decisions with better prospects can lead to a sense of personal success and fulfillment.
- You can learn to manage your behavior so that it's congruent with what's most important to you at this stage of your life.
- You can minimize inner conflict by understanding which inner motivations competing for your attention take precedence over others.
- You can manage stress and conflict with others by knowing what issues connect with values you are willing to go to the mat for, and which issues you can let pass by with minimal engagement on your part. In other words, clarifying your values priorities provides key insights for knowing which battles you are going to fight and why. You will also be more adept at identifying which issues you are going to minimize or ignore, and your reasons for doing so.

Begin the following process by first prioritizing what have been your core values in your "Current Life Chapter." Then proceed to your desires for the "Next Life Chapter." You might want to work with pencil and have a good eraser nearby, since you're likely to be making changes as you think about your choices.

Begin by reviewing those values that you rated 4s in Part I for selecting your "top 10." Draw on your intuition in completing this process and "trust your gut" in selecting your choices.

Part II: Prioritizing Your Personal Success Criteria

Current Life Chapter	*Next Life Chapter*
1.	1.
2.	2.
3.	3.
4.	4.
5.	5.
6.	6.
7.	7.
8.	8.
9.	9.
10.	10.

Directions for Part III

Step 1: From those core values you prioritized in Part II under " Next Chapter of Your Life," list your top seven values on the chart in Part III, "Applying Your Criteria for Personal Success."

* Record your top seven values in the space "Bedrock Values for Assessing How Successful You Will Be in the Your Next Life Chapter."
* As you transcribe this list, you might want to think through your values priorities again and put them into your own words.

Step 2: This step asks you to determine how fully those values you have identified as top priorities in the next chapter of your life are being met in the current chapter of your life. Use the following scale in making your determination:

Rating Scale

+ + value fully satisfied in current situation
+   value mostly satisfied in current situation
+ − value moderately satisfied in current situation
−   value mostly unsatisfied in current situation
− − value completely unsatisfied in current situation

Step 3: Focus on the column headed "What Has Defined Your Sense of Success in the Current Life Chapter?" Use this column to determine as best as you can the degree to which a core value is currently being satisfied.

* If you have rated the value as being either partially or fully satisfied in your current situation, try to identify the conditions, situations, and actions that have proved satisfying.
* An example is provided for what a completed matrix looks like. For Bernard, for example, completing his personal success matrix helped him examine his current life situation and determine what would provide future fulfillment.

Step 4: Focus on the column headed "What Has Been Missing in Your Current Life Chapter that Would Provide You with a Fuller Sense of Success?"

* Use this column to determine, as best you can, what it would take in your current life situation to more fully satisfy your core values.
* You might again find Bernard's sample profile to be helpful. It follows the form that you will use for "Applying Your Criteria for Personal Success."

Part III: Applying Your Criteria for Personal Success

Priority	Bedrock Values for Assessing How Successful You Will Be in the Next Life Chapter	Rating	What Has Defined Your Sense of Success in the Current Life Chapter? (conditions, situations, actions)	What Has Been Missing in Your Current Life Chapter that Would Have Provided You with a Fuller Sense of Success? (conditions, situations, actions)
1				
2				
3				
4				
5				
6				
7				

Bernard's Example

Priority	Bedrock Values for Assessing How Successful You Will Be in the Next Life Chapter	Rating	What Has Defined Your Sense of Success in the Current Life Chapter? (conditions, situations, actions)	What Has Been Missing in Your Current Life Chapter that Would Have Provided You with a Fuller Sense of Success? (conditions, situations, actions)
1	Living and growing spiritually	+	Involved in a church with an active adult education program. Reading and discussions with wife and friends.	A disciplined meditation agenda to quiet the mind and experience a sense of inner calm and stillness.
2	A committed love relationship	+ +	The relationship with my wife is a source of great satisfaction in my life. It's something we both work at and neither takes it for granted.	While being confident of our mutual love, I appreciate our needs for separate interests and also for continuing to explore and discover new areas of mutual interests.
3	Enjoying my family	+	Relish and enjoy our kids and grandkids. Love watching and helping the grandkids learn and grow.	With kids and grandkids in different areas, providing equal time and attention is challenging.
4	Using and developing my top talents and strongest interests	+	Have enjoyed using and developing my creative and coaching abilities in work with adults and in writing.	While I feel my writing skills have been improving, I've been falling behind in the creative applications available now with the Web.
5	Work I enjoy	+ –	Enjoy my work in coaching adults and creating useful resources. Growing weary of the travel and time away.	Looking to create some new ventures in which I can contribute creatively but be at home more.
6	Having fun with good friends	–	Have a great group of friends and growing number of friendships in our new community.	We enjoy time with friends, which is an important need. But want to better balance that with time for ourselves.
7	A home in which I feel at ease and comfortable	+ +	Love our new home and enjoy my wife's artistic enhancements.	Would like more time to putter around the yard and do some light gardening.

◆ **Interpreting the Sample Criteria Application**

Take a look at Bernard's sample for ideas on how a completed report might look. The sample report reveals two ways in which the process was helpful to Bernard and can be for you:

1. Examining your current life situation helps reveal what may satisfy your core values priorities in the future. In that regard, note from Bernard's sample report that a value of "Using and developing my top talents and strongest interests" has been partially met in his current life situation. He has met these needs by using his coaching abilities in his work with adults and by developing creative abilities through various writing projects. He plans, therefore, to continue with these kinds of activities in the future. It's just that Bernard will be doing these things on his own from here on, rather than as part of a full-time employment situation.

2. Your current life situation may also provide insights into what's been missing and what might have provided deeper satisfaction. Bernard, for instance, realized that his top value priority of "spirituality" was being only partially met and concluded that a disciplined meditation practice could more fully support that core value. Based on that realization, he started participating in a local Buddhist meditation group and weekly yoga classes. He also decided to explore more options within his own faith tradition and accepted an invitation to meet with a men's breakfast group on a monthly basis.

Bernard wanted to make some minor adjustments but felt that he didn't need to make any major changes at this point. If most of your values priorities are currently being satisfied, you might want to continue in your current situation, perhaps with some fine tuning here and there.

Or if your values priorities are being met but life circumstances have dictated the necessity for change, you might want to recreate something fairly similar to what you already have, as much as is possible within the parameters of your current life situation.

However, should your core values for the next chapter of life be completely unsatisfied in your current life, you would want to look at ways you could restructure your current conditions, situations, and actions.

◆ Planning Together

If you are in a committed relationship and intend to remain so, a discussion with your mate about your values priorities assessment is in order. For a fruitful discussion, you would want your partner to complete the core values assessment process before the two of you compare and discuss your results. Both of you should be prepared for a rich and lively conversation!

From my experience in conducting many life-redesigning workshops, I've witnessed some rather animated interactions between partners reacting to differences noted in each other's core values priorities. One such discussion involved a wife demanding to know from her husband why relationship was number one on her list but did not even appear among his top priorities. Surprised by her reaction, he responded that since he was already in a committed relationship, it didn't occur to him to list it as a priority. His response did nothing to mollify her. In fact, it raised her hackles even more.

"If you don't think our relationship important enough to identify it as a top priority," she said, "how likely are you to give it much time, attention, and nurturing commitment?"

The husband finally saw her point and put "relationship" at the top of his core priorities. He had never intended to slight their relationship, but he had taken it for granted in his list of priorities. He had also allowed his introverted nature to blind him to the fact that just having good intentions is not enough. He also needed to let people—especially his highly extroverted wife—know what his intentions were. But, most of all, he needed to be expressly clear with himself about what he valued most. Otherwise, things that were of lesser value to him would slip in and take precedence by default.

If we are not consciously aware of our real values priorities, we tend to overlook them in favor of what has our attention at the moment. Relationship tends to be one of those overlooked areas that don't make it on our to-do lists. That's especially true for those of us who've been in long-term relationships.

Regardless of how long you've been in a particular relationship, if it truly matters, you and your partner could probably benefit from a healthy dose of renewal as part of a senior life rejuvenation effort. Life circumstances change dramatically when your career and family issues no longer demand your full attention. As part of your adjustment to new circumstances, you don't want to fall into the trap of ignoring or trying to change your partner instead of the two of you working to change your life together. Nor do you want to miss the fun and fulfilling experience of seeing how you both have grown and matured, and how you can find new ways to share your dreams for the future.

◆ Summing Up

Graduating from a full-time work commitment invites a life redesign. Undertaking this process confronts us with the challenge of determining what will make our future—especially the next chapter of our future—fulfilling. Living a richly fulfilling life is a matter of making choices and taking actions congruent with our core values. We're unlikely to feel highly successful if we are not achieving what we value most dearly.

Unfortunately, most of us pay little conscious attention to our personal values in the course of daily life. Most of us have felt pressured to subsume our individual values to those of our social institutions and cultural norms in order to make it in the world.

The transition into senior life offers a rich opportunity for greater freedom of choice. But achieving this new freedom requires that we consciously reassess and clarify our values priorities. Our personal values tend to change and evolve over the years so that few of us in our fifty-plus years are motivated from the same values that motivated our behavior earlier in life.

If you want real satisfaction and fulfillment in the next chapter of your life, you need to place a high value on values clarification.

CONNECTING YOUR
TALENTS TO INTERESTS

"I hadn't thought of myself as a creative person because I've never been particularly good at art. But now I see there are many ways of being creative and I don't have to continue in civil engineering just because I'm good at math and science."

—CIVIL ENGINEER SHIFTING TO LANDSCAPE ARCHITECTURE AS A
RESULT OF REASSESSING HER INTEREST-BASED TALENTS

"It's really difficult determining what other interests would enable me to use my talents differently after working for 35 years in a managerial capacity."

—EXECUTIVE CONTEMPLATING HIS RETIREMENT OPTIONS
AND LOOKING FOR SOMETHING MORE THAN GOLF

"Have fun. Have more fun than any team in the tournament. People perform better when they're happy."

—JIM LARRANGAGA, BASKETBALL COACH OF GEORGE MASON UNIVERSITY'S
2006 NCAA CHAMPIONS, *AARP MAGAZINE* (January/February 2007)

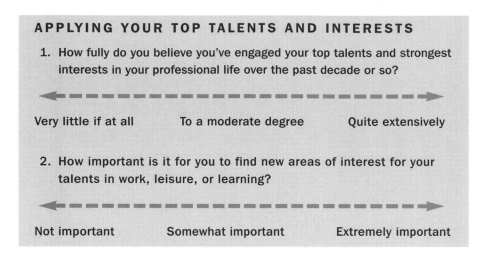

APPLYING YOUR TOP TALENTS AND INTERESTS

1. How fully do you believe you've engaged your top talents and strongest interests in your professional life over the past decade or so?

Very little if at all   To a moderate degree   Quite extensively

2. How important is it for you to find new areas of interest for your talents in work, leisure, or learning?

Not important   Somewhat important   Extremely important

◆ Reassessing Your Talents

Twentieth-century intelligence tests created the spurious impression that a number could gauge an individual's capability. Thanks to the limited dimensions of intelligence measured by all those tests, many of us came to believe that only a small percentage of us were highly intelligent, that quite a few of us were pretty dull, and that most of us fell into a bell-shaped curve of mediocrity.

How intelligent you considered yourself to be, based on this old way of measuring and reporting I.Q., most likely had a huge impact on your sense of self-esteem. On the one hand, if you came away with a score that signified you as having a high I.Q., you may have found yourself proudly parading around as one of the gifted few. If, on the other hand, you were one of the many whose scores indicated mediocre intelligence, you tended to function in ways consistent with the expectations of mid-range intelligence. And if your scores fell into the below-average range, you may have been placed in special programs with other "slow learners" or students with "special needs." Wherever your scores landed in the spectrum, you probably thought that you had been pegged for life as being categorically brilliant, mediocre, or dumb.

A friend recently demonstrated the impact of I.Q. scores on self-image. In an experiment in a graduate psychology course he was teaching at The Johns Hopkins University, he administered an intelligence test to his students and then, unbeknownst to the students, arbitrarily assigned I.Q. scores to their test results. He awarded no score higher than 105, even though these were bright students. In the next class session, he handed out the fake test results and then asked the students to stand in the appropriate corner of the room based on their I.Q. score. Even though he had assigned no score above 105, most of the students went to the corner designated for scores of 130 or above. Had you been in that class, which corner would you have gone to—the high I.Q. corner, or one designated for mediocre scores? The point my friend wanted his students to understand was how strong the impact of an I.Q. score can be on us all. Of course, these students may have ignored the false I.Q. scores because they already knew what their actual scores were and/or went to the corner that matched their perceptions. Whatever their motivations for ignoring the false-score test it brought home in a dramatic way the impact an I.Q. stigma can have on one, especially in the formative years. Understanding this was especially important for these students, since most of them were already teaching or would be in the near future.

If you believe you are highly intelligent, chances are you are going to perform that way. If others believe you are highly intelligent, chances are that they are going to treat you as such. Well-documented research shows that run-of-the-mill students whose teachers believed them to be highly intelligent significantly outperformed similar students who had teachers who believed them to be average students. From countless examples such as these, we have come to realize that our potential cannot be determined by a number. Yet we let numbers supposedly relating to intelligence affect our self-esteem and our performance, even though we all know of individuals who broke through the burden of being branded as "average" or "below average." Einstein, a name virtually connoting "genius," was labeled as a dullard by his teachers in his early school years. Although not a genius, perhaps, by Einsteinian measures, Ed, my roommate during my senior year in college, had had his application for admittance to the university turned down because of low SAT scores. Being a very persuasive guy, however, Ed was able to convince university officials to admit him on probationary status. He graduated in business administration with high honors and went on to obtain an MBA and pursue a highly success career in finance.

Recent research in the psychology of human potential is dramatically changing our views about individual capabilities. The emerging view is that everyone is talented, but we are talented in different ways. It follows from this expanded view of human capability that we all should be able to find the unique path in life and work that develops and uses our special endowments. To me, this revisionist view of unique giftedness seems intuitively correct. I've seen many examples of the difference in quality of life that we can make by shifting from work for which we are moderately suited to work that is a good match for our talents and interests.

Each of us is a one-of-a-kind creation. Every one of us is a composite of countless varieties of genetic combinations, stretching back into ancestral infinity. So, for instance, once upon a time if you united a Celt with Viking, the result was progeny never before seen on the planet. Then over hundreds of generations, if you mixed the offspring of that union with marauding Mongols and Visigoths, stirred in some Normans, and sent them to America, where they mixed with Germans, Ethiopians, Persians, and Native Americans, you would end up with someone like you and me.

Some of us carry genes from masters at cave-wall painting, and others are genetically descended from experts at slaying mastodons. There has never been another person exactly like you on this planet. So why do so many of us conform to such a few general paths in life, developing similar competencies, acquiring similar bodies of knowledge, and pursuing similar career trajectories? What happened to our instincts for hunting mastodons? Who remembers how to transform a buffalo skin into a colorful garment? Who carries the instinctive ability to design frigates that can overtake and subdue pirate ships?

In spite of our uniqueness, few of us have had the opportunity to develop and apply the gifts arising from our unique heritage over eons of time. Of course, once in a while a Galileo or Mother Teresa or Oprah Winfrey comes along. Most of us, however, allow the world we live in to squeeze us into a limited number of prescribed molds. In school we all had to take the same courses, read the same books, pass the same exams, compete for the same colleges and jobs. We even had to learn to play games the same way—I never saw anyone play football using a tennis ball, or hook the ball through the goal posts with a golf club. Cheerleaders do set routines, and we all cheer in unison at the same things.

◆ Time for the Real You to Stand Up

Our jobs and the culture of our workplace required that we apply prescribed skill sets and accommodate our personalities to business needs. I've counseled many former IBM employees who were never comfortable with the corporate culture of sameness that they felt they were forced to accept. But I've also heard the same complaint from clients who worked elsewhere. Just as clients from IBM may have protested their "professional dress code" of blue shirts and dark suits, some of my clients from the U.S. State Department say they never want to see another white shirt or dark suit. Corporate culture determines more than our work wardrobes, however. If you wanted to design cars for a large manufacturer of automobiles, you may have developed your skills in auto design with little regard to what your special gifts might actually have been.

Back in the 1960s, I became a naval officer at a young age. Given the draft, my only choice about serving in the military was which branch of service I wanted to pursue. In my youthful ignorance, I thought the Navy would be better suited to my undergraduate degree in geology. And, besides, I liked the Navy's uniforms for commissioned officers better. So, to make a long story short, I ended up 10 years later with competencies I would never have dreamed of acquiring—namely, getting men to do things they didn't particularly want to do, like moving airplanes about an aircraft hangar deck without smashing high-ticket weapons into one another. Little did it matter that my talents ran in a different, more creative bent. Like everyone else, I pretty much did what I needed to do to make it in the world in which I found myself. My unique gifts and talents lay buried beneath the demands of my daily responsibilities and survival. Simply put, I needed to make a living, take care of my family, and find ways of fitting in.

Throughout our early and middle adult years, few of us found time to investigate and explore what our unique gifts even were. Not until we turn fifty-something do most of us have the time and inclination to really define our unique gifts and explore fulfilling ways of applying them. Then, as we begin to enter our senior years, many of us finally have the opportunity to reinvent ourselves. In fact, many of us have expanded options for choosing where and how we will apply our talents in work, play, and learning. But this involves determining which talents we want to continue putting forth as our strongest suits, which we want to discard or park off to the side, and which we want to pick up and explore. It's time for the real you to stand up.

◆ Reinventing Yourself Around Your Unique Talents

What do you excel at? What would you like to do more of? What have you excelled at in the past? What do you want to do a whole lot less of? Are there talents you would love to develop and activities you might enjoy but never had time for? Consider questions such as these as you graduate into senior life and reinvent yourself. If there is one thing I hope you'll remember from this book, it is this:

> ***You don't have to continue doing something***
> ***just because you happen to be good at it!***

Let's say, for example, that you are a senior finance specialist and are really good at it, but you often find yourself daydreaming about climbing Mount Kilimanjaro and organizing safaris. Pay attention to your dreams. They are worthy of serious attention. It's all too easy to discount such images as nothing more that diversionary efforts of the mind to entertain you when things get a bit too routine. In fact, such mental images just might be messages from your inner self, communications from a deep wisdom center suggesting new life ventures. Don't let complacency and a fixation on what's practical overrule your fantasies. I've seen too many individuals, especially men, who've had successful careers, disregard their daydreams and slip into the life of a consultant because it seems easier or more practical to continue the same kind of work they were doing. Becoming a consultant is, of course, commendable if what you have been doing is a passion. If you're doing what you love, why stop? But to continue in something you're less than excited about simply because you are good at it would be like eating the same meal night after night simply because you think you can't fix or afford anything else. Such limited dinner fare not only becomes tasteless but nonnutritional.

Reinventing yourself is risky and challenging, but taking on a new challenge can also be immensely rejuvenating. When was the last time you took on an engaging challenge, one that involved some adventure and risk? How did that feel to you at the time? What was your reaction to it in retrospect? Let's face it, you and I are not going to be around this old planet forever. We don't know if we have 10 or 20 or 40 more good years. Although two or three decades may seem long from the vantage point of the current moment, when I look back at my life, I see the decades speeding by at an ever-increasing rate. You owe it to your future self to reinvent your life in a way that will provide the future you with a sense of joy, accomplishment, and fulfillment.

If you have progressed this far in the book, you have already taken some big steps toward self-reinvention. You have engaged in some vision work, considered in what ways you will want to remodel your identity, and reassessed and possibly even reordered your values. Proceeding from here involves deciding which talents you want to feature in your new life. It's time to specify which talents you want to leave out, which you want to develop in new ways, and which you want to move from the background to the foreground.

Talents are potentials that come in three general varieties: learning capabilities, natural abilities, and personality endowments. What you know—or your accumulated knowledge—is a function of your learning capabilities. Some of us can learn calculus, some trapeze artistry, and some slapstick comedy so funny that the audience can only gasp in laughter. The types of knowledge you have accumulated, along with the know-how you've acquired, indicate your particular style of learning. For example, you might have learned a lot about plant biology or baseball and know how to identify all the trees in the forest or how to figure out the batting average for every major league player. But you may not have the natural abilities or talents to grow award-winning roses or pitch for the Boston Red Sox. We come hardwired into the world with our talents and have life experiences that present us with choices and opportunities to develop them or not.

The same is true for learning capabilities. Some of us may be better equipped to learn about the photosynthesis of hybrid roses because we came endowed with a natural bent toward the kind of mathematical calculations needed to be a botanist. Or we could have been endowed with the proverbial green thumb—an inherent sense of the sun, soil, and moisture conditions needed for growing perfect roses. Same with baseball. I know a young man who was born with the ability to do large computations in his head and can recite baseball statistics ad infinitum. But, no matter how hard he worked at it, he'd never be a major league pitcher because he just wasn't born with the kind of athletic ability that is required for striking out a great batter when all the bases are loaded and it's in the ninth inning of the last game of the World Series.

Personality-wise, some of us are gregarious, some congenial, some intrepid, and others soulful. The better you understand the strengths of your personality, the more effective you can be in capitalizing on your natural gifts. We'll explore that in more detail in the next chapter. For now, let's focus on assessing what natural talents you have developed and might want to continue using (possibly in new ways), those well-developed talents you want to discontinue, and what's lurking inside ready to be brought into the light of day.

◆ Motivating Your Talent

The emerging view of human intelligence is that it consists of a broad array of different talents, as opposed to some universal type of general ability. Determining your real capabilities, therefore, is more complex than simply administering an intelligence test and deriving an I.Q. score. Talents also spread across an array of abilities, from left-brained analysis to right-brained intuition, from facilities for relating to people to learning languages to shooting balls through hoops.

But it's not just what you're good at that defines your personal gifts; it's also a matter of connecting what you are interested in with your talents. You may be built to be a world-class swimmer, but if you hate the water, you aren't likely to win an Olympic medal in swimming. The same is true for just about any type of human capability. For example, I worked with a client who was a brilliant accountant. She graduated with high honors, earned an MBA from a top university, and moved into a lucrative position. There was just one problem—she hated her work and had to undertake a career move to do something that was a better fit for both her talents and her interests.

TALENT MOTIVATED BY ENERGY

I refer to this combination of talent and interest as *motivated strengths.* When you combine talent and interest in anything you do in life, whether work, learning, or leisure, you are going to be more energized, more engaged, more persevering (it's hard to stop doing what you love), and more successful.

Over the years in my counseling practice, I've developed an organizing structure that has helped hundreds of individuals better understand and capitalize on their unique endowments of talent and energy. This structure separates strengths into six styles based on brain dominance (left/right brain thinking preference) and the characteristic ways in which people express their styles. A more detailed explanation of this process is available in my book *Will The Real You Please Stand Up?* I have also included a brief adaptation of the process here for your convenience.

The first feature of my organizing structure deals with dominance. One of the many amazing features of the human physiology is that many parts of the body come in sets of two—eyes, ears, arms, legs, and kidneys, for instance. We also have two hemispheres of the brain, left and right. Most of us develop a dominance of one side of the body over the other. Some of us are right-handed and some left-handed; some of us have right-eye dominance and some left; and some of us are more adept in right-brain functions and others in left. *Brain domi-*

nance refers to the fairly recent discovery that most of us develop a preference for using one side of our brains over the other. Logical, objective thought process is the realm of the brain's left hemisphere, while nonlinear, subjective, and intuitive thought is the specialty of the right. This concept of brain dominance, as I've come to understand it, is based in large measure on my study with Ned Herrmann, whose work is described in his books *The Creative Brain* (Lake Lure, North Carolina: Brain Books, 1988) and *The Whole Brain Business Book* (New York: McGraw-Hill, 1996).

The second feature of my organizing structure has to do with how people tend to focus and concentrate their energy. Have you noticed that some of us always seem to have our heads in the clouds? Those of us with this kind of focus may not even see you when we pass you in the hall because our energy is focused inward. It's not that we don't like you or aren't interested in you—it's just that our thoughts are focused in the frontal lobes of the cerebral brain, which we have engaged to solve some problem. With this inward focus, we're probably not paying much attention to what's happening in the here and now around us. We are the *mental cerebrals*. If you happen to be one, get your head out of the clouds right now and pay attention to what you're reading.

Another way in which some of us are focused is in what's going on around us, especially in our attention to others. Pass one of these folks in the hall or on the street and you know that they know you're in their world. They may smile at you, say hello, or simply acknowledge your presence with a knowing glance. These are folks who need people, who interact with people, and who tell career counselors that they want a job working with people. I refer to those of us in this style as *relationals*. Their interpersonal relationships form the primary interest in their lives. If you fall in this category, you don't want to end up spending your time in solitary research.

A third way in which we concentrate our attention and energy is in body-oriented activity. These are the *kinesthetics*, or activity-oriented individuals. They tend to be more attuned to their bodies and more action-oriented than those of us more intent on a life of the mind or interacting with people. A kinesthetic would much rather throw a ball than talk or think about it. When it comes to ballgames, the kinesthetic would rather play or be an active spectator, while the relational person would probably rather coach the team or use the game as a way to socialize with friends. The cerebral would probably prefer to invent a game or conduct a statistical analysis of it.

SIX STYLES OF MOTIVATED STRENGTHS

Combined, the brain dominance and energy focus dimensions generate six styles, as shown in Figure 7-1. Let's look at each style in more detail.

Analytic Thinker   Individuals favoring this style are most comfortable in the world of objective facts, analysis, abstract conceptualization, and cerebral problem-solving. They seek to understand their world through careful mental concentration based on the interaction between cause and effect. Their motto might be: All things can be understood through science. They are likely to see a world based on the laws of physics. They tend to mistrust intuition and the mystical because those realms are not rational. They also tend to be critical in their approach to life and work. They have a passion for rational thinking, attempting to discern what is true and what is false through detached logic. If you engage them in a problem, they can't leave it alone until they can find a reasonable explanation or a logical solution.

FIGURE 7-1. SIX STYLES OF MOTIVATED STRENGTHS.

	Left-Brain **Objective Rationals**	**Right-Brain** **Subjective Feelers**
Cerebral *(Mind-Oriented)*	Analytic Thinker	Mystical Intuitive
Interpersonal *(People-Oriented)*	Coordinator-Organizer	Nurturer-Inspirer
Kinesthetic *(Activity-Oriented)*	Artisan-Craftsperson	Playful Performer

Coordinator-Organizer   Those of this persuasion are most comfortable in the objective world of facts, information, and data. They have a passion for the practical and the efficient and distrust the intuitive and/or the emotional. They are motivated by productive, planned-for outcomes. Their motto would be: Develop a plan and work the plan. To achieve a desired outcome, they would organize people or resources to accomplish projects within a prescribed time frame and/or ensure that policies and procedures are followed. They like being in positions of control where they exercise authority over programs, projects, resources, and people. In work they are oriented to business situations involving management, administration, contracting, purchasing, or finance. In leisure life they gravitate toward coordinating events, managing things, and organizing people. If you give them a problem to solve, they will don their business hat and devise a practical solution, probably in consultation with a few authoritative sources.

Artisan-Craftsperson   These are activity-oriented individuals energized by hands-on tasks that involve practicing a trade (mechanics, carpentry, landscaping), executing a technical skill (computer operations, medical technology, masonry), or performing in physically demanding occupations (competitive sports, military special forces, construction work). Artisan-Craftspeople exercise patience and discipline in doing physical things involving coordination, strength, and attention to detail. They tend to be good at trouble-shooting, fixing, building, executing manual operations, or performing technical activities. They might be found operating heavy equipment or complicated machinery. This might be their motto: Just git `er done. If you give them a problem to solve and if it involves some kind of physical or mechanical challenge such as hanging a door or fixing an engine, they will find an ingenious way of doing it. If, however, the problem involves some kind of a personal issue, they are likely to tell you to mind your own business.

Mystical Intuitive   Individuals favoring this style enjoy and feel comfortable in the subjective world of ideas, possibilities, conceptualization, and imagination. They feel a strong proclivity for expressing themselves in writing, music, dance, art, or some type of creative entrepreneurial venture. They tend to trust intuition over analysis and look for truth from the inner realm of knowing rather than the outer world of facts and data. Their motto might be this: The world and its creator are wonderfully mysterious. If you give one of these folks a problem to address, be ready for out-of-the box ideas originating from the abstract inner realm of intuition.

Nurturer-Inspirer   Individuals preferring this style favor the subjective world of values, feelings, and ideas. They have a passion for working with people. They tend to be warm and friendly and are often charismatic individuals with strong convictions regarding human rights and equality issues. With robust personalities and astute communications skills, they often gravitate to situations where they can influence the intellectual, emotional, physical, or spiritual development of others. This could be their motto: Of the people, with the people, and for the people. If you give them a problem to solve, they're likely to engage a group of people in a discussion of the issue.

Playful Performer   These are individuals who are energized by work and leisure activities that involve learning and performing routines. Playful Performers love to be engaged in an active performance that brings something alive. They tend to be sensuous, sentimental, impulsive, and spontaneous. They enjoy entertaining others, have a good stage presence, and instinctively understand how they impact others. They tend to make decisions based on their personal values, drives, and emotional make-up, rather than from detached logic. Their preference for people interaction and activity inclines them to occupations such as entertainment, customer service, coordinating public activities, and nontechnical sales. Their motto might be: Let me entertain you! If you give them a problem to solve, they will want to have fun with it, probably drawing on a proven method but adding a playful nuance to it.

Assessing Your Motivated Strengths

This assessment is designed to help you determine what strengths you might want to continue using, which it's time to abandon, and which underutilized strengths you might now wish to develop. This assessment is organized into three parts:

1. Review the individual strengths within each of the six styles to determine your current level of competence in using the strength.
2. Rate how much you believe you would enjoy using this strength in the future.
3. Determine what future actions to undertake with these strengths.

Use the following rating scales for making these assessments:

Rating Your Competencies

Talent Rating

0   1   2   3   4   5   6   7   8   9   10

Completely   *Moderately*   *Highly*
unskilled   *skilled*   *skilled*

Rating Your Enjoyment Potential

Joy Rating

0   1   2   3   4   5   6   7   8   9   10

Total lack of   *Moderate level*   *High level of*
enjoyment   *of enjoyment*   *enjoyment*

Use the following descriptions as aids in determining what suggested actions to undertake.

- Feature (F): those you rated 7 or higher in both the Talent and Joy columns.
- Develop (D): those you rated 7 or above in the Joy column, but 5 or lower in the Talent column
- Minimize (M): those in which you are highly competent but have little interest
- Avoid (A): those you rated 5 or lower in both Talent and Joy

Analytic Thinker Style	Talent Rating	Joy Rating	Suggested Action
Quantitative work: studying things statistically through numbers and hard data			
Analyzing: understanding and solving problems by breaking things down into fundamental elements			
Investigating: conducting detailed examination or inquiry into the facts to discover the truth of something			
Abstract problem solving: posing hypotheses about why something might be as it is			

Analytic Thinker Style	Talent Rating	Joy Rating	Suggested Action
Intellectual curiosity: being intensely interested in the phenomenon of things—a mental explorer			
Evaluating: forming, reassessing, and reforming opinions based on observing things in practice			
Objectivity: having ability to perceive, describe, or react to something logically via the facts without being influenced by personal feelings or preconceived notions			
Dispassionate decision making: having ability to step back from situations to evaluate and select options strictly on the basis of hard reason			
Scientific observation: using scientific methods to study something by carefully controlled observation			
Deductive reasoning: having ability to draw sound conclusions from an examination of the facts			
Technical or scientific writing: preparing carefully researched and precisely detailed reports and position papers			
Researching: conducting a study of a problem situation by uncovering and examining all available facts and data and their probable implications			
Diagnosing: identifying the cause and effect of something by careful analysis and interpretation of available facts			
Prognosticating: predicting the future likelihood of something based on trend analysis			

Coordinator-Organizer Style	Talent Rating	Joy Rating	Suggested Action
Administering: overseeing the affairs of some kind of a business or social program			
Coordinating: managing and bringing together a complex enterprise involving people, activities, and resources			
Executing: carrying out an activity, a plan, or policy; moving a plan into action; getting things going			
Planning ahead: making preparation or arrangements for the future			
Business acumen: having ability to make quick, accurate judgments involving business and organizational matters			
Inspecting: critically examining an organizational process to assess its compliance with expectations			
Budgeting: allocating the available resources to accommodate the needs of a particular operation			
Detailed follow-through: assuring that a task, plan, or situation is progressing in an orderly manner			
Prioritizing: ability to understand the relative urgency of things and rank them in order of importance			
Time management: organizing your time to effectively accomplish an agenda within a prescribed time frame by minimizing distractions			
Supervising: taking charge of a group or team of people to ensure that a task is adequately accomplished			
Logistics management: overseeing projects to assure goods and services arrive where and when needed			
Policy planning: establishing procedures governing the actions of individuals, groups, or organizations			
Directing: controlling individuals, groups, or teams by providing instructions, directions, and guidance			

Artisan-Craftsperson Style	Talent Rating	Joy Rating	Suggested Action
Physical dexterity: being skilled in physical movement, especially in coordinated use of body and hands in manipulating objects			
Operating equipment: skillfully working with various types of equipment, apparatus, tools, machines or instruments			
Mechanical intelligence: being adept at understanding how things work mechanically and how to use tools safely and cleverly			
Technical problem solving: excelling at finding the cause of technical problems and figuring out how to fix them			
Constructing: being good at building things, knowing how to make structural things with quality and efficiency			
Workmanship: being skilled in the artisan crafts; adept at producing high-quality products			
Handcrafting: having ability to skillfully make things using manual skills and artistic inclinations			
Performing to specification: accomplishing technical work according to a plan or compliance with instructions			
Quality control: maintaining equipment, materials, tools in top working condition			
Gardening: having a green thumb; exceptionally adept at growing healthy, vibrant plants			
Precision manual work: performing exacting work requiring keen hand-eye coordination and self-control.			
Crafting: being skillful at making attractive things by hand			
Repairing: fixing something broken, damaged, or deteriorated; restoring something to good condition			
Remodeling: renovating or altering the structure or style of something such as a building, room, vehicle, or furniture			

Mystical Intuitive Style	Talent Rating	Joy Rating	Suggested Action
Creating: drawing on the imagination to invent things, generate ideas, and engage in out-of-the-box thinking			
Originality: departing from traditional or previous forms; bringing new ideas, concepts, or other mental creations into existence			
Conceptualizing: imagining how seemingly disparate things could fit together in a big picture perspective; seeing patterns and associations			
Imagination: having ability to form images and ideas in the mind in novel ways—minds-eye inventiveness			
Vision/envisioning: having ability to anticipate possible future events and developments			
Intuition: being aware of or knowing something instinctively without having to see or calculate it—inner knowing without benefit of conscious thought			
Subjective interpretation: understanding things through feelings rather than from rational analysis			
Original composition: creating an original work of art or innovative work of some kind through the sheer power of imagination			
Speculation: skilled in guesswork, drawing on intuition to devise possible explanations for a certain phenomenon and developing hypotheses			
Creative problem solving: generating numerous ideas, usually of a nonlinear sort, to solve problems			
Hypothetical thinking: developing imaginative reasons to explain why something could possibly be as it is			
Inventiveness: creating new things, ability to draw upon the imagination to create or design new things			
Mystical thinking: delving into the mysterious, the supernatural, or that which defies all objective logic			
Clairvoyance: ability to see and know things beyond the range of normal human perception			

Nurturer-Inspirer Style	*Talent Rating*	*Joy Rating*	*Suggested Action*
Enlightening: expanding minds through imparting knowledge, know-how, and wisdom			
Counseling/coaching: helping others improve their performance, problem solving, and decision making			
Nurturing/empathizing: supporting others with compassion and relating to their feelings			
Persuasive writing: ability to influence people's views and opinions through the power of the written word			
Championing a cause: ability to create enthusiasm and commitment from others for a heartfelt cause			
Communicating with impact: ability to deliver presentations that produce emotion-generating reactions			
Healing presence: a natural ability to comfort, console, and heal through the power of compassion and empathy			
Active listening: ability to deepen interpersonal communications by reflecting what you've heard, responding both to the verbal and nonverbal			
Consensus building: getting people with different views to invest in and commit to an idea, action, or plan			
Compassion: attending to others in genuine, loving appreciation for who they are and their circumstances			
Facilitating personal development: ability to motivate others to be and become their best			
Change catalyst: influencing change in individuals and groups through gentle persuasion and subtle creativity			
Humanitarian idealism: seeing goodness in the human heart and being gifted in helping others improve their lives			
Mentoring: drawing on the wisdom of years to assist, support, and nurture those younger and less experienced			

Playful Performer Style	Talent Rating	Joy Rating	Suggested Action
Entertaining: engaging others or an audience by providing amusing or interesting material			
Performing: showing good stage presence, able to project an image that engages the attention of an audience			
Composing: fashioning artistic works that entertain, such as music, dance, poetry, drama, and comedy			
Physical grace: having fluidity of movement that enables one to excel in physical activities such as dance and sport			
Culinary arts: showing a flair for cooking that stimulates the senses, delights the eye, and engages sensuous feelings			
Hosting: possessing a gracious presence that makes people feel welcome, comfortable, and special			
Promoting: having a natural ability to market, advertise, or promote a product, cause, or organization			
Improvising: possessing a talent for thinking quickly and creatively without preparation or scripted text			
Negotiating: interacting intuitively and creatively to achieve agreement on disputed issues			
Emergency responding: being adept at spontaneously reacting quickly and effectively to unexpected and urgent situations, remaining calm in the process			
Comedic sense: seeing the funny side of things and being able to amuse others through spontaneous interaction and a keen sense of humor			
Joviality: having ability to completely lose the self in the current moment; showing full enjoyment and cheerful absorbance of the gifts of the present			
Resourcefulness: having extraordinary ability to get things done in uniquely creative ways			
Flexibility: being able to change or be changed according to current circumstances			

Prioritizing Your Favorite Talent Groups

Based on your assessments in the six groups of skills, determine which are your favorite talent groups. Rank them from your most favorite (#1 group) to your least favorite (#6 group).

After ranking these groups, make a rough estimate of how much you would like to be using these talents over the next three to five years in work, fun, and learning.

Talent Group	Your Priority Rating (1 to 6)	Approximate Percentage of Time You Hope to Use This Talent Group in the future
Analytic Thinker		
Coordinator-Organizer		
Artisan-Craftsperson		
Mystical Intuitive		
Nurturer-Inspirer		
Playful Performer		

Summarizing Your Assessment Results

Use the following chart to summarize your results from the Motivated Strengths Assessment.

Capitalize on These Strengths	Develop These Strengths
Minimize These Strengths	Avoid These Strengths

Applying Your Motivated Strengths

The following chart is provided for help in generating ideas in how you might wish to apply your preferred strengths in your future work, leisure, and learning. Check off the items that are of interest to you.

Sample Work/Volunteer/Learning/Leisure Activities for Left-Brain Styles

Analytic Thinker	Coordinator-Organizer	Artisan-Craftsperson
❏ Study science and history. ❏ Read and/or write detective stories. ❏ Join a chess club, play chess online. ❏ Study the stock market and invest with care. ❏ Teach math, science, or history. ❏ Join archeological expeditions. ❏ Become a member of a science or intellectual club (Mensa, American Historical Association). ❏ Consult with a think tank in your field. ❏ Write articles for science and history publications. ❏ Join a professional association. ❏ Devise computer systems for groups and businesses of interest. ❏ Develop mind games involving math, history, and/or science. ❏ Take up astronomy. ❏ Become a tour guide at a science or history museum. ❏ Conduct research for a professional association. ❏ Trace and record the family lineage. ❏ Join a computer information network or design Web pages.	❏ Assume a management position with a civic organization or social club. ❏ Become involved in local politics, run for office, volunteer to support a political campaign. ❏ Take on a position of responsibility in a professional association or community service group such as Boy or Girl Scouts. ❏ Work as a volunteer with the handicapped. ❏ Teach a course in a business area related to your field of interest. ❏ Become a board member of a bank, auditing firm, or school district, or an officer/elder in your church. ❏ Consult with the Small Business Administration. ❏ Chair a fact-finding committee. ❏ Volunteer work at a hospital or health clinic. ❏ Become a nutrition consultant. ❏ Start a business selling antiques, heirlooms, or classics you value. ❏ Work as a logistics expert with a police or fire department.	❏ Buy and repair antique furniture for fun or profit. ❏ Join a motorcycle club. ❏ Compete in a clay pigeon shooting association. ❏ Restore classic cars. ❏ Take up scuba diving. ❏ Start a landscape, lawn maintenance or I-Can- Fix-It business. ❏ Knit, crochet, sew, cross-stitch, quilt. ❏ Take up sailing. ❏ Assist in a greenhouse or plant nursery. ❏ Start a bike repair business. ❏ Teach courses in cooking, gardening, car or home repair. ❏ Start a business repairing old homes, building boats, or restoring antique clocks or cars. ❏ Pilot your own plane and/or glider, take up fly fishing, guide hunters into remote areas. ❏ Compete in physically engaging sports such as racquetball or golf. ❏ Do carpentry work with Habitat for Humanity. ❏ Learn glass blowing. ❏ Make jewelry or yard sculpture.

Sample Work/Learning/Leisure Activities for Right-Brain Styles

Mystical Intuitive	Nurturer-Inspirer	Playful Performer
❑ Study abstract art, ancient music, or dance. ❑ Study the desert mystics, Buddhism, or other enlightenment and intuitive disciplines. ❑ Take-up a disciplined meditation practice. ❑ Write original works of fantasy along the lines of *Lord of the Rings, Star Wars,* or the Harry Potter series. ❑ Create original works of abstract art for fun and profit. ❑ Visit/explore/write about mythical and mysterious places such a Findhorn, the Delphi, the Pyramids, or Machu Picchu. ❑ Study and teach a psychic discipline such as ESP, telepathy, or clairsentience. ❑ Invent and design original games that enhance intuition and creativity. ❑ Design and sell clothes, toys, or art objects for those with a flair for the creative and unusual. ❑ Become certified as a spiritual director/coach and set up a practice. ❑ Start a business to help create homes in line with people's spiritual orientations.	❑ Read psychology, human development, self-help, biographies, spirituality. ❑ Assume a leadership role in a cause you care about. ❑ Undertake a career change in a helping profession such as counseling, ministry, art therapy, life coaching. or vocational rehabilitation. ❑ Study, teach, write in a heartfelt subject area in the humanities, the arts, literature, or psychology. ❑ Take up a healing practice such as massage therapy, Reike, or aromatherapy. ❑ Write for a publication, Blog, or organization committed to personal development and mental/emotional health. ❑ Work with an institute involved in self-help education, healing, and life enhancement therapy, such as the Canyon Ranch, Omega. and Esalen Institutes. ❑ Do advocacy and/or personal care work for Hospice, disaster-relief counseling teams, or grief support groups. ❑ Volunteer for groups that help migrant workers or single moms.	❑ Teach and/or study music, sculpting, ceramics, pottery, dance, painting. ❑ Compete in ballroom dancing. ❑ Volunteer teaching for young children. ❑ Become credentialed as a mediator in an area dear to your heart. ❑ Undertake a new career as a nurse, physician's assistant, or social worker. ❑ Train in and/or teach yoga, physical fitness, or a martial art such as tai chi, karate, or tae kwon do. ❑ Master a musical instrument and join a group for pay or play. ❑ Become a tour guide at an art museum or for an organization such as Elderhostel. ❑ Perform in local theater productions. ❑ Compose music, poetry, and/or plays. ❑ Master conflict resolution and negotiation skills and join a team doing work in these areas. ❑ Create toys for kids or design and carry out engaging activities for those confined to nursing homes.

◆ New Directions for Old and Underdeveloped Talents

A statement I made earlier in this chapter bears repeating at this point: You don't have to continue doing something just because you happen to be good at it! I know many people who have been successful in making a shift in the way they develop and apply their talents. Let me share a few examples to help spur your thinking about how you might use your own talents in new ways.

Ted's Mystical Intuitive talents have been highly developed in his 30-year career as a writer and an editor for the National Park Service. Even after all those years in the "writing saddle," he still loves to use his talent and skills for crafting clearly articulated prose. But he has also become a bit weary of confining his creativity to governmental structures. To remedy that and to provide a freer reign for his humor and creativity, he has found a way to use his creative talents as a journalist in a whimsical column for a community-based news magazine and as a poet who has been published in a number of publications. His gift for tongue-in-cheek commentary and satirical poetry has earned him the well-deserved reputation for being the town wit. As his government career becomes past tense, he is looking forward to being able to devote full-time to his passion for poetry and penchant for "reporting all the wit that causes a titter in print!"

Marla decided it was time to retire after 30 years of exercising her talents as a Nurturer-Inspirer teaching in the public school system. Before she made the big retirement decision, however, she had learned that a routine bone scan showed that she was in the early stages of osteoporosis. She took up yoga as part of her new health initiative and found that she loved the actual practice of it and the wonderful effects it had on her body and mind. She also began to realize that she had a real talent for the practice of it and soon became a serious student, eventually becoming a certified teacher herself. It wasn't long before she retired from teaching social studies to middle school youth and began teaching yoga to adults of all ages. With her contagious enthusiasm and honed teaching skills, she quickly became a popular, well-respected yoga instructor and now recently opened her own studio.

Marla's genuine delight in all her students is clearly evident, but she has a special place in her heart for her elderly students at a nearby retirement community. She feels good about being able to help them improve their mobility, overall physical health, and emotional well being. In addition, since retiring, she now has time to exercise her Playful Performer talents with an English folk dance group that performs for fun and entertainment at community events. Today, Marla is a vibrant personification of health and well-being and is having a great time helping others to feel great. What more could any Nurturer-Inspirer ask for?

Dianne is a dentist—or I should say, *was* a dentist—who after many years of tending teeth as Analytic Thinker and Artisan-Craftsperson decided that it was time for a new and different use of her time and talents. She has enjoyed transferring her gifts for analyzing and appraising and her skills for working with detail to a new venue—owning and operating a home accessory store specializing in vintage furniture, house and garden decor, and anything else that strikes her eye for the well-appointed home. She is also having fun in using her latent talents as a Playful Performer and Coordinator-Organizer to make her shop a popular stop for shoppers who like unique boutiques.

Fiona, a highly competent Coordinator-Organizer, decided to take an early retirement from her senior executive position with an international development organization to pursue a new endeavor as a Nurturer-Inspirer. In her role at the top of a large operation, she realized that she was enjoying coaching and mentoring her staff and other employees more than tending to her corporate management responsibilities. Prodded by that realization, she began to explore new career possibilities in the helping professions and eventually chose to pursue a social work degree. Although she had to face the incredulity of friends and associates who were shocked that she would even consider such a shift, she stayed true to her new course and enrolled in a graduate school program that would support her new career vision.

Today Fiona is a social worker pursuing her passion for helping international workers transitioning into the culture, customs, and legalities of a foreign culture. She enjoyed her years in the hot seat as a corporate executive, but she has no regrets about leaving her high-paying, high-stress position behind. The last time I talked with her, she said that she receives infinitely more satisfaction from helping one client at a time than she ever did in helping a large corporation make the bottom line.

Mike, at the age of 58, decided it was time to try something dramatically new and different. After a long and successful career as an international economist, he negotiated for a buyout from his company to try his hand at organic beef farming. His talents as an Analytic Thinker had been well-developed and applied as an economist working with entrepreneurial sectors of developing nations, but he had always harbored a secret desire to try out his own entrepreneurial talents and apply his Artisan-Craftsperson skills and Coordinator-Organizer abilities to a new venture. Currently he is five years into his new venture and is thoroughly enjoying the outdoor life that comes with raising choice cattle and managing a business that caters to discerning buyers. As an economist, he earned a generous income for working with leaders in the public and private sectors. Now, as his own boss, he is barely squeaking by financially, but has never been happier or healthier. He expects to turn the corner profit-wise soon, but he says his real payoff is the new experience and knowledge he is gaining, plus all the organic beef he can eat on the side.

◆ Roundup Time

In your fifty-plus years, you are probably well positioned to make some life/work/leisure adjustments in order to play to the unique talent strengths you have that are energized by passion. Are you ready to let go of some of the things at which you have become rather adept but no longer particularly enjoy? Or would you like to use a well-developed talent in a new way or try out a talent you have not had an opportunity to develop previously but might now enjoy? At this stage of life, not only are you a person of many talents, but also you have most likely identified some uniquely personal interests. Do these talents and interests support and enhance who you are becoming? If not, this may be the best time of your life for connecting a talent, whether currently developed or not, with something that you value and that provides you with an energizing sense of enjoyment.

When you think about it, a phrase that many life-development counselors and coaches, including myself, often use—*follow your passion*—is rather passive. Your passion is not, after all, something you follow around from field to field as you try to round it up and herd it into a pen. Your passion is nothing less than YOU—it's the ultimate expression of who you are. As dancer/choreographer Martha Graham said, "There is a vitality, a life force, an energy, a quickening that is translated through you into action, and because there is only one of you in all of time, this expression is unique. And if you block it, it will never exist through any other medium and it will be lost. The world will not have it. . . . You have to keep yourself open and aware to the urges that motivate you. . . ."[1] In other words, the world needs *your* YOU-niqueness, and only you can bring it to its full expression. But doing so means that you must actively go for it!

---

1. Agnes de Mille, *Martha: The Life and Work of Martha Graham*, (New York: Random House, 1991), p. 264.

RELATING AND BEHAVING
DIFFERENTLY AS A SENIOR

"It was okay to be a jerk 10 years ago, but it's not okay to be a jerk now."

—RETIRED LAWYER TURNED ARTIST RECALLING WHO
HE'D BEEN AND WHO HE'D BECOME

"I came home from my last day at work feeling free and happy. Then my wife informed me she'd also retired. Suddenly I faced a new reality—who's going to fix my dinner now?"

—PHYSICIST RECALLING THE DAY HE RETIRED

"I'm bossy by nature, I love to run things, to stir things up and get results. After 30 years in this organization, however, I'm ready to retire and move onto something new. But who will I boss around—my dog? And how can I satisfy my need to achieve real results when I leave this organization?"

—FEMALE EXECUTIVE PONDERING HER NATURE AND NEW OPTIONS

REFLECTING ON YOUR PAST AND PRESENT BEHAVIOR

1. How effective do you consider your behavior to have been over the past decade in supporting your success at work, at home, and in relationship?

←- →

| Leaves a lot to be desired. My behavior always seems to get in the way of being my best at work and in relationship. | Fairly well overall. Some improvements on my part could have been beneficial for others and myself. | Highly successful in all areas. I get along well with most people in most situations. My actions have produced success and earned respect. |

2. Considering the behaviors that have become your accomplished way of doing things, what changes might be in order as you graduate into your new, senior chapter of life?

←- →

| A number of changes are needed to have more fun, get along better with others, and succeed in my aspirations for the future. | It's a mixed bag—some aspects of my behavior support the kinds of results I desire and some do not. A few modifications here and there might be in order. | My behavior serves me extremely well in all avenues of my life. It's been a key to my success in the past, and I see no need for change. |

◆ When Old Behaviors Don't Work

At work we learned behavior that was essential for career success. Over time many of us adopted whatever behavior was needed to be successful as a results-oriented executive, critical analyst, or creative problem solver. Then there are those of us who may have acquired behavior patterns that enabled us to just show up and do whatever was prescribed for the day. Regardless of which kind of behavior worked for us, the fact that it worked effectively reinforced it, and eventually it probably became habitual.

In our relationships we also tend to take on predictable patterns of relating and behaving. We may have adopted certain roles at home: soccer mom/dad, social secretary, chauffeur, bookkeeper/financial planner, or maintenance engineer. Whether we are single or partnered, with or without children, we have all developed ways of handling household chores; and, in the process, we have established methods, manners, and relationships to meet our needs and manage our lives. Life evolves into a comfortable routine. Then we get older and, like it or not, change happens. Our bodies change and require more maintenance work. Kids leave the nest and certain roles are no longer needed. We become grandparents and take on new relationships with our children and grandchildren as we fall in love again with those cute little darlings. Our parents pass on and we become the oldest living members of our families. Eventually, we retire from the careers and jobs that once filled our days. Things we once enjoyed become routine. Boredom sets in. Then, to top it off, our life mates start behaving in ways we find unsettling.

We may find that some of the actions and behaviors that helped us get ahead at work don't necessarily achieve the same results in our home or social life. Take, for example, the manner in which an executive who is a no-nonsense decision maker is accustomed to listening and responding to the ideas of others in the workplace. An executive must learn to listen to ideas with an ear cocked to what's being said, an eye on the time, a nose sniffing out commercial possibilities, and unfaltering knowledge of the company's needs and bottom line. An executive has to make quick judgments on the merit of a new idea, decide what actions are practical, and provide incisive direction.

Executives earn high marks for decisiveness, strategic thinking, and fast-paced behavior at work. But the same behavior at home, in casual interactions with family and friends, may brand the "old exec" as an insensitive and arrogant bore. How many times, for example, has an executive been told by his or her spouse that it's not the exec's precious advice that is needed at home? Nor does the exec's spouse want to know how to fix a problem, thank you very much. Although the corporate world rewarded the exec for issuing directions and fixing problems, at home the exec may have to learn to listen with empathy and respond with compassion if a nurturing relationship is to be part of life's senior chapters.

Individual work settings demand certain kinds of behaviors for successful performance and for fitting into a particular culture. Accommodating to certain behavioral patterns in work, however, can become so programmed that the fact that they carry over into other areas of life is inevitable and, in some cases, regrettable. In fact, we may eventually adjust so well to behavioral expectations in the workplace that our self view becomes synonymous with our work persona.

An economist I counseled grew so accomplished at the critical behavioral demands of her work that she critically analyzed everything, including her relationships, her adult kids' behavior, even the meal set before her. You name it, she could, and did, give a resoundingly critical appraisal. Her style of behavior drew the attention she needed to have an impact within her organizational setting and earned her the reputation for such an intimidating work style that she could even scare the pants off a U.S. Army general. But even though this behavior worked in her organizational setting, her intimidating behavior made her a failure in her daily life: She couldn't keep a husband (three had left her), she had no friends, and she believed her daughter had come to hate her.

Another manager I worked with became so successful at work in directing others, delegating, and providing corrective feedback, that in retirement he tried to use the same kind of behavior to produce the same "successful" results at home with his new wife. Guess what happened? He learned the hard way that behaviors responsible for success in organizational life may undermine success in senior life.

Reassessing our behavioral patterns of the past and undertaking beneficial adjustments may go a long way in increasing joy and fulfillment in senior life. Unfortunately, changing behavior is easy to talk about but difficult to do, especially when a particular type of behavior has led to career success. After all, the "right kind" of behavior gets reinforced in innumerable ways in the workplace. Certain behaviors earn you promotions and others get you fired. Some behaviors lead to acknowledgment and others to sanctions. Managers go to leadership training to improve their workplace behavior. Annual performance reviews and 360-degree feedback from associates alert managers to how well they're performing prescribed behaviors. But our behavior at home and in social situations, where we don't receive written performance reviews, is often more difficult to alter than what we do at work, even when a breath of fresh air is in order.

Take, for example, a recent and close-to-home situation for me. My wife, Pat, made a suggestion to our book group at a recent meeting. She suggested that we change some established behavior patterns so that the women would not always be the ones who see to the meeting arrangements and prepare the dinners, as it has been in the past. I must admit that we men pretty much just show up at the appointed time and place, indulge in good wine and food, and enjoy the conversation, often dominating it since the women are busy getting dinner ready. My wife, a strong feminist, suggested, in a nice way, that the roles we had come to accept and perpetuate were actually sexist behaviors and that we might want to consider how we could make some changes to equalize the workload and responsibilities involved in getting 10 people together for dinner and discussion.

The group's reaction to Pat's proposal was not met with overwhelming approval. In fact, her proposal sparked some heated discussion. For one thing, as you might guess, the men were not overly enthusiastic about the idea. After all, we'd grown comfortable with the way things were, and we would just as soon not change a good deal, right? What was surprising, however, was that one or two of the wives also immediately expressed antagonistic feelings to the idea of changing our customary way of doing things. They didn't trust their husbands' cooking and said that their husbands would just make a big mess in the kitchen. Besides, they added, the guys had other things they needed to be doing instead, like taking care of outdoor chores. It should be pointed out that everyone in the group is over fifty and no longer needs to work full time. Moreover, everyone is healthy and highly educated and has multiple options for engaging in enjoyable hobbies and interests. Moreover, we all consider ourselves to be progressive, inclusive, and open-minded. Yet even the suggestion that the five couples consider a minor behavior change provoked strong reactionary pushback.

With that in mind, how difficult might it be to change some of the role-bound behavior you've accepted and grown used to over the years?

◆ Changing Behavior for a New Kind of Success

When we transitioned from adolescence into full-fledged adulthood, we learned to make some major behavior modifications. For most of us, that involved becoming less narcissistic and more responsible. For most of us, that also entailed joining the work world and becoming dependable team players who could and did produce the results our employers wanted. We settled in and became comfortable with, or at least tolerant of, work-conditioned life as we proceeded through the long journey of adult life. Then, eventually, we graduated into senior life and found ourselves once again required to make some major adjustments to our behavior. But this time we may need to do the opposite of what we did upon entering adulthood. Instead of accommodating to a results-focused lifestyle, we may need to let go of a work persona and learn how to be more comfortable with who we naturally are.

For many of us, such a transition is difficult to contemplate, let alone make. It's not easy to walk away from years of being oriented to productivity, deadlines, and other business-related stresses. That's especially true for those of us who have successfully achieved high organizational status and impressive professional identity. As one of my clients said, "How do I deal with no longer having my business title backed by the authority of the organization when I have important calls to make?"

We soon discover that behaviors required in the corporate world aren't always appropriate to our new status in life as seniors. We need to learn how to relate to others without the power and influence of our success in the corporate world. We may need to learn how to be less intimidating, less critical, and less focused on the bottom line. Our priorities may become oriented to being a more loving presence to others, being less concerned about influencing others for some specific purpose, or impressing others with our work-based knowledge and professional expertise. We may even want to relinquish our focus on advancement altogether. In the process, we may discover how glad and grateful we are for the opportunity to be less conforming, more creative, and fully cognizant of joy in the moment.

Getting to that point is usually not easy, however. After all, the reason we've gotten extremely good in our ways is that we've been practicing them for decades. Yet change is not only possible but assured—if we develop a vision of what we want and exercise the will to grow into it. The behavior we've grown accustomed to was learned to begin with, and the behavior we want to develop can also be learned. It may help to keep a simple three-step process in mind. First, know what behavior you want to change. It's impossible to change any behavior beyond your awareness. In organizational settings, regular performance reviews helped to make you aware of strengths and shortcomings. Furthermore, the reviews often came with specific recommendations of what you needed to do to meet goals and expectations. Once you graduate from organizational life, however, you will probably need to find other avenues for determining what behaviors are now constructive and which, if any, could benefit from change. You might want to ask others on a periodic basis for feedback and then stake out some time for genuine, unhurried self-reflection.

Awareness is the first step. But awareness by itself is not enough. Step two is recognizing when you are engaged in, or about to engage in, an action you wish to modify and then manage to stop yourself on the spot from proceeding down the old pathways—before you make that wrong turn. An example from my own personal experience may serve as an illustration. I recently became aware of a tendency to "uhm" when giving a presentation. The person providing me with that feedback indicated that my "uhmming" was distracting to the audience. I was kindly encouraged to cease and desist with . . . uhm . . . my "crutch." At first I was shocked and took a little "uhmbrage" at this feedback, for I had been totally unaware of my proclivity. I checked with others to see if I was indeed guilty of this public speaking sin. I was. So it wasn't long before I began to take this valuable feedback to heart. When I became conscious of this tendency, I was then able to start working to eliminate it by recognizing when I was about to "uhm." I also became aware of how easily this little speaking habit of mine had been picked up by some of our grandkids!

Obviously, the second step, recognition, is critical for modifying behavior. But once again, it in itself is not sufficient for change. The third step is substitution. You must develop a new behavior to substitute for the old one, and you must learn to substitute the new behavior each and every time you catch yourself about to repeat the old behavior. In my case, I found that substituting a silent breath or two for every "uhm" I was about to utter soon pretty much eliminated my old tendency.

Awareness, recognition, and substitution—they each involve attention, intention, and practice. Each of these steps may take some time to implement and master. In the meantime, we inevitably go through some awkward stages in the process of refining our skills in recognition and substitution. We may fumble and be slowed down as we consciously recognize and substitute new behavior over and over again. Eventually, however, we master the new behavior and it becomes a new, more productive action that we perform without thinking. I'm looking forward to graduating to "non-uhmer" status. What's on your behavior modification agenda?

◆ Divesting Old Relationships and Building Social Capital

The workplace fulfills many important relationship needs. In addition to providing us with a sense of professional identity, a mission to perform, and a business persona, work brings us together in affiliation with others, necessitates communicating with others to produce desired outcomes, and provides built-in mechanisms for achieving self-esteem. By its very nature, the workplace offers a basis for social interaction, from small talk over coffee to gossip around the water cooler to networking lunches with colleagues. We meet new people through business interactions, learn to solve problems together, and share special occasions such as office parties, birthdays, and holiday events. Our work-based relationships may go back many years, perhaps even decades. Saying goodbye to these relationships for the last time when we retire can be nostalgic but also disorienting. At a deeper level, we may find that leaving those associations behind also leaves us without a way to satisfy many of our needs for affiliation.

In my own situation, I recall the sadness I felt in saying goodbye to friends and colleagues when I retired from directing a college counseling center to tackle life as a freelance consultant. In a way, I felt that I was abandoning the staff I'd hired and worked so passionately with in creating a highly successful program. That was more than a decade ago, and I still think about my old colleagues, the good times we shared, and the challenges we weathered. Like most of us when saying goodbye to our colleagues at work, I promised to stay in touch. And I did, for the most part, on an occasional basis. But those old relationships are never the same. As time passes, we make new friends, develop new interests, and move further and further away from the old life. Then one day we learn that an old work associate has passed on and is no longer with us.

Recently I attended the funeral of one of my revered long-time colleagues, a kind and gentle soul. John was an extraordinary counselor who contributed much to thousands of individuals. Many old colleagues, now retired, came to John's funeral to pay their respects to our old friend. Seeing these old colleagues was poignant and heartwarming. We hugged, recalled old times, cried, and looked at pictures of our younger selves happily working together and enjoying each other's company. Where did all those years go? What happened to our youth and grand ideas? As I thought about all the mixed emotions I was feeling that day, I realized how easy it would be to stay fixed in the past, to keep reliving our old highs—and lows—again and again. But we need to move on, create new friends, and find new ways to be among the living wherever we are.

As we grow older, our friends and relationships become even more important than they were earlier in life. In her book, *My Time: Making the Most of the Bonus Decades after Fifty,* Abigail Trafford talks about building "social capital" in the bonus years of life after fifty. In other words, we need to develop a social network capable of sustaining us through our senior years. Of course, a social network, much like a professional network, is a two-way street. We need to travel in both directions—to give at least as much as we get. A group of friends and like-minded individuals who stay in touch can support one another, offer help when needed, and provide the kind of assurance that only comes from being connected to a social community.

Trafford cites research that shows that not having close friends may, in fact, be a health hazard. Research shows that those who are more socially isolated are also more likely to die prematurely, before the average lifespan indicated by current mortality statistics. Trafford concludes that "the relationship between isolation and risk of death is so strong that it stands out whether or not you smoke, drink too much alcohol, eat a lousy diet, or lead a sedentary life." It seems that those with few friends are not only likely to die sooner but are even more prone to the common cold. There's little doubt that a strong connection exists between the quality of one's relationships and the ability of one's immune system to ward off physical and mental health problems.

A general sense of happiness also, it turns out, is directly linked to the quality of our relationships. Dr. Dan Baker, director of the Life Enhancement Program at Canyon Ranch, is a leading researcher in the field of "happiness" psychology, also called *positivism*. In his book *What Happy People Know: How the New Science of Happiness Can Change Your Life for the Better,* Baker concludes that a key to health and happiness is doing what we love and being in loving relationships. Baker, whose work is based on years of first-hand experience and direct research with hundreds of individuals, concludes that to be happy and healthy we need to learn to love ourselves and to love others. By self-love he is not referring to narcissism or egotism. What he is referring to is appreciating the miracle of life that each human being represents and the value of living in gratitude for this incredible gift. It's hard, possibly even physically impossible, to be in a loving relationship and be generally unhappy. Of course, we are never ecstatically happy every moment. Baker is talking about a general attitude in life.

A general attitude of happiness, according to research cited by Baker, cannot be divorced from loving relationships; they are by far more important to our state of happiness than money, power, fame, physical attractiveness, or anything else. Because relationship is such an important need, there are two critically important steps we are well advised to do when leaving the workplace.

The first is to say goodbye to old friends and old comrades. This may be harder than we imagined, even when we've been coveting the day of our departure for years. For instance, I find that 15 years after leaving the college where I worked for so long, I now not only have fond memories of colleagues I enjoyed but also of those I disliked! From the wonderful vantage point of hindsight, I can see that even the colleagues I found difficult and irritating contributed to me and others in ways that I hadn't realized at the time. For one thing, they provided me with opportunities for seeing myself differently. For another, their behavior often prompted me to be more resourceful in accomplishing the job. And last but not least, I learned how to be more compassionate and skillful in dealing with those who seemed to stand in the way of my lofty goals. I also learned that sometimes they had good reasons for their opposing viewpoints and that a note of grace and humility on my part could go a long way in creating a happier, healthier, and, in the end, more productive workplace. It is important to acknowledge the gifts of all those you've worked with over the years as you say goodbye. "Goodbye," then, does not mean "good riddance." The word *goodbye* is, after all, a contraction for "God be with you."

After the fond goodbyes of step one, we find ourselves confronted with the second step: to move on and create new relationships in our new settings. Relationships are, as Abigail Trafford points out, investments in social capital. We need friends to celebrate the sunny days and be there for the cloudy ones. An expanded network of friends can open up new avenues of rich possibilities available only through synergistic interaction with others. Developing new relationships, however, requires both interpersonal skills and intentionality. Those of us who are shy or highly introverted may find that making new friends is more challenging for us than it is for those who are gregarious and extroverted. Extroverts appear to be comfortable interacting with just about anybody anywhere. For them the challenge is to be selective enough in creating new friendships to achieve the depth needed for real bonding, the kind that comes with a commitment to be there with another in times of travail as well as joy.

There is nothing richer than a deeply loyal friend when you're in need of empathetic understanding, someone to stand by you as you walk through a trying time, to listen to your stories of the grandkid's latest antics, or to share your hopes and dreams for the future. In-depth relationships may actually be easier for introverts to develop than extroverts, even though extroverts may make a larger number of friends faster and more easily than introverts. Introverts, with their natural inclination toward self-reflection and ear for inner dialogue, tend to prefer a few in-depth relationships—in contrast to the wide variety of casual friends that extroverts enjoy. What may be a problem for introverts, however, is sharing enough of their precious inner life with new folks in new situations so that they can move to the deeper levels of trust required for truly supportive friendship. Introverts may also find it more challenging to find people who have similar interests, since introverts don't make a point of being in as many places where they will meet as many people as do extroverts. Joining a group or an organization that connects with personal interests, such as signing up for an educational tour on archaeology or becoming a member of the local Rotary Club, may help introverts—and extroverts—find new friends and develop new relationships.

Of course, *new* does not always mean better. It just means "now." And the "now" that you are currently experiencing has, of course, grown out of the past. In talking about the importance of developing new friends and relationships, I am not advocating that we sever all our old relationships. You may find that many old friends and colleagues will always be a part of your life, whether they are physically present or not. We are, as the poets tell us, part and parcel of everyone we've ever met.

I find this realization to be especially meaningful as I celebrate my seventieth birthday. Perhaps I've been going through a life-review process that is part of entering a new decade, but lately it's been important for me to reconnect with old friends and colleagues and recount the old times. My wife has teasingly cautioned me more than once to beware of lapsing into what she calls "the VFW syndrome or old-man phenomenon" of sitting around and rehashing the days of yesteryear. I hear her. But I also know that life review with trusted "buddies" is important; it helps us make sense of what our life has meant. It gives us a way to stay connected with our roots. Old friends can never be replaced, and some of us are fortunate enough to keep old friendships alive and vital throughout our lives. But like it or not, none of us is the same person we once were; old friendships must also change and grow if they are to keep their significance. For one reason or another, not all old friendships will make it with us into our senior years. Those that do will probably have changed enough over the years to qualify them as new.

◆ Relationship Challenges in Senior Life

In addition to saying goodbye to old relationships and generating new social capital as we enter the senior years, it is also important to give personal relationships the attention and care they need to grow and blossom. Growing older together can deepen the love and appreciation life partners have for each other, but entering a new stage of life changes ways of being together and tends to create new challenges.

Through my experience in working with hundreds of individuals entering their senior years and transitioning into new lifestyles, I've observed several common problem areas for partnered couples of all kinds. Although I have used a male/female model for most of the couples in the brief scenarios that follow, I have found from my counseling practice that many of the same issues, in one form or another, also apply to nontraditional couples such as gay, lesbian, bisexual, and transgendered (GLBT). One issue, for instance, that is universal to all couples is the question of where to live. The next chapter deals with the potential problems that can arise when you and your partner have different preferences about where to live. But there are other challenges that you may not expect. I've listed some here. As you read the list, note which ones could apply to you:

- They were initially attracted by differences in their temperaments and personality styles, but since settling into the everydayness of partnered life, they've been working to change one another to fit their image of what the other should ideally be. Now that they are retired, they have more time to devote to the job of changing one another.

- He's an extrovert who needs a great deal of social interaction, and she's an introvert who treasures solitary time and solo endeavors. He wants more social interaction, while she's seeking more quiet time to hear her own voice and do her own thing.

- She's taking off with a new career, while he's leaving his career behind and looking forward to their having more time together in his retirement.

- She's become more assertive and far less accommodating, while he's become softer, gentler, and more compassionate. Now that they are spending more time together, they are beginning to realize they don't know each other as well as they thought they did, and they're not sure that they like who the other is becoming.

- A couple is in a new relationship after each has lost a former spouse/partner to divorce or death. One wants to remarry immediately and/or set up housekeeping together as soon as possible. The other wants a close relationship but is not ready to remarry and/or share a home with someone else now or possibly ever.

- One partner has created a busy post-career lifestyle that includes lots of social, recreational, and volunteer activities, while the other partner, who is just retiring, has never had time or interest in doing that. The socially busy partner is frightened and intimidated by the prospects of a partner who has few plans for retirement other than the two of them doing things together.

Of course, not all couples will experience all or even any of these scenarios, but reviewing them might help alert you to areas worthy of serious discussion. Identifying and discussing areas of critical difference and planning ways of creatively addressing them can make a world of difference in rejuvenating your primary relationship.

Had Thad realized his wife Nina's need for emotional support and for finding a meaningful outlet for her intellectual talents, they might still be together. As it turned out, he was too focused on his career to address the serious problems that had been developing in their relationship. Nina had given up a good job and her professional career to follow Thad to Latin America for an interesting opportunity to cap off the senior stages of his career. For the first year, Nina did fairly well in the new setting, enjoying their beautiful home and acquainting their teenage daughter with the new culture. But then the daughter was off to college, and Nina felt the need to do something worthwhile. She had also begun experiencing resentments about giving up her career to support Thad's. Thad, meanwhile, was enjoying the high esteem, along with the great salary and perks, that came with his prestigious position. For him life was good, and he remained blissfully unaware of the deep troubles that were brewing at home.

Thad's good life came to a sudden, crash ending. It started when headquarters decided to close the Latin American office he'd been running for the past seven years and retire him from the company payroll. The good news was that Thad came away with a nice retirement package. But now, minus the work that filled his days with purpose, he was suffering the loss of identity that had made him feel important in the community. That, however, was not the worst of it. There was still a bigger loss to come, one that shook him to the core of his being. Seeking consolation from his wife about his loss of job and identity, he found that she was far from sympathetic and used the occasion to announce that she was leaving. She had had enough of playing second fiddle to a husband preoccupied with work and had accepted a position with a nongovernment organization. She was moving on—without Thad. Thad sought reconciliation and pleaded with Nina to try marriage counseling. But for Nina, it was too late. She could no longer see a future with Thad.

The last time I saw Thad, he was understandably depressed. He saw a dismal future for himself: a lonely man with nothing better to do than to spend his days sipping espresso at local bistros gossiping with other old codgers (the *old-man phenomenon* I mentioned earlier in this chapter). However, I'm fairly confident that Thad, who is well educated, urbane, well heeled, and handsome, will eventually create an interesting new life. But first he needs to come to terms with what he has lost: his wife, his work-based identity, and the affection of his daughter, who blamed him for the failed marriage. Thad came to realize how important his wife and family life were, but too late. In retrospect, he realizes he'd been seduced by the lure of a posh job and a high-flyer lifestyle that blinded him to what was really important. We can't roll back the river: What is done is done. But we can hope that Thad and others like him find the resilience necessary to navigate the dark days ahead and develop the resources needed to chart a meaningful new life.

Work can be a gratifying way to use our talents and energies. It can also blind us to things we need to pay attention to. If we're not careful, we may find it easier to find solace in work and career identity than to deal with difficult relationship issues. Unlike many problematic situations at home, work can provide fast solutions and quick rewards. We may even use it as a convenient escape from family conflict. Avoiding difficult issues in our relationships, however, may result in the loss of our closest and dearest loved ones.

PARTNERS WITH PYGMALION PROJECTS

Do you recall what you sought in a relationship back in your courting days? Were you looking for the love of your life, someone to have fun with, an intellectual partner, or someone who stirred your hormones into hyperactivity? Reflecting on what drew you to your partner (or partners, if you've had more than one), would you say it was the attraction of opposites or your similarity in interests?

While most of us had some idea of what we wanted in a love relationship, there's a strong probability that neither conscious choice nor random romance was entirely responsible for who we ended up with. In his excellent book *Please Understand Me II*, psychologist Dr. David Keirsey discusses four general styles of temperaments and their proclivities in relationship attractions. Kersey's styles are similar in general to the personal strength styles discussed in Chapter 7. Keirsey concludes that the attraction of opposites probably is involved in one's choice of mate(s), but only to a degree. Other, stronger dynamics are probably also at play in bringing our partner(s) and us together. Those forces, however, operate at the subterranean level and involve psychic dynamics that are usually beyond our conscious awareness or control. Furthermore, these subconscious impulses continue operating over the years in our primary relationships. Although differences may be an initial attraction, these same differences can, over time, become sinkholes that drain a relationship. For this reason, we want to become more fully aware of our subconscious inclinations so we can exercise fuller conscious control over them, especially if we want our relationship to bloom into its full potential in the senior years.

Based on some 50 years of observing human nature, Keirsey discovered that styles like the Analytic Thinker and the Mystical Intuitive and their close cousin the Nurturer-Inspirer tend to attract one another as life mates. The reason for that affinity, Keirsey speculates, is twofold. The more obvious reason is that these styles share in common an abstract style of thinking, which puts them on the same wavelength both in worldview and mode of communications. If we dwell most comfortably in the abstract sphere of possibilities, sky-blue concepts, and broad generalities, we want and need to interact with someone comfortable in that realm. The most likely outcome for an abstract thinker attempting to romantically relate to a down-to-earth, more concrete thinker is mutual frustration. The two styles are virtually worlds apart. Those of us with styles oriented toward practical thinking (Coordinator-Organizer, Artisan-Craftsperson, and Playful Performer, as discussed in Chapter 7) tend to become irritated and impatient with the "weird ways" of an abstract thinker.

Abstract thinkers relate far better to other abstract thinkers, and more literal thinkers to other literal thinkers. The attraction of opposites operates within each of these parameters, however. Abstract thinkers are not all alike, but the differences between abstract thinkers are still less than they are between an abstract thinker and a literal thinker. Analytic Thinkers, therefore, are drawn like butterflies to pollen to the romantic flair, emotionality, and idealism of Mystical Intuitives and Nurturer-Inspirers. In turn, Mystical Intuitives and Nurturer-Inspirers are seduced by the Analytic Thinker's orientation to the life of the mind, along with the calming affect of their well-reasoned approach to things.

Similarly, those of the literal temperament (the order-loving and convention-preserving Coordinator-Organizer and the living-in-the-moment Artisan-Craftspeople and Playful Performers) are drawn to differences within their styles. Coordinator-Organizers may seek to balance the serious and pessimistic side of their nature with the playful, adventure-loving, physically active Artisan-Craftspeople or Playful Performers. Artisan-Craftspeople and Playful Performers, by contrast, are prone to complement their preference for living in the moment with the planning, organized, and dependable ways of the Coordinator-Organizers.

Regardless of what brings partners together initially, eventually the aura of romance begins to fade as couples find themselves in the trenches of daily life. The dreamy-eyed projections of love and lust give way to the real person we have chosen as a life mate. When that happens, it's human nature to take on the task of changing our partner into a better person. This practice, in fact, is so well-known that comic stories have evolved about this tendency.

For example, there's the story about the young bride-to-be who's so nervous about the intricacies of the upcoming marriage ceremony that she seeks help from her minister in getting things right. Attempting to relieve her stress, the minister assures her that the ceremony can be broken down into three easy-to-remember phrases. First, he says, is the exchange of vows, to which she will simply state, "I will." Then it's the altar, where she and her betrothed will go to kneel for the marriage prayer. After that, it's the wedding hymn. While the hymn is playing, she will exit the church as a married woman hand-in-hand with her new husband. The wedding day came, and the bride had a case of nerves. Recalling the advice of the minister as she marched down the aisle, all she could think of was, "I will, altar, hymn. I will, altar hymn. I will alter him."

Keirsey refers to this tendency to reform our mate as the *Pygmalion Project*. That's in reference to Pygmalion, who in Greek mythology was king of Cyprus and fell in love with the goddess Aphrodite. He so longed for his vision of her as the perfect woman that he created a statue of her and ended up falling madly in love with his creation. As you might guess, he discovered how challenging it was to have a warm and fulfilling relationship with a hunk of stone. Fortunately for Pygmalion, Aphrodite saw his predicament, took pity on him, and brought his creation to life as the beautiful Galatea. As the story goes, they were united in marriage and lived happily ever after.

Like Pygmalion, we also tend to fall in love with our own concocted ideals, which get projected onto someone we find romantically attractive. Then that person becomes the "object" of our love instead of the genuine human being he or she really is. In the early stages of romantic love, our emotions often make it difficult to know exactly whom it is we have fallen for. But time eventually dispels our romantic projections and opens our eyes to the actual person sitting across the table from us. In this awakened state, it is a rare person indeed who likes and accepts absolutely everything about the actual person.

Also like Pygmalion, we might find that our love projections are so powerful that we can't resist trying to alter our mate into our image of perfection. Efforts to change our mate are likely to center on making our mate more like our own self. We want our mate to take on our own traits of temperament. In that regard, Coordinator-Organizers may chide their fun-loving, happy-go-lucky Artisan-Craftspeople or Playful

Performer to become more responsible, more thrifty, more punctual, more planning, and less preoccupied in the physical world of the here and now. Playful Performers and Artisan-Craftspeople are likely to grow weary of their Coordinator-Organizer partners badgering them to become more responsible, and may begin to urge them to lighten up, have more fun, and to stop taking life so seriously. The feeler types, the Mystical Intuitives and Nurturer-Inspirers, grow weary of their Analytic Thinker's cold detachment and rational approach to everything and soon demand more warmth and empathy. Analytic Thinkers may become disenchanted with the emotional, cheerful ways of the Mystical Intuitive or Nurturer-Inspirer and try to turn their unrealistic optimism, "Pollyannaish" idealism, and all that touchy-feely stuff into cautious skepticism and rigorous logistics.

Full-time employment and the demands of daily life limit the time we have to alter our mates. Then along comes retirement, freeing up needed time for the job of changing our partner into the person who fits our image of the perfect mate for us now. But our efforts to change our mate are more likely to produce detrimental and unintended results than to culminate in a better partner. Let's face it—the more someone tries to change us, the more likely we are going to be resentful. Nagging someone to change only results in making one feel unappreciated and diminished. Persistently unwelcome efforts to change another eventually force one to become hardened to ongoing criticism, rebel against the criticisms, or give in to passive compliance to the demands. Winning the battle to change another succeeds only in unwittingly transforming that person into a resentful automaton or someone quite different from the person we once loved and respected. Who wants to be married to a lapdog or a dispirited individual? Who wants to stay married to someone who abuses his or her integrity as a human being? We may find that our partner has simply had enough and needs to end the relationship to restore the individuality and regenerate the self-confidence she or he once had. Since divorce has become more socially acceptable it's a more frequently chosen option for couples of all ages, including those in their senior years. Should living together become habitually more negative than positive, a couple is well advised either to seek ways to renew their mutual love and respect or to have the courage to end the relationship.

CHANGING THE BEHAVIOR BUT NOT THE PERSON

Although efforts to change our mate are ill advised, modifying bad behavior can be a necessity. But we need to remember the distinction between personality and behavior. Behavior is what we do and how we act. Personality is who and what we are. We have little choice about our personality since we come hardwired into this world with proclivities to certain traits and temperaments. And, in that regard, you're okay and so am I. The way we express our proclivities grows out of our life experience—good experience can bring out the better parts of our personality, and bad experience can elicit the opposite. We have little control over our personality or life experience, but we can change our behavior, for better or worse. Many psychologists believe that there is both a Hitler and a Mother Teresa in us all. But we do not need to exercise our potential for Hitlarian behavior; we can choose to behave more like Mother Teresa instead. If we so choose, we can learn to manage the broad panoply of behavior we are all capable of, from the constructive to the mundane to the destructive.

The temperament of an Analytic Thinker is intellectual, critical, and thoughtfully careful. To be anything else, a person with this temperament would have to be somebody else. Should an Analytic Thinker's behavior turn noxiously critical, however, such behavior would be destructive. A Nurturer-Inspirer who permits unmanaged emotions to erupt in rude or uncivil outbursts is also out of line. By nature a Playful Performer is fun and lighthearted and enjoys living life fully in the moment. Regardless of this inclination, however, the Playful Performer's personality does not come with a license to be irresponsible and undependable. The more duty-oriented and convention-conscious Coordinator-Organizers have no authority to impose their rules of conduct or personal morals on others. Bad behavior is bad behavior. Temperament or personality style is not an excuse for behavior that is destructive to others.

No one's behavior is beyond reproach, and just about anyone can benefit from behavior modification improvement. Refusing to change bad behavior is a sign of a serious self-esteem issue or an overly inflated ego. Either of those afflictions bodes poorly for good relationship. Of course, neither you nor I can improve any behavior beyond our awareness, and a lot of our behavior falls in that range. We can unwittingly offend someone without even realizing it. For instance, it's not uncommon for an abstract thinker to pass friends by without seeing them or to overlook the newest acquisition of a partner. That's because abstract thinkers are usually so absorbed with a mental challenge that takes them far away from the here and now that they are often completely unaware of what's happening right around them. In colloquial jargon, we may refer to this type of personality as "the absent-minded professor," a label that has sometimes been applied to me. In fact, one of the gifts I received for my seventieth birthday was a sign that says, "I smile because I don't have the slightest idea what's going on." So far, I haven't hung it on the wall with my other counseling credentials.

Understanding how our mate's behavior is affected by temperament helps us realize that a behavior that is different from what we expect or desire does not necessarily grow out of negative intentions. By contrast, it's also important to remind ourselves how our temperament leads to behaviors that affect others, especially those whose relationship we value. We want to act in ways that support our relationships. But even in the most valued of relationships, we may find it necessary to provide feedback to help someone become aware of the impact that certain behaviors have on us, both positive and negative. Tactfully providing feedback to counter bad behavior may prevent a relationship from going sour.

Incidentally, giving feedback is not the same as giving advice. Feedback holds a mirror up to someone so that that person sees himself or herself through the eyes of another. Advice involves telling others what we think they should do. Good feedback can be invaluable. Most unsolicited advice falls on deaf ears.

For relationship enhancement, it always helps to acknowledge the finer aspects of another's personality and find reasons and occasions to celebrate that special person's uniqueness. It also helps to respond to good behavior with appreciation. When it comes to undesirable behavior, we have to decide whether it's better to ignore or confront it. Some behavior may be better ignored than rewarded with attention. There is still a bit of the adolescent in all of us, no matter what our age. But with the wisdom we've gained from parenting, grandparenting, and other life experience, we know that what we pay attention to is what we get.

So if your partner is acting like an irritable adolescent and begging for a fight, are you better off to indulge that behavior or ignore it? Or if your partner has an annoying habit like playing the TV too loudly and your repeated requests to lower the volume are ignored (or unheard), do you seek a quiet spot of reprieve and wait for the right time to acknowledge your partner for having the volume at a tolerable level? Or do you confront adolescent behavior with more adolescent behavior by turning off the TV, taking the remote control, and smashing it to pieces? If your partner continues to make decisions for you both without your input, do you offer praise when you are included? Or do you need to consider the consequences of ignoring decisions made without your input?

At this stage in life, most of us have long ago learned how to reward good behavior and discourage unwanted behavior. But is it possible that over the years you have developed a pattern of responding more to your mate's negative traits than to the positive ones? How often do you tell your mate how much you love and respect him or her? What did your mate do today that you appreciate? How specific and affirming can you be? How enthusiastic and romantic?

◆ Feedback and Behavior Modification

You are your behavior, or so it's been said—and it's true, to a degree. If the sum of who you are equaled your behavior, however, you would be totally transparent and completely predictable. The truth is that others can observe only your behavior—not what generates it. They can't see your values, temperament, attitude, and what's playing in your emotional center—all of which work together, to a greater or lesser degree, to generate your actions at a particular time. Sometimes we act out of a reasoned, conscious choice, and sometimes we react to the stress of an emotional situation. At other times, probably most of the time, we are not fully conscious of our behavior and go about things in a programmed way that has become habitual. We act like a machine in motion. It is the machine in motion, no doubt, that people generally associate with behavior that appears to equal the sum of who we are.

The truth is that others don't see our behavior; they see their perceptions of our behavior. Most people think perception occurs in the eye of the beholder, but actually it's a phenomenon occurring in the observer's brain. All input from our senses is translated into meaning within the brain. Observation, therefore, is a perception of the mind rather than an actual viewing of the outer world. Whatever meaning we attribute to our perception is unique to our own personal filtering system. That's the reason that four individuals viewing the scene of an accident invariably give four different accounts of what they saw. We attribute meaning to what we see and interpret our sensory impressions into a particular context that has been created by our values, temperament, programming, attitudes, and experiences. So, for instance, we see the sun come up and say, "Oh, it's going to be a good day." Or we see an angry colleague and assume that the colleague is experiencing marital discord, work-related frustration, or something else that we have come to associate with this colleague's anger. We all make assumptions about what we see and hear, and, in the process, we sometimes err in judging a person or situation.

You can't, of course, control the assumptions others make about you. But you can manage your behavior, and you can manage the assumptions you make about the behavior of others. If you really want to improve the quality of your relationships, you'll want to be careful about the assumptions you attribute to the behavior of those you think you know well—your loved ones, friends, and associates. You'll also need to be more aware of how your behavior affects others.

By the time we graduate to senior life, we've become well practiced in our particular brands of behavior. But if we are still basically healthy, we are still capable of improving our behavior at any age, especially if we're willing to seek and pay attention to honest feedback. You need to know, for instance, if you are acting in a way that appears critical, insensitive, arrogant, or overpowering. It's equally as important to hear feedback about your behavioral strengths. What is it about the way you project yourself in the world that works? Is it a smile that lights up the room? A laugh so infectious it makes others smile inside? Or do you listen to others with such sincere authenticity that it leads them to deeper levels of understanding and insight? Living without feedback would be like walking around town with our bare bottoms showing, oblivious to the fact that others are surprised to see that we're not wearing any pants.

There are four kinds of feedback: good, bad, affirming (confirms what you already know), and dissonant (the kind that bowls you over in surprise). Good feedback comes from accurate perceptions truthfully reported. Bad feedback is heavily biased; it is based on input that is either deliberately negative or contains more of the presenter's projections than accurate perceptions. It's important, therefore, to be curious about feedback but not overly gullible in your reactions. I always advise clients to seek feedback but to be discerning about what you take to heart; check it out with other sources before you commit to a behavior modification agenda.

Feedback that agrees with what you already know about yourself is validating, but may not provide much help for improving your behavior. Tough feedback, the kind that's difficult to give and uncomfortable to receive, is often the kind that presents the most potential for improving performance. In psychological lingo, we refer to this kind of feedback as *cognitive dissonance,* which means that the feedback you receive runs disturbingly counter to the way you see yourself.

Take Michael, for instance. One day he is confronted by his wife, Arlene, that she finds that having any kind of a serious discussion with him is exceedingly frustrating because, she says, "You always look at me critically in any serious discussion and argue with everything I say." This comes as shocking news to Michael. His perception is that he's been earnestly trying to be helpful by listening critically to what's being said and to provide her with another, more expanded view of the situation under discussion. Clearly there is a huge perceptual incongruity in what

Michael sees himself doing and what Arlene perceives. Arlene is obviously misinterpreting Michael's actions and intentions, but Michael is also not aware of how he is contributing to that misperception. It turns out that the way he draws his brows together and squints his eyes when he's listening to her signals a negative attitude in her understanding of body language. Michael needs to hear and heed what Arlene is saying because his behavior is unintentionally creating havoc in their relationship. And Arlene needs to understand that her interpretation of Michael's body language may not always reflect his intentions.

Critical information that comes as a surprise may make us uncomfortable. A typical response for anybody receiving disquieting feedback is to argue and react defensively. To illustrate the point, Arlene's perceptions in this example are based on inaccurate assumptions about Michael's behavior. But if Michael chooses to react to Arlene's misperceptions in an angry, defensive mode, his behavior will probably escalate their conflict. And if Arlene chooses to attack Michael for his confusing, albeit unconscious, use of body language, she will be setting up dynamics that make it difficult for Michael not to react defensively. Then the likely outcome will be a heated confrontation over who's right and who's wrong. Such a conflict could even end up seriously hurting their relationship—especially if it becomes a pattern for dealing with disagreements in their relationship.

Rather than reacting defensively, Michael could choose a productive response instead. He could, for instance, say something like, "Wow, thanks for that feedback. I must admit that I'm shocked but so glad you told me—I had no idea how my behavior was affecting you. The last thing I want is for our conversations to be a source of conflict in our relationship." After that acknowledgment, Michael could then ask Arlene to help him understand exactly what he's been doing to cause her to misunderstand his intentions and what he might do in the future to make their discussions more positive.

CREATING BETTER RELATIONSHIPS

Although feedback is a powerful technique for improving relationships, few of us are good at giving or receiving feedback. Most of us didn't learn effective feedback techniques from our families or through our life experience. My role model for dealing with marriage conflict was a father angrily stomping out the door while my mother was left fuming at his unreasonable behavior and refusal to deal with conflict. So instead it simmered underground, an earthquake waiting to erupt. In school, I was far more likely to learn quadratic equations than how to receive and deliver behaviorally enhancing feedback. And it hasn't been until the past decade that I have seen the corporate world come to realize the important link between improving human interactions and productivity.

Thanks now to 360-degree feedback, leadership training, and coaching resources, behaviors that lead to poor performance, mediocre productivity, and low morale can be addressed and frequently improved. But we still don't have ready access to these kinds of performance-improvement resources in our personal relationships and home life. Outside of the help available to some of us through professional therapists and counselors, we have to manage own behavior enhancement agendas.

To make your home life happier and your relationships more fulfilling, consider undertaking your own interpersonal and relationship improvement plan. A good beginning for such a plan is to seek a better understanding of your behavioral patterns and the perceptual impact of these on your partner, family, and friends. Find out what's working (relationship enhancing) and what could benefit from improvement (relationship negatives and neutrals). There is really only one way to obtain accurate information of this type—by talking directly to each person who is important to you. Talk to each person individually at a time and in a safe place that is comfortable for both of you. Do not resort to hearsay by asking Gene what Sarah really thinks of you; that will only triangulate communications and create complicated dynamics, not to mention the likelihood that such second-hand information usually has less veracity. Authentic feedback comes from primary sources, not secondary resources.

For genuine feedback, you might approach someone in the following way: "I'm undertaking a personal behavior review and would greatly value your feedback for that purpose. I want you to know that I highly value my relationship with you and want to do whatever I can to be more supportive and affirming. Since I can only see my actions from the inside, I can't know how they may be affecting you. I'm hoping there are things I do that support you and our relationship and am quite sure there are also things I could improve. Could you help me with some feedback? For instance, in your opinion, what do you see as the positives and the negatives of my behavior in our relationship? It would help if you could be as specific as possible, because I really care about you and want to be a positive presence in our relationship."

Be sure to ask for help in picturing what improved behavior might look like and how you might more fully contribute your strengths. And remember to acknowledge your appreciation for all feedback, positive and negative, even if some of it stings a bit. You will eventually get over the sting and can use its unpleasant sensations in the meantime to make you aware of some things you hadn't noticed before. Being stung could even be the truth that sets you free. The only way you can improve your relationship and enjoy its fullest potential is to know the truth—or, in this case, the perceptual truth—and such knowledge doesn't come without some risk on your part.

In receiving and giving feedback, remember that it's really difficult to see another person's intentions. All we can really see is the behavior to which we attach our assumptions. If others misperceive your behavior, find out why and what you can do to modify your actions in a way that they can more correctly "get you." Watch your own tendency to jump to conclusions about others when they are talking with you. Remember, as Michael and Arlene discovered, that some of us are completely unaware of our body in certain situations. Test your assumptions before acting on them, and if others mistakenly accuse you of being angry or irritable or anxious, ask them what you're doing that causes them to see you in that way.

As a personal example, I recall an occasion when my wife, clearly peeved over my actions, confronted me about being rude and angry in a discussion we were having. Since I wasn't aware of being either rude or angry, I was both startled and dismayed by her misperception. My first reaction was to get angry and contentious with her. Then, fortunately, I remembered my feedback training, so instead of angrily denying her perceptions, I responded by saying that I was surprised I'd given her that impression and asked her to demonstrate what I was doing that caused her to see me as rude and angry. With that she scrunched up her face to mimic how I looked and imitated my words and intonations. That turned the tide on a situation teetering on the verge of breaking down into an angry flare-up. I saw how ridiculous I looked from my wife's perspective, and her playacting struck a funny chord in both of us. We broke out in uproarious laughter that broke the tension of the moment.

Laughing has many healing properties, especially if we can laugh at ourselves. Had I followed my first inclination to argue and retaliate in that situation with my wife, we would probably have ended up in an angry stalemate. Ever since that encounter, however, I've been working to relax my facial expressions, to soften my stare, and speak in a gentler, more civil tone when we're engaged in a disagreement. I know disagreements are not going to go away. I'm continuing to work on recognizing and better managing my nonproductive tendencies in these kinds of encounters, and wherever possible, to see where the potential for humor might work its transforming wonders. I know that my behavior will never be perfect as a husband or person, but every little improvement helps. From systems theory we know that introducing energy into a system changes the system, so any improvement made in a relationship has a multiplier effect. The more positive energy we infuse into a relationship, the more positive the dynamics of the relationship are likely to become.

CONFRONTING BAD BEHAVIOR

A rule of thumb in giving feedback is to let the other person know exactly which actions have been offensive and exactly how they have offended you. Then describe what more acceptable behavior might look like. How, for instance, would you respond to your partner's saying, "How can you be so incredibly stupid?" You would have every right to react in anger to a comment that puts you down as a person rather than addressing a particular offensive behavior. You also would be justified at being especially upset if the comment had been delivered in a situation where you felt publicly humiliated. Every molecule in your systemic conditioning might cause you to respond in kind with a biting retort. But while you might momentarily satisfy a thirst for revenge, you would also probably escalate an unthinking, unkind, and unfortunate comment on your partner's part into a full-blown confrontation. While that might feel gratifying at the time, it would most likely work against your overall goals. To constructively confront bad behavior, consider responding with something that describes your feelings and your limits without demeaning the other person.

For example, you might say, "John, I strongly resent both your words and the sentiment. I'm not stupid and I am extremely angry that you have seen fit to insult my intelligence. I want you to know that I will not sit here and let you talk to me that way and in that accusative tone. You don't have to agree with me, nor would I want that. But you have no right to call me stupid. If I've said or done something to make you angry, I'd like to know what it is and talk about it. But I'm not going to tolerate your putting me down and calling me names. If you persist with your insults, I'm finished with this conversation. If you are ready to be civil with me, and to apologize, I'm willing to continue the conversation. What do you want to do?"

No one should be the victim of persistently bad behavior. Of course, we all have our bad moments, and none of us always acts and reacts in best form. An occasional slip into bad behavior is humanly unavoidable. If our actions hurt or offend another, there is only one appropriate thing to do—apologize and make whatever amends might be in order. Should we become aware of habitually engaging in offensive behavior, however, we need to devise a way to stop it and replace it with better behavior. If we need help to do so, there are personal coaches, therapists, pastoral counselors, or wise friends we can call on. In the end, there is no positive payoff or possible excuse to continue bad behavior. Behavior that is harmful to another hurts everyone involved, undermines a relationship, and may even turn love to hate.

When we are subject to someone else's bad behavior, how do we go about finding an appropriate response on the spot? What can we do to help bring attention to the behavior in a way that results in positive change? Responding appropriately when we're angry takes emotion management. I've often found it helpful to engage in something that forces me to pause, such as counting to 10 or taking some deep yoga breaths. This allows my intelligence and analytical skills to catch up to my emotions. Then I can develop an appropriate response. The pause is important because the reactive brain (the fight or flight mechanism) responds impulsively and instantaneously. A disciplined pause provides time for the slower-responding thinking brain to assess the situation and give us options for choosing intelligent behavior.

Becoming victim of repeated bad behavior can eventually destroy a person's sense of personal worth, so it is vital to address destructive actions and situations. But it is also important to go about it in a constructive way. We all have a right to be who we are and to develop our inherent talents and gifts to the fullest as long as we are not subjecting others to bad behavior. We do not have the right to demand that our partner change the core of his or her being in order to conform to our ideal of what the perfect mate is like. That would be disabusing the personality and temperament that makes your partner unique.

◆ Parting Ways

Much as we might hope for it, not all marriages are made in heaven; in fact, some become a living hell. Should you find yourself in an unrelentingly negative relationship that's beyond fixing, ask yourself what keeps you from leaving. Life is just too short to suffer unremittingly in an unredeemable situation.

An abusive relationship saps vitality and can keep you locked in the dark side of your personality. There are all kinds of abuse. Emotional torment can be as harmful as physical abuse. Being ignored and denigrated as a person can be as deadly as being bound or beaten.

If you can't fix a relationship, you need to fix the situation. I don't believe we were put here to suffer, and I don't believe we earn points in the afterlife by staying in a toxic situation. We're here, I believe, to realize our fullest potential, to enjoy the gift of life, and to share our God-given talents. If you can't achieve that because of the relationship you're in, it's time to move on. It's not a failure to leave an abusive relationship. The real failure would be in remaining in a situation that undermines your ability to grow and to enjoy your short run on the stage of life.

I know that leaving is easier said than done. It took several years, for instance, for someone my wife and I care deeply about to do what she needed to do. This was a situation where two adults in their fifty-plus years married too quickly on the rebound from previous relationships. Nadine, whose husband had been killed in a tragic accident, was lonely and anxious to find a compatible relationship. She is a highly active extrovert who feared that being a single woman would keep her from having the kind of social life she wanted. Then along came Devon. He quickly swept her off her feet. He was handsome, charming, and attentive, showering her with gifts and showing great pleasure in the physical activities she so enjoyed. But Devon, it turned out, had a rather shoddy track record with women. He had been in one failed relationship after another and always ended up blaming the other person for things not working out. None of this came to light, however, in the rush of courting and the excitement of a new relationship. Then, much to the amazement of those who knew them, they married within a few months of meeting each other. Their rationale for the rush into marriage was that they were well-seasoned adults who knew what they wanted. They enjoyed each other's company, and they wanted to be married. So why wait?

Within a few months of being married, however, they quickly began to realize that while they enjoyed many of the same activities, they had distinctly different values. Their values were so far apart, in fact, that they soon found themselves in constant conflict. That's when Nadine began to realize that the person she thought she was marrying was not the person she'd actually married. As Nadine began the slow, painful journey of trying to find out who Devon really was, she discovered his trail of broken relationships and experienced his abusive nature. She realized she had make a big mistake in not taking the time to get to know Devon and his history apart from his own embellished narratives about himself as a hero who always came to the rescue of those in need, especially attractive damsels in distress. Eventually, the relationship became so contentious that Nadine had to free herself from a highly abusive situation. The divorce ended bitterly, with fights over the smallest of details and at great personal and financial costs to Nadine.

Devon moved onto another relationship well before the divorce was finalized. Nadine, however, while freed of that relationship, required years to heal and redeem her sense of self-worth. That experience made her both wiser and more cautious. She no longer feels she needs to be coupled to have a complete life. While she still enjoys relationships with men, she has a full life on her own. She has become more independent and has found new and interesting avenues for enjoying her life. You can bet that should any relationship ever develop into the potential for marriage or cohabitation, Nadine will take plenty of time to know what she is getting into. If she does remarry, which is doubtful, it will be only if she finds a thoughtful person who is genuinely loving, kind, and compatible with her deeply felt values.

Deeply held values not only shape our beliefs and behavior, they can also lead to lifestyle choices. Sometimes the radically different lifestyle preferences of two people cannot be bridged with material changes. Take our friends Kevin and Mavis, for instance. They found each other in their senior years, both having left unfulfilling marriage situations some years earlier. Kevin is an artist who loves people and enjoys a simple, unfettered lifestyle. Mavis, who met Kevin at one of the many workshops he conducts, is a wealthy bon vivant who has always appreciated the luxuries of an upscale life. But despite (or maybe because of) their contrasting lifestyles, Mavis found Kevin to be intriguing; through various devices, she ingratiated herself into his affections. Eventually she lured him away from his unconventional way of life into her "pink palace" and a high society lifestyle, where she introduced him to the yacht set and country club community. Kevin found this amusing for a while, joking that his yacht was the small plastic variety he kept moored in the bathtub.

Their differences in lifestyle and aspirations, however, soon began to create some friction. Kevin was an early riser who was often found in the local coffee shop, hanging out with artists and shopkeepers involved in the local arts scene. Mavis was used to sleeping in late and beginning her day at lunchtime with her bridge set. The rest of her afternoon was often spent managing and preparing for her social schedule. Even though she eventually gave up many of her social engagements to have more time to paint with Kevin, it soon became apparent that there were other, deeper incompatibilities that were not so easily fixed. For one thing, Mavis wanted to travel and see the world. She had a vision of their buying a villa somewhere along the Mediterranean coast, where they would enjoy the good life, seeing the sights and enjoying fine food and drink. Kevin had already done a lot of traveling and was now interested in being part of a community and spending more time with kids and grandkids. He had never been one for living high on the hog in the first place, and was even more averse to doing so now because such a lifestyle was detrimental both to his physical and fiscal well being. When it became obvious that neither was willing to significantly change their ways, nor able to change their interests, it was clear that going their separate ways was the best solution. They cared about each other, but they did not love each other's lifestyle, and that was certain to always be a bone of contention. Both have gone on to enjoy the lifestyle that nurtures the unique style of each. Kevin is a gregarious center for the local arts community and enjoys time with his grandkids. Mavis still paints, but she moved to an upscale retirement community where she enjoys the luxuries that she can afford and can have a comfortable base from which to travel in style.

Ending a relationship can be extremely messy and difficult. There are all kinds of religious and social strictures against divorce, and our cultural conditioning may leave us with a heavy sense of guilt when we leave a marriage or long-term relationship, especially one that involves children and grandchildren. Sometimes it takes more gumption and courage to end a relationship than to tolerate a bad situation. While the decision to leave a relationship should not be taken lightly, neither should the choice to hang on to a bad situation. Deep pain in a relationship is unlikely to heal of its own accord. When a relationship becomes painful, we need to do what we would if we had a toothache—seek the services of a qualified professional for help.

◆ Love Alone Is Not Enough

It's no news to anybody who has ever been in a relationship for more than a week, well maybe a couple of months, that nobody lives happily ever after. Relationships take work, which means communicating, understanding, empathizing, and being willing to give and receive support. Even a strong relationship encounters conflict. Partners in a strong relationship, however, know how to manage conflict and use it as a learning experience for improving trouble spots. Partners who want their relationship to grow have the courage to step out of their comfort zones and creatively explore new ways of relating. As their understanding of each other deepens, their capacity for intimacy is also likely to expand. But all of this requires trust. Partners must trust each other enough to bare their souls without fear of ridicule or concern that the disclosure of vulnerabilities will ever be used against them in any way. This means that both partners must take responsibility for creating a safe, supportive environment.

The bond of a nurturing relationship grows out of love, compassion, and taking delight in each other. If a long-term relationship has become routine and boring or, even worse, unfulfilling and abusive, both partners need to embark on some serious work. It's easy to blame a partner for all the ills of the relationship, but there is a high probability that it's not just one of the partners who needs fixing. More than likely, both partners need to reexamine their priorities and make some changes in their behavior and lifestyle choices. Perhaps the relationship just needs a little touching up here and there, but if a major overhaul is required, it may be time to invest in joint counseling sessions or a retreat that focuses on relationship issues. Even in the face of serious difficulties, however, you still have choices about how to respond to various challenges. Although it usually takes more effort to respond to difficulties with love and grace than with anger and moroseness, an affirming approach helps to create the kind of safe atmosphere that nurtures healing and growth. If you value your relationship, you need to be proactive in keeping it fresh and fun and mutually supportive.

GUIDELINES FOR RELATIONSHIP MANAGEMENT

Sustaining a loving relationship means constant communication, and that means work, especially during transitions. From my years of counseling experience, I've found it helpful to remind clients of a few simple but frequently overlooked pointers when one or both partners are going through a transition. First and foremost, it's important for partners to allow each other to be who each of them is as a unique individual and to support each other in becoming the best that each can be. That means riding the crests as well as the troughs in the course of each other's growth and the relationship as a whole. It also means relaxing and enjoying those graceful glides on glassy seas when things go your way. But it's unrealistic to think that you can be ecstatic about your relationship all the time. As the old song says, some days are diamonds, and some are dust.

A second pointer is to remind yourself of the jewel-like qualities of your partner and your relationship, especially during those times when the glitter is gone. Generating a clear picture of the precious gems of your relationship into a "love vision" can help you keep the positive aspects of your relationship in mind. Bring your love vision out and shine it up on a regular basis, even more so on the dark days. Share your vision with your partner. It's difficult to see the shiny facets of a loving relationship if you shut them up in a closed box. Talk about things that matter on a daily basis. If you wait for the perfect time to share something important, you may end up being too late.

A third pointer is to take time to acknowledge your partner for a specific attribute or action. Make sure your acknowledgment grows out of an understanding of who your partner is, not who you want him or her to be. We talked about this danger in relation to the Pygmalion Project earlier in this chapter. So, for example, you wouldn't want to continually acknowledge your infectiously romantic and extroverted mate for restraining her feelings in social interactions just so you don't have to deal with your own easily aroused feelings of insecurity and jealousy. Instead, look for ways to acknowledge her unique ability to engage others in interesting, animated conversation. You may, in the process, learn something about your mate and yourself. In appreciating the gifts of your partner, think about what you would be missing if your partner were suddenly absent from your life. One day that could be the reality. Be sure, therefore, to treasure the unique vitality of your relationship before you have to deal with your final day together. You might find that the next time a reactively critical comment comes to mind, you are more likely to replace it with a positive affirmation.

To move your relationship to a fuller level of nurturing support, explore together what makes you happiest, what you both remember as the fondest joys in your relationship, and what you can do to help each other live a life of meaning, purpose, and gratitude.

SOME FINAL TIPS FOR REGENERATING YOUR RELATIONSHIPS

Many of my clients have found the following 10 guidelines to be helpful for enhancing relationships in senior life:

1. *Renew affiliations.* Look for and create new relationships to replace those workplace affiliations you leave behind as you graduate from full-time employment to a new chapter in your life. Who

will be the "central characters" in your new life? What major and minor themes of this chapter will your new affiliations help you develop?

2. *Share your thoughts and feelings.* Take time on a regular basis with your partner to discuss what's on your minds. Communicate daily at a set time, perhaps over morning coffee or evening cocktails. Make a weekly date for more extensive sharing of what you both are thinking and feeling. Think of these as relationship deepening meetings. Be bold in discussing your concerns, joys, hopes, and dreams. Make a point of not interrupting each other as each of you takes a turn talking while the other is listening. If you don't understand something your partner is saying, wait until your partner is finished and then go back to points you would like to clarify or explore in more detail. Save the gripes and blaming sessions for another time.

3. *Practice gratefulness.* As the day winds down, take time with your partner to review three things for which you are grateful from that particular day. As you enjoy the big and little things of each day, note the blessings that have come your way. Don't allow a list of criticisms on your mental balance sheet to outweigh the daily blessings. And please don't wait until it's too late to let others know how grateful you are for the gifts of their presence. Counselors and ministers are trained to listen for two key themes in the life stories of those who have entered their final days: grace and gratitude. Those who die well are often those who have lived well; they have seen grace at work in their life, and they are grateful for the gift of grace and life itself.

4. *Examine assumptions.* We all make assumptions that become the basis for how we operate. But take the time to find out whether you and your partner are proceeding on the same the assumptions. You can avoid an emotional train wreck by clarifying the assumptions that each of you has about a certain situation or each other and then adjust your behavior to achieve mutually agreeable outcomes.

5. *Practice empathy.* Empathy is a process of really listening to another as if you were in that person's shoes. Ask yourself what it really is like to be that person in that situation. If you find yourself giving advice, you've moved away from empathy into the unsolicited imparting of your views. Save your advice for those occasions when someone specifically asks for it, and then you

may want to dispense it gingerly in carefully measured spoonfuls, especially when it comes to advising someone else on self-improvement. In fact, you may want to stay away from the latter entirely, even when your advice is solicited. Use the opportunity instead to offer questions that could help the other person figure out what the best course of action for that person appears to be at that time.

6. *Give each other space.* Too much togetherness can become suffocating. Look for things you enjoy doing together and those you enjoy doing separately. Create a room of your own or some individual space, even if it's just a corner desk in the bedroom or a workbench in the garage. We all need a place to engage in uninterrupted solitude.

7 *Seek feedback.* Ask those who know you well for feedback on your behavior. Ask them to describe your current behavior in terms of what works well and what might be improved. Create a personal development plan that capitalizes on your behavioral and attitudinal strengths; then start working on developing one or two areas at a time where improvement is in order.

8. *Invent new behaviors.* If you're stuck in old behavior patterns that are not achieving the results you want, why continue them? Some of the behaviors that worked well in your organizational career may not be productive in your new lifestyle.

9. *Practice optimism.* If you are a brilliant critic or a mastermind at seeing the flaws in things, it may be challenging to adopt an optimistic approach to life. But your health, longevity, and relationships will all benefit from doing so. It's emotionally draining to be in relationship with an eternal pessimist. That does not mean that you must be the eternal Pollyanna, always gleeful and above the bad things in life. But let's face it—most people find that it is simply more pleasant, more energizing, and more hopeful to be around positive people. It is also kinder to yourself to assume a generally more optimistic nature; otherwise, you're likely to pass right by all the lovely roses because you're focused only on the thorns.

10. *Celebrate your one-of-a kind partner.* Develop and carry around in your mind the love vision you have of the unique person you are blessed to be with as a mate. When your mate engages in bad behavior, as he or she inevitably will, address the behavior but not

the self-worth of your partner. Don't forget to address your own bad behavior! Remember that we all slip into bad behavior at times. If the behavior is not part of an abusive pattern, address it, forgive it, and move on. Be kind and gracious to your mate and to yourself.

COMING HOME: RELOCATING TO THE GOOD LIFE

"I'd move out of the city in a heartbeat to a quiet country setting with a great golf course, but my wife is a big-city girl and absorbed in her career. Because I love my wife and want to remain married, I'm just going to have to live with traffic and congestion and deal with the situation the best I can."

—RETIRED PROFESSOR WISHING FOR A PASTORAL SAILOR-GARDENER LIFE

"I think I must have been something like an army scout in a past life because all I want to do is travel and explore the world. My husband hates to travel, however, so I have to find other ways to keep myself interested and occupied."

—RETIRED PROFESSIONAL WOMAN SUBSTITUTING A NEW CAREER
FOR PREFERRED INTEREST IN TRAVELING

"My husband wants to retire in Wilmington, North Carolina, but that won't work for me. Because it is stretched out along the coast, I'd only have about 180 degrees of operating room. I want a home in downtown Raleigh, NC, where I can have 360 degrees of operating room to meet people and develop new friendships."

—HIGHLY EXTROVERTED COMMUNICATIONS PROFESSIONAL EXPLAINING
HER REQUIREMENTS FOR RETIREMENT LOCATION

◆ The Good Life and Where to Find It

Where do you find the good life for enjoying your senior years? A seemingly infinite number of commercials tell us that the answer is the perfect retirement community. All you need to do, such commercials advocate, is move to the right location and there you'll find happiness. Of course, that location just happens to be the one being promoted by whatever particular advertisement catches your attention. Those ads, featuring pictures of rolling golf courses and smiling seniors sipping drinks around a pool, can be rather seductive. Should you find such pictures beckoning you, remind yourself that you're looking at paid advertisements. Commercial ventures invest huge sums of money promoting the concept that happiness is to be found in a particular location. If golf and the clubhouse lifestyle is what you are looking for, then just about any place with eighteen links and a climate congenial to year-round golf may do just fine. But if you're one whose interests range beyond golf, it's highly unlikely that a perfect place for you is going to be found from seeing an advertisement or reading a list of the top 10 places to retire. If you're seeking life fulfillment, you'll need to find a location where you can do and be your best, and that is an individual proposition.

An old saying about the relationship between self and location cautions, "Wherever I go, there I am." We can't run from our emotional problems or our personal fallibilities for the simple reason that we take ourselves wherever we go. It's also true, however, that some places are going to be far more compatible than others to who you are and who you're becoming. Choosing where you are going to live in the fifty-plus years without considering the important aspects of life fulfillment could lead to frustration.

To illustrate that point, imagine a couple who chooses an apparently great location on the basis of a brochure promoting "the ideal retirement community." Then, after moving to this special place, they discover that this ideal retirement community is not what they had hoped for at all. They had envisioned a place where they could be engaged in a progressive community, associating with an environmental action group, teaching courses in their favorite disciplines, and playing prominent roles in civic affairs. But instead of a small college town with a strong community ethic, they find miles and miles of villas, golf course fairways, and nearby strip malls.

Before you can understand what an ideal or even a suitable retirement location might look like, you need to clarify your aspirations and goals for senior life. So why, then, does choosing the right location seem to be such a driving force for so many retirement planners? Probably because dealing with a concrete choice such as location is much easier than struggling to define something as intangible as your ambitions for a fulfilling life. Location is important, but the one you choose must be congruent with what is going on to make your life rich, full, and satisfying.

DONNA AND FRANK'S EPIPHANY

Frank, a psychologist, and his wife, Donna, a college professor, decided the time had come to retire and move to a place with a year-round warm climate. They were sure that the perfect place was a quaint little town in the Carolina hill country they had discovered in their earlier travels. Satisfied that they had found their retirement heaven, they quit their jobs and retired to the little Carolina hill town. They had fun settling in and renovating the adorable country cottage they'd purchased, and they enjoyed sampling local restaurants and setting out to make new friends. What they soon discovered, however, was that making new friends in this small, rural community was more challenging than they had anticipated, even for Donna, a gregarious extrovert who had easily made loads of friends wherever she had lived. But folks in this community had lived in the same place forever and were both reserved and mistrustful of strangers. Still, they assured themselves, there were many benefits to living there, such as that tasty southern food found in the local restaurants, mild winters, a low crime rate, and lots of beautiful countryside to explore.

As time passed, however, they both began to realize that while all of that was great, it was not enough to keep them from becoming bored. There wasn't much to do around the area for two professionals who had enjoyed busy careers that fully engaged them in the lives of others. Of course, there were plenty of great books to read, and they had plenty of time to meditate and enjoy long walks along the picturesque country lanes. But soon enough, the days began to grow too long, and they got tired of hanging out by themselves 24/7. They also found out that their new retirement location got pretty hot in the summer, especially for folks who had grown up in Maine.

Finding and relocating to their little bit of heaven represented a major lifestyle change on their parts, one that had seemed like a good choice in the spur of the moment. They had invested a great deal of money, time, and creativity in renovating their new home to accommodate their needs and tastes. But now each was wondering how to tell the other that this little piece of retirement heaven was boring as hell. Each of them was secretly feeling fickle and wondering what in the world they had spent all that time and money on just to be unhappy.

HAPPINESS IN SENIOR LIFE

Let's take a moment here to review just what *happy* might actually mean in senior life. The dictionary defines *happy* as "feeling or showing pleasure or contentment." Another definition is "slightly drunk." Happiness, for most people in senior life, seems to be something beyond contentment, or even being slightly drunk, for that matter. Happiness, as a general state of mind, is in knowing that you're living your life in a way that is fulfilling. That usually necessitates a sense that you are growing in some way, contributing some value, and that your being in the world counts for something. Happiness, for most of us, is not likely to come from material things or activities we engage in simply to fill up our time.

Eventually, Donna's disillusionment with the place reached such a point that she decided to risk Frank's ire and admit that she simply was not happy with this life. To her surprise, Frank admitted he'd also begun feeling much the same way and was relieved that Donna had broken the ice on the subject.

After some soul searching and hours of discussion, they elected to sell their little cottage in the sun and move to a place to which they felt drawn, Portland, Maine. Something in their early roots seemed to draw them back to Maine and city life. It turned out that Portland was much more compatible with who they were and what they wanted to do. They quickly settled into Maine life and soon found themselves busy with the kinds of things they liked to do. Frank renewed his psychologist's license and opened up a part-time counseling practice. Donna, who had always loved pretty things, opened a shop selling second-hand knick-knacks. These, however, were not just any knick-knacks; they were little treasures obtained from the attics and basements of little old ladies who had stored them away for decades. The nature of this work enabled Donna to meet and interact with all kinds of interesting people who enjoyed her company so much that they looked for other little treasures and told their friends about her. Soon Donna had a thriving little business, which she pursued more for fun than money. Frank also enjoyed helping out in the shop and occasionally joined Donna on her treasure hunts, although he let Donna do all the talking, at which she excelled. They set up shop in the basement of their attractive little home, which had once been owned by a sea captain, and there they enjoyed cleaning up their little treasures and restoring them to their former glory.

In addition to their work, they found an active church and joined the choir; both loved to sing and had great voices. They took advantage of the rich cultural life in Portland, with season tickets to the theater and roles in amateur theater productions. A nearby health club provided Donna with a place to swim laps and be on the senior women's aquatics team. They knew that winters in Maine could be long and cold, but with a crackling fire in their fireplace, and the option of deciding whether or not they wanted to venture forth on brusque, snowy days, they were grateful that their life was so rich and full. Frank found that he could even have an occasional glass or two of wine with dinner without losing control. As a psychologist, he determined that his former alcoholic tendencies had been an escape from a life that had grown dreary. In their new retirement home, however, he felt so rejuvenated that he no longer needed booze to cheer his spirits.

◆ Critical Issues in Your Relocation Choice

What are your priorities in a suitable location for your senior years? Do you want to be in a place where you can thrive and be your best? Or are you looking for a final resting place? Are you rooted to the place you've lived forever? Or are you more of a traveler who would be happier on the road? Is your ideal location one where you can get a good latte at an outdoor street café when the weather is nice and then lock the door to your place and head south when snowflakes fly? Do you yearn for the clean air and quiet countryside, or the hustle and bustle of city life? Have you always wanted to study philosophy or world history but were either too busy or too inconveniently located to do so? What or who is going to determine your location choice? Will you let the inertia of the past keep you right where you are, or is your wanderlust likely to take you on trips of adventure around the globe?

It would be wasted money and time if you progressed this far in this book and then ended up in a location lacking the essentials required for self-realization. The issue to consider at this point is where fulfilling places to live are likely to be for you and, if you are partnered, for you and your partner together. Look over the following list for ideas in assessing which criteria are most essential for your location choice.

Clarifying Your Location Priorities

Here's a three-step process for approaching this task:

1. Check all options that seem important to you.
2. Circle the seven you consider to be the most important in your future.
3. Prioritize your circled choices from most important to least important.

❑ Access to cultural activities (the arts, museums, historical places)

❑ Adult education opportunities (college or university learning access)

❑ Access to nature: hiking, biking, canoeing, birding

❑ Climate: mild, sunny, four seasons

❑ A "happening" city

❑ A quiet country setting or rural community life

❑ Affordability: cost of living (real estate, taxes, goods and services)

❑ Entertainment: good restaurants, sporting events, local theater

❑ Topography: mountains, ocean, water, desert

❑ Geography: the United States (south, north, west, Midwest, New England, Mid-Atlantic), Latin America, Canada, Europe, Asia, Pacific Islands

❑ Proximity to grandchildren, family, and friends

❑ Personal growth: yoga, martial arts, health spas, fitness centers, spiritual retreats

❑ Quality health care facilities

❑ Recreation: boating, fishing, golf, tennis, camping, hiking, biking, skiing

❑ Work opportunities: access to consulting, part-time jobs, new careers

❑ Volunteer possibilities: opportunities to work for worthy causes

❑ Cultural flavor: country, rural, urban, suburban, progressive, fast-paced, sedate, conservative, ethnic orientation, cross-generational, restricted to 50+

❑ Types of people: multicultural, well educated, artsy, quaint, wealthy, middle-class, yacht club members, golfers, friendly, tolerant, liberal, conservative, rugged, down-home

❑ Religious/spiritual options: places to practice your faith or spiritual discipline

❑ Convenience of location for caring for aging parents or other family and friends

❑ Other: _____

_____

_____

◆ Resolving Differences in Location Preferences

The choice of where to live in retirement can be difficult enough for an individual but even more so for those planning together. How do you resolve dilemmas like the following, where two partners in a committed relationship are literally and figuratively miles apart in where they want to live?

- She wants to relocate closer to the kids and grandkids. He prefers moving to Mexico, where they could make their retirement dollars go further than in either the high rent district they now reside or that of her location preference.

- He loves to travel and wants to see the world. She wants to stay home, tend her garden, spend time with her friends, and enjoy quality time with the grandkids.

- She wants to move to a new place, make new friends, and start a new life in a new location. He wants to stay in the home where the trees and shrubs he planted 30 years ago are now maturing, where he has the perfect workshop, and where he can mentor new members of the civic organizations that he has led to prominence over the years.

- She loves the city life. He's been dreaming of retiring to a quiet community with a golf course and a few good restaurants.

- He wants to teach his favorite discipline part-time in a university town. She wants to buy an RV and hit the road.

- He wants to purchase his own plane and fly rescue missions with the civil air patrol. She wants to run a B & B in the historic countryside in a no-fly zone.

- She wants to build a brand new home requiring little upkeep in a new, upscale community. He wants to buy and restore an old home in a historic district.

These are just some of the challenging situations faced by many couples in determining an ideal location for their senior years. Resolving these differences in a way that both partners come out winners takes creativity, a willingness to engage in serious problem solving, and a mutual respect for each other's differences. Failing to do that can have serious consequences in a relationship—the more accommodating partner may simply give up his or her aspirations and begrudgingly go along with the other's dream program, or both partners may remain so intransigent in their positions that they are forced to go their separate ways.

In my years of working with hundreds of fifty-plussers, I've seen an interesting variety of ways that different people have dealt with such issues. In one case, the wife, who as a young child was forced to flee Vietnam with her parents, yearned to return to the land of her birth to experience life in twenty-first century Vietnam. Her husband longed to buy a villa on coastal Salerno and immerse himself in the rich cultural heritage of this part of Italy. Further complicating the situation was that their adult kids had no intention of moving to either place; they were staying in the good old U.S.A. The couple eventually resolved their dilemma by agreeing to live in Vietnam for five years and then transition to Italy. They also planned to make frequent visits to the United States to be with their kids and to help finance an annual family gathering at some convenient location.

Paula and Robert worked out a different kind of solution to their different preferences for a retirement location. Paula was a retired lawyer and an introvert who insisted they relocate to a quiet community and build a lovely home in the woods. Robert was a gregarious extrovert and retired State Department diplomat who wanted a condo in the downtown area of a bustling city, one with an international orientation such as Washington, D.C., London, or Paris. Because they had already spent their busy career years in the city, Robert decided to be magnanimous and honor Paula's wishes. The search for the right location eventually led to buying property in the woods on a high bluff featuring a beautiful panoramic river view, where they built a lovely, energy-efficient home in a Japanese motif.

Paula was happy there with their two dogs, miles of country lanes to walk, a modern kitchen from which to create culinary delights, a nearby university where she could take a course or two in a subject she wanted to explore, and the few interesting friends they found tucked away in the wooded hills. Robert tried to be happy there, but soon found the community much too small for his extroverted ways and attraction to city life. To accommodate his needs, they traveled frequently to places like Paris, London, and Madrid. But Robert found he needed more than an occasional trip to satisfy his need for the buzz of city life.

They resolved their dilemma by buying a second home, a condominium in the heart of Buenos Aires. At least three or four times a year, for extended periods of time, you can find Robert there enjoying the city's extroverted people and rich, colorful heritage. Sometimes Paula stays at home with the dogs, and other times they take off together on an international adventure. They have come to appreciate and honor their differences and, in doing so, have found a compromise that works for them. They also found an unforeseen bonus in that after they've been apart, homecomings are like mini-honeymoons.

But compromise is not the answer for everyone. Art and Janet were unable to settle their differences in location preference by working out a mutually agreeable compromise. Janet, a therapist with a thriving practice, is a declared "big-city gal." It's in her blood; she was born and reared in London. Art grew up a country boy in Oklahoma. They met in London, where Art had been on assignment, and soon fell in love and married. Then they moved to Washington, D.C., so that Art could accept a professorship at an area university. In Washington, Janet stayed home to raise a family and took a part-time job as a secretary. Eventually, however, Janet realized she needed something more in her life and undertook a mid-life career change to become a therapist. She developed a successful practice just as Art, an avid golfer, retired from teaching and was eager to move to a sedate golfing community, away from city congestion. But Janet had no interest in letting go of her practice and even less interest in leaving the city life she found energizing.

When Art and Janet found themselves in a dilemma where compromise did not appear to be an option, they had to do some serious coming to terms with what they now wanted from each other and from this new chapter in their lives. From Janet's perspective, the compromise had already occurred, years ago. She had left London to move to a new country to be with him. She had supported him through graduate school and had been the primary caregiver for raising their children. He had had his turn. Now it was her turn to develop her professional identity. And now that she finally had the means and freedom to enjoy the cultural opportunities around them, she wasn't about to give them up.

They stayed in the city. Art loves his wife and wants to remain married to her, so he has looked for ways that he can enjoy their urban location. He has also found ways to enjoy the countryside on his own. Every once in a while, he throws his fishing gear in the back of his old pickup and takes off for some trout streams in the hills. In addition, he and Janet have fun traveling together, frequently with another couple they enjoy. Meanwhile, Art says, hope springs eternal, since there is always the chance that Janet will retire at some point and maybe even change her mind about the country. Of course, the question still remains as to whether this big-city girl could ever be happy in a pastoral community, miles away from shopping malls and, even more important, the new grandkids that are now an important part of their lives.

◆ **Finding a Mutually Satisfying Location**

These examples represent three different approaches to addressing differences in preference locations:

1. *Slingshot,* where first one partner's wishes are accommodated and, then, later, that of the other partner
2. *Compromise,* in which both partners' wishes are met to a considerable degree, although neither gets exactly what he or she wants
3. *Accommodation,* where one partner is committed to a particular location and lifestyle and can't be happy in another situation. The other partner is left with one of two choices: deferring or departing.

Of course, not all couples in their senior years have acutely differing views on relocation. Some may find themselves perplexed instead by the huge number of possibilities available. Choosing from such a wide range of options can be overwhelming. In fact, some find the task so bewildering that they simply stay put or get seduced by one of those high-powered ads touting the perfect retirement community. Should you find yourself in such a relocation quandary, there is a reasonable way to address the problem. It's a joint planning process that takes into consideration the top interests of both partners for making a mutually agreeable choice. I can vouch for this process because it's how my wife and I found a location ideally suited to our unique desires for this chapter in our lives. I owe Dick Bolles thanks for the basic idea for this process, which is described in his book *The Three Boxes of Life and How to Get Out of Them.* "Finding Your Ideal Location" can help you find and work through multiple options for honing in on the place that works best for you.

Finding Your Ideal Location

Step 1: Each partner should do step 1 separately and not in consultation with the other. Use the "Clarifying Your Location Priorities" that you completed earlier to come up with a list of your top seven location preferences. Think in terms of the kinds of places you prefer, not in relation to specific places. So, for instance, for this section you might list "a high desert community with a New Age orientation" rather than Sedona, Arizona.

Step 2: Once again, each partner does this part separately. Use the table labeled "Part I: Prioritizing Your Location Preferences" to list your top seven locations.

Step 3: Now get together and review the types of locations each of you has listed as your preferences. See where the two lists overlap and differ. Highlight similarities and discuss differences to determine if these are severe (city versus country) or minor (condominium requiring little upkeep versus freedom to explore interesting places in the world).

Step 4: This step you will also do together. See where you can agree on your joint priorities and merge your lists into one that lists the top seven for you as a couple. Use "Part II: Joint Preferences and Interesting Options" to write down your merged list. For differences in the order of your priorities, you could engage in further discussion to clarify and/or compromise, if possible. Or, if the differences are minor, you could just flip a coin to see whose entry goes first and whose next.

Step 5: Now develop a list of about 20 locations that could meet your jointly established criteria. If specific places don't readily come to mind, try to recall and list interesting places you have visited. You could also peruse maps and travel books for options, brainstorm ideas with friends and associates, and search Google.com for specific ideas like "universities offering coursework in Asian studies" or "small towns on big rivers" or "historic areas in the Northeast."

Step 6: Research and explore your list of location possibilities. Whittle your list down to around 10 places of greatest interest and make plans to visit and explore them first-hand together.

Step 7: After you've researched and visited the 10 or so places on your list of possibilities, you are now ready to sit down together and assess how fully the locations on your list are likely to satisfy your joint criteria. To do that, use a 10-point scale to rate each place, with 10 fully meeting all of your criteria and 0 meeting none of them.

Step 8: After arriving at your top choices, consider another visit of several days at your locations of top interest. You want to do everything you can to make a well-informed choice. If possible, visit your top choice(s) a number of times, at different times of the year, so you can see how seasonal conditions might affect you (too hot and humid in the summer, too crowded with tourists in the fall, too cold and closed up in the winter, too near a flood plain in the spring).

For an example of how this process can work, read the case study following Part I and Part II to see how my wife Pat and I found our ideal location and dream home.

Part I: Prioritizing Your Location Preferences

Ranking	Partner A	Partner B
1		
2		
3		
4		
5		
6		
7		

Part II: Joint Preferences and Interesting Options

Ranking	Combined Options	Possible Locations	Rating
1			
2			
3			
4			
5			
6			
7			

PAT AND DAVE EXPLORE AND IDENTIFY
THEIR LOCATION PRIORITIES

As I approached my late fifties, I found that I had reached a plateau in my career as a college administrator and needed a new vision for re-generating my life and work. It was time, I concluded, to leave my job and reestablish myself as a management consultant and life coach. Additionally, I had grown weary of big-city suburban life and hoped to move to a smaller community that had a "core" to it, a place possessing a community identity and spirit where interesting things were taking place. In discussing this with my wife, Pat, a public relations administrator in her early fifties, I found that we agreed that the time for change was ripe for us both.

Although Pat had an excellent job that paid well and came with some nice benefits, it had some real downsides. She'd become worn down by constantly seeking to make people happy, listening to incessant gripes both from her staff, who wanted and deserved better pay, and from clients who always wanted more publicity. Pat had always longed to study art and launch a new career as a watercolor artist. Over the years, she had dabbled in painting and had taken an occasional lesson here and there from a friend who happened to be a master painter and a great teacher. But work and family responsibilities had always kept her too busy to pursue her real passion in art. Now, however, the kids were on their own and she was also ready for a change in work and location.

The suburban area in which Pat and I lived was adjacent to a major city with superb cultural activities. We enjoyed visiting museums, taking in the art scene, and attending concerts and plays at nationally known performing arts centers. We were also located within a 20-minute commute to work, and our kids were within easy visiting distance. However, we were becoming more and more fed up with urban sprawl, noise, pollution, and bumper-to-bumper traffic. The negatives had come to outweigh the positives; we were ready for a genteel, pastoral lifestyle. With this in mind, we began visiting various places to check out what each had to offer in the way of lifestyle and work opportunities. Our financial situation was such that we both needed to continue generating some income, and we both wanted to continue working.

Over the years we visited many appealing places. Now that we were serious about a change, however, we realized a need to establish some jointly determined criteria for making our choice. To do that we decided to individually define our preferences in writing and then to narrow these down to our top seven priorities. Incidentally, there is no magic in

seven. It's just that that seven priorities is about all that an individual or
a couple can effectively juggle at a time. When Pat and I each finished
a list of priorities, we recorded our priorities in two different columns
on one sheet of paper to see and discuss areas of difference and agreement. The results of our efforts are shown in the following example.

Example: Pat and Dave Identify Their Preferences
Part I: Prioritizing Your Location Preferences

Ranking	Partner A Pat's Preferences	Partner B Dave's Preferences
1	Beautiful place in the Blue Ridge Mountains or on the coast of Maine. A small attractive town.	Small to mid-sized town with attractive, historical, tree-lined streets and good restaurants. Community great for walking and talking.
2	On or near a river, lake, ocean or bay, with a four-season climate, but lots of sunshine.	On a body of water or scenic river where I can canoe, kayak, and walk in nature.
3	An arts community where I can associate with and learn from other artists and show my paintings in a gallery.	Near a good college or university with an adult education program for part-time teaching and where I can study history and world religions.
4	Close enough to kids and grandkids for frequent visits but far away enough to prevent built-in babysitting.	Progressive community of well educated people where I can have interesting discussions over coffee and get involved in a book club.
5	A liberally progressive Protestant church involved in social justice and an active adult education program.	Population base where I can do some consulting and pursue a life-coaching practice.
6	Outdoor recreation opportunities such as hiking, biking, and kayaking.	Near enough to kids and grandkids for visits but too far for frequent babysitting.
7	Near a city with great cultural opportunities (theater, museums, arts).	Availability of civic-based community associations such as Rotary, Elks, or Lions Clubs.

Finding Home

Reviewing our two lists of location priorities provoked some interesting discussion. Both of us wanted to live in a small town, one having a feeling of community involvement that was progressive and brimming with interesting people and activities. But there was a challenge in meeting Pat's desire to be in an arts community combined with my need to establish a consulting practice. Merging our two lists into one necessitated confrontation and compromise. For the most part, however, we found our conversations to be enjoyable, even when working out our disagreements. Sometimes we took time out and let things settle before resuming our discussion. Often these timeouts provided new information leading us to make adjustments to our lists. Eventually, our discussions enabled us to create a joint list of merged priorities.

Our joint list served as the basis for identifying suitable locations. We proceeded with the next step in the process by reminiscing about interesting places we had been and interesting places we had heard about. We also pored over maps and sought input from friends and associates. That produced a lengthy list of 30 interesting places, both near and far. Then we began to whittle our list down to our favorite 15 places.

But you can't live in 15 different places; we still needed to find a best-fit situation. To do that, we used the 10-point rating scale suggested in step 8 of "Finding Your Ideal Location." Applying the scale proved easy for familiar locations, such as Walpole, New Hampshire. This quaint New England village we had explored while visiting friends in the area. We loved the natural beauty of the area and were intrigued by the interesting people who lived there. Yet we gave Walpole a rating of only 7 for one important reason: it was too far away from our kids and the grandkids we hoped soon to be on the scene. We also ruled out the vibrant, picturesque town of Northfield, Minnesota, for the same reason, even though we liked that the town was nestled among wooded hills along a river and was home to two excellent colleges. Minnesota also had a certain pull for me, since I was born and raised there and still had family and friends in the area. But besides being too far from our children, Pat felt Northfield was just too cold and too far away from her beloved Appalachian Mountains and Celtic heritage. Northfield, therefore, came out a mere 6 on their joint rating. (A 4 for Pat and an 8 for me equaled a joint score of 6.)

When all the results were in, a surprising winner emerged. Had you asked us about Shepherdstown, West Virginia, a few years prior to our seriously beginning a relocation search, we might have looked puzzled and wondered where in the world it was! When we visited the lovely old colonial town on the bluffs of the Potomac River, however, it was love at first sight. We found a community not only with a lively cultural life, a thriving college, and first-class restaurants, but one that was pleasantly situated along some of the most scenic mountain and river trails in the United States and was enthusiastic about artists of every color and stripe. It even had the kind of vibrant faith community that Pat and I had been looking for, was close to a commuter train that would enable me to trek into Washington, D.C., for my growing consulting practice, and was only a few hours' drive from our children.

Example: Pat and Dave Find Their New Home
Part II: Joint Preferences and Interesting Options

Ranking	Combined Options	Possible Locations	Rating
1	Small to mid-sized attractive town, tree-lined streets, in the Blue Ridge Mountains or on the coast of Maine.	❏ Ashville, NC	9
		❏ Walpole, NH	7
		❏ Ithaca, NY	8
2	An active arts community where Pat can associate with and learn from other artists and show her paintings in a local gallery.	❏ Amherst, MA	6
		❏ Shepherdstown, WV	10
		❏ Charlottesville, VA	8
3	A population base that might benefit from Dave's career management and executive coaching services.	❏ New Haven, CN	7
		❏ Cincinnati, OH	6
4	Close enough to kids and grandkids for frequent visits but far away enough to prevent "built-in" baby-sitting.	❏ Unity Village, MO	6
		❏ Dartmouth, NH	6
		❏ Burlington, VT	6
5	Near a good college or university where Dave could teach part-time and study history and world religions.	❏ Middlebury, VT	7
		❏ Waterford, ME	7
		❏ Portland, ME	6
6	On or near a scenic body of water and in the countryside with good hiking, biking, and canoeing options.	❏ Northfield, MN	9
		❏ Lexington, VA	
7	Progressive community of educated people with strong civic groups, tolerant faith communities, and interesting book clubs.		

◆ Connecting Heart to Home

When you take action in pursuit of a heartfelt desire, look for new doors to open, often in totally unexpected ways. At least, that's what happened to us once we resolved the question of where to live. As we were researching our ideal location, we were also envisioning the kind of home we wanted. That vision had been evolving when one day, standing on a scenic overlook of the Potomac River at Shepherdstown, our dream crystallized. Our dream home would be a comfortable house located on a high wooded bluff with an expansive view of the river and hills beyond. As you might imagine, such a place would not be easy to come by anywhere or anytime, let alone in lovely little Shepherdstown, which had become a magnet for folks retiring from big-time jobs in Washington, D.C., and Baltimore. The earlier arrivals had pretty much bought up the river property in the area, and new folks all seemed to be looking for any that might remain. Most of these folks had deep enough pockets to buy just about anything that suited their fancy. Not so for us, however. We thought that, even in the unlikely event that we found a place to match our dream, such a place would not be anywhere within our means. But sometimes dreams come true, and so it was for Pat and me.

It all happened in an extremely serendipitous manner. Pat described it as "a miraculous convergence of forces" that she and I could never have made happen ourselves—or even foreseen happening at all. What happened was this: After deciding that Shepherdstown was where we wanted to be, we spent weekends in town looking around and meeting and talking with the locals. On one of these occasions, we were having dinner with a new acquaintance when Pat casually mentioned that we would move to town in a blink if we could find a place in the woods with a great river view. As it happened, this was exactly the right person to say that to at exactly the right time. Our dinner companion informed us that her father had just decided to sell his place on the river—but it wasn't on the market yet. Shocked, I asked to look at the property and arranged a visit first thing the next morning. One look at the place, located on a high bluff looking down on a panoramic view of the Potomac River with the Blue Ridge Mountains off to the west, and we knew that this was everything we had dreamed of, and more. Without a moment's hesitation, we approached the owner about the prospects of purchasing the property.

It soon became clear, however, that Bob, the owner, was not going to sell to just anybody. In fact, Pat and I later discovered, there had been many people inquiring about the property over the years, but Bob had been unwilling to sell for various reasons. In discussing our interest in the place with Bob, we realized that he was conducting an interview to determine if we were the next "right" stewards for this special place. The place, with its magnificent natural beauty, had meant a great deal to Bob and his family for many years. In fact, Bob explained that the tall arching trees in the woodlands around the house had been his sanctuary. He didn't need to go to any established church, he said, because just sitting on the hillside or walking in the woods was the "most religious experience" he could possibly imagine.

Pat and I also felt that we were walking on sacred ground, but could we pass Bob's "test"? During the course of our conversation with Bob, we experienced something that Pat later said was "the moment when she heard the click." It turns out that I had majored in geology at the university where Bob had established the geology program so many years before. In fact, Bob's best friend there had been my academic adviser. Apparently, the geology connection did it, because Bob agreed to sell the place to us—on three conditions. One was that we agree to the price he had decided upon. Without even thinking about it or knowing if we could afford it, Pat and I agreed on the spot to a price that turned out to be extremely reasonable for such a valuable piece of property and one that, miracle of miracles, we could afford. The second condition was that we would take care of the six-toed, feral cat that lived in the shed but loved to rub Bob's legs. Of course, this condition posed no problem for us; we were delighted that a built-in cat came with the place. But we weren't prepared for the third condition. Bob wanted us to promise that his ashes could be scattered along the river's edge of his old property when he passed-on. It turns out that Bob's health was failing and that was a primary reason he'd decided to sell the property at this particular time. To tell you the truth, we were already growing fond of Bob and hated to think of his not being around. So, although we hoped we wouldn't have to fulfill this condition for a long time, we were perfectly agreeable to this request and took comfort in the idea that these beautiful woodlands and the coursing river would be home to Bob's final remains. The place had been the culmination of Bob's dreams, and now Pat and I were inheritors of the dream. We bought the place on the spot and never looked back, except to say, "Thanks, Bob."

That was a several years ago, but we are still astounded by the fortuitous circumstances that landed us at our dream home on the nation's capital river. What are the odds of our talking to one of the few people who knew that the decision to sell that particular property had been made the day before? What caused us to mention our interest in such a place at such a particular time? Even stranger, why was it that we had intended to visit Shepherdstown on three separate occasions, but each time had to reschedule? Had we come on one of those earlier dates, the property would not have been for sale. Had we come even a day after it became public knowledge, it would have quickly been sold to an eager buyer. Serendipity happens. But in this and most cases, it's important to have a vision of what you want so that you recognize fortuitous circumstances when they are presented to you. Had Pat and I not crystallized our vision, we would not have known what to ask for and never would have recognized this particular place as our dream place.

When Bob passed away a few years later, his family carried his ashes out to his former sanctuary and scattered them along the river's edge. He will always be part of that special place, and we will always be grateful for the opportunity to have succeeded him for nine wonderful years as stewards of the dream.

◆ Dreaming and Acting

"Where does this road lead?" asked Alice of Wonderland to the Cheshire cat. "Where do you want to it to go?" the grinning cat responded. Well, you know the rest of that story. If you don't know where you are going, how will you know where to go—or even when you're there, for that matter? This is just as true for locating the best place for your next chapter in life as it is for choosing a mate, finding the ideal job, or realizing any special dream. I'm of the opinion that if the Creator didn't want us to envision our heartfelt aspirations and translate them into achievable goals, she would not have provided us with the ability to dream and devise intelligent plans.

You need to be willing to dream if you want to define and pursue a passion, and that requires an optimistic outlook on life. Pessimists tend to discount such an activity as a waste of time. To a pessimist, dreaming only sets you up for disillusionment and false hope. Yet many studies over the past several years (see Martin Seligman's and Dan Baker's books listed in the Reference section) reveal that optimistic individuals are more likely to be successful in their work and life than pessimists. It's been my experience in counseling hundreds of individuals over the years that those willing to step outside the routines of their daily lives and allow themselves to dream new visions for their futures put themselves on paths that enable them to realize their dreams. One true-life story after another confirms that when you're on the right path, fortuitous opportunities often come your way. Of course, when they do, you need to recognize them and have the courage to take whatever risks are necessary for acting on them.

Pat and I had no time to consult a financial planner or check area real estate prices to see if Bob's offer was practical and realistic. But we had spent lots of time dreaming, discussing, exploring, and working out exactly what we wanted. When our dream place was presented to us, we recognized it and jumped at the opportunity, trusting our sense of Bob's integrity and our intuition that we could make it work. And we did. Our dream place became a kind of retreat center—not only for us and our children, but also for many family members, friends, and colleagues. We loved sharing the place and our dreams, and over the years many other dreams were hatched on our deck as the sun set over the Potomac or in our great gathering room as the last embers in the fireplace burned low. Yet had we not acted quickly on the opportunity of a lifetime, we would still be saying "if only. . . ."

We will never regret going for our dream. In fact, we soon expanded upon our dream with an addition that doubled the size of the funky little post-and-beam house that came with the property. But over the years, as we kept investing more and more time, energy, and resources into our property, we also learned that it's important to know when to let go of one dream and embrace another. Eventually the 12 acres of woodlands that had been our dream place became more of a responsibility, both physically and fiscally, than we wanted to manage as we moved into our sixties and seventies. In addition, with the arrival of grandkids on the scene, we grew increasingly concerned about the hazards of the precipitous cliffs that lined our property along the rocky edge of the river. So, with heavy hearts, forward-looking vision, and a sense of relief and excitement about the next step, we sold our dream place to a younger couple who seemed "just right" for that special neck of the woods.

At this point you may be wondering why you should even bother to go through the process outlined in this chapter for prioritizing your location preferences. After all, as the stories of two couples featured in this chapter—Frank and Donna and Pat and myself—illustrate, our dreams—even those that have been carefully and lovingly hatched—don't always have long life spans. Like Frank and Donna, you may miscalculate and overidealize certain elements of your dream. Or, like Pat and me, you may find that the dream for one stage of life doesn't always fit the next. Things change. As British economist and social philosopher Charles Handy wrote in *Beyond Certainty: The Changing Worlds of Organizations*, "Things do outlive their purpose, and what was once sensible may now seem crazy. We do not have to be slaves to our history."[1] Although Handy was writing about the purpose of an organization, I believe that his comments also apply to individuals. Organizations, like the people who compose them, are living, breathing, and evolving organisms, and that means change is always in progress in us and around us.

Pat and I will always be grateful for the nine wonderful years we had at our dream place and regard that time as one of the highlights of our lives. But we are also every bit as grateful for where we are now. What we realize in retrospect is that if we hadn't gone through the process that enabled us to recognize and realize the dream place of our fifties, we wouldn't be where we are now—in a lovely place that embodies our dreams for this chapter of our lives. Fifteen years ago we couldn't have foreseen living in a villa in a winding golf course community that caters to people of all ages. For one thing, the section where we live wasn't even built then. Even more to the point is the fact that, at the time, Shepherdstown wasn't even on our map of possible future locations. We had to go through the process to discover that. We had to live on our little tract of West Virginia woodland to learn that, in addition to our other concerns about constant upkeep and safety issues for the grandkids, we really missed the social interactions and amenities of a planned community.

We did not make the decision to sell our dream place lightly. We had celebrated many of life's special markers there—weddings, birthdays, graduations, Pat's ordination, and unforgettable holiday gatherings. At first, we had a hard time envisioning ourselves anywhere else. Once we made our decision to sell, though, we knew we were on the right track. We felt we didn't need to go through the formal process for prioritizing our location this time since we both wanted to be in Shepherdstown. And after exploring new developments in the area, we soon decided upon our new neighborhood and began the process for building a customized villa, one that enabled each of us to realize some new dreams— for Pat, her own artist's studio; and for me, a game room large enough to accommodate a regulation-sized pool table. Our earlier dream made the next one possible. Indeed, we've been fortunate that, for us, our earlier dream has truly been a gift that keeps on giving.

What's next for you? Have you crystallized a dream? Where is your dream place? What serendipity is coming your way? Are you ready to act on it?

---

1. Charles Handy, *Beyond Certainty: The Changing Worlds of Organizations* (Boston: Harvard Business School Press, 1986), p. 58.

SUSTAINING VITALITY: MANAGING YOUR CHANGING SELF IN A CHANGING WORLD

"I find that having a goal that's a bit dangerous is important to keep me going. The danger is not necessarily a physical one, but one that pushes me to achieve something new where success is not guaranteed."

—SIXTY-EIGHT-YEAR-OLD RETIRED PHYSICIAN ENROLLED AS
A UNIVERSITY FRESHMAN FOR A BACHELOR'S IN MUSIC

"My parents both retired and waited to die. This wasn't the ticket for me. Until my last breath, I want to be engaged in life. So I started taking yoga classes and began a new business helping clients redecorate their homes to be in harmony with their soul's desire."

—SIXTY-FIVE-YEAR-OLD EXECUTIVE COACH HAVING TO RECREATE
A NEW LIFE BECAUSE OF A HEALTH PROBLEM

"I realized eleven years ago that if I suddenly dropped dead in my boots I would feel incomplete. It was then that I decided to sell my law firm and explore what I needed to develop in myself."

—SIXTY-EIGHT-YEAR-OLD ATTORNEY WHO FOUNDED A WASHINGTON, D.C.,
LAW FIRM AND THEN RETIRED TO BECOME AN ARTIST

ASSESSING YOUR PSYCHOLOGICAL AGE

1. How old do you currently feel in terms of your health, mentally and physically?

◄━━━━━━━━━━━━━━━━━━━━━━━►

| I'm like an old car in need of major overhaul | It's variable, with good days and bad. I'm like a good car with a lot of miles on. | I'm feeling zestfully youthful, like a high-powered sports car ready to zoom. |

2. How might you characterize your potential for living zestfully in the future?

◄━━━━━━━━━━━━━━━━━━━━━━━►

| Don't want to be bothered. I'm like an old horse—put me out to pasture and let me graze. | It's there, but I could use a big dose of vitamins to get me up and going again. | No doubt about it, I'm fit as a fiddle and ready for playing some new tunes. |

◆ Staying Young at Heart and Sound of Mind

I love the word *vitality*. It's a quality I enjoy in others and wish for in myself. Have you ever noticed how a vibrant individual radiates energy that creates enthusiasm in others? The dictionary defines vitality as the "abundant physical and mental energy usually combined with a whole-hearted and joyous approach to situations and activities." A second definition describes vitality as "the nonmaterial force that distinguishes the living from the nonliving."

I don't know about you, but I'm hoping that I will be perceived as clearly distinguishable from the "nonliving." I have known individuals, however, whose energy level is so low that you can barely distinguish them from the nonliving. To me, vitality represents an energizing life force within us that radiates outward to those around you. I've seen vitality in people from the age of 9 months to 90 years. Two role models come to mind for vitality in senior life—Maggie and Joe.

I'm going to Maggie's ninetieth birthday party tonight. Maggie's invited a few hundred of her closest friends to celebrate this milestone with champagne and hors d'oeuvres. Maggie is a bit of a legend around Shepherdstown. I'd heard about Maggie a dozen years ago when my wife and I moved to town. I first met her when I was out walking one day and encountered this attractive, platinum-haired, and distinguished looking lady who was on a casual walk about the community.

She greeted me with an engaging smile, proffered a friendly hello, and introduced herself as Maggie. We chatted a few moments and then continued on our separate ways. But after a few steps she turned back with a grin on her face and said, "Now you can tell people you've met Maggie." Since then, I've had the good fortune to meet and talk with Maggie on several other occasions, including the time when she treated Pat and me to dinner at the country club she owns.

You never know when Maggie might appear; she's always on the go. I was out working in the yard one sunny afternoon when I heard a warm, friendly voice say, "I love to see people out making things pretty." Conversations with Maggie can run both wide and deep with this wise and worldly woman. So I stopped pulling weeds and asked if she was out inspecting the neighborhood. "Yes, indeed," she said, "I like seeing what's going on." Soon we were talking about life in general. Maggie said she loves her life for many reasons, a primary one being that she loves people, and there are people everywhere. That's Maggie, and you can't help but love her. She has a grand life, but not because of a grand lifestyle. Although she is a woman of considerable means, she has weathered many of life's trying ordeals, including the death of her beloved husband and father of their four children. Yet she always seems to have a glowing countenance that conveys her passionate engagement in life. You can see it in her eyes, hear it in her voice, and experience it in her presence. I hope that Maggie is going to be with us for a long time.

Joe is another individual with an energizing presence. Joe's been a good friend for about 25 years. Joe is one of those people who knows everyone—and everyone knows Joe. I recall being with him on a cold winter's morning at a remote place on the Maine coast when a lone car pulled up and two guys got out. One of them looked over in our direction and yelled, "Hey Joe!" Turns out they had taken one of Joe's famous art workshops some years back.

Joe is a master artist, art teacher, storyteller, and community builder. He loves life, enjoys people, and has friends everywhere. In fact, he has so many friends that once in a while his wife wants the two of them to go someplace where no one knows him so she doesn't have to share him with a multitude of friends. Joe knew the perfect place—Las Vegas. No one could possibly know him there. As they were getting on the plane to Vegas, however, the pilot poked his head out of the cockpit and yelled, "Hey Joe!" Turns out that in times of airline layoffs, this pilot had worked at the local meat market and had been Joe's butcher.

Wherever he goes, he brings people together. In Shepherdstown, in addition to being a gallery owner, he was also the cartoonist for the local paper and started a Friday artists painting group, of which my wife is honored to be a member. His motto for life is to live light on the planet. He stays flexible and has no trouble moving onto new things when the occasion warrants. "I'll see you when I see you," he says. He left a college professorship when he felt the administration had become more interested in dollars than students. He left Shepherdstown when the town's administration seemed to be more interested in bowing to the demands of developers than in meeting the needs of local residents. When he served on the town council, he was committed to community-oriented values like making the town a friendly place for children, seniors, dogs, and cats.

In his new location he has worked to create an atmosphere where the community supports artists and the artists support the community.

At the age of 76, Joe is as lively as he was at 50. He even looks the same. He is an energy source and coach/advocate who's constantly involved in causes bigger than himself. He has fun in pretty much everything he does. His humble beginnings never kept him from being successful or joyful. If you ever happen to be in Easton, Maryland, stop in at the Sharp/Mayer Gallery for an engaging visit and visual treat. No doubt you'll leave with a gorgeous painting and a new friend.

Maggie and Joe have a special kind of vitality that is worth a fortune. They haven't discovered the fountain of youth, but they know what the potent elixir is for living to the fullest—keeping a youthful zest for life. Although both Joe and Maggie are gregarious extroverts, it's far more than their friendly nature that's at the source of their abundant energy. As far as I can tell, they are curious about nearly everything. They never stop learning, and they are truly interested in and care about people. They aren't afraid to say what they think about matters that are important to them. They have a great sense of humor and love to laugh with people, but never at them. In fact, they would be quick and direct in expressing their displeasure at anyone ridiculing another. They always make time for family, friends, and themselves.

While they enjoy relationships and meeting new people, neither Joe nor Maggie, as my friend John says, "make themselves a bowl of candy for the world to eat up." They love life but are not afraid of death. They know that life is not a bowl of cherries, but they deal with what comes their way with resilience, grace, and wisdom. They treasure their memories of the past but live their lives going forward and don't get stuck in the past. They are optimistic and have plans, hopes, and aspirations for the future. They take care of themselves physically, mentally, emotionally, and spiritually; and encourage others to do the same. Joe is always recommending self-development books to his art students and friends. Maggie always has a new scheme for making the world around her a kinder, more beautiful place for people, plants, and animals—especially her beloved bluebirds. For me, and many others, these two individuals are inspiring role models for sustaining vitality in the senior years.

From folks like Joe and Maggie and hundreds of other people I've worked with and known, I've observed seven principles that play a key role in sustaining vitality throughout the senior years. You may come up with some others, but I'm providing these so that you'll at least have a starting point:

Seven Principles for Senior Vitality

1. Free yourself from fears about death and dying.
2. Manage your mental, physical, and spiritual wellness.
3. Be and remain resilient as you encounter life's joys and tribulations.
4. Stay engaged in community; belong to something you enjoy.
5. Do something dangerous.
6. Grow into and stay true to your unique nature.
7. View your life as an interesting story. Be the author of your future.

How do you incorporate each of these principles in your life at present? How would you like to integrate them in the future? What other principles would you add?

◆ Desperately Denying Age

Chad came to see me ostensibly about retirement, but it soon became apparent that his retirement plans were pretty well crystallized. He was going to spend part of his time consulting in the area of his expertise, allot some time to community work through active engagement in the Rotary Club, and have fun with friends on the tennis court and golf course. It wasn't retirement in itself that concerned him; it was the changed behavior of his wife. It seems that his 56-year-old wife Susie had taken up biking in a big way. Biking had come to dominate her life to the point of being a fetish. She had taken up bike racing and had become so good in amateur racing in women's events that she'd moved on to racing with the men. Her weekdays were devoted to training and weekends to racing. Competitive biking had become so important that she did not want her husband to retire for fear that he would disturb her racing regime.

It wasn't just the racing fetish that bothered Chad so much, however; it was his concerns that she was having affairs, or at least one affair—with one of her male biker friends. Chad's growing concern was based on telltale signs such as numerous, exceedingly long phone calls to her male friend and her attempts at keeping them a secret from Chad. There were also frequent racing excursions that kept her away for several days at a time, and a sudden interest in the massive use of anti-aging creams. Chad believed that Susie's affairs and biking fetish were desperate attempts to deny and stave off deeply disturbing fears of growing old. Maybe she thought that by staying in tip-top condition, hiding wrinkles, and proving she was still attractive to men, she could remain eternally young.

As you might imagine, Chad was distraught and anxious to determine what he could do about the situation. He considered acting out of hurt and anger. But after we talked about his feelings and options, he realized that he continued to love his wife, though not her current behavior. He also felt that she was not trying to hurt him personally, but was reacting, instead, to a terrifying fear of growing old and losing her feminine appeal.

As a couple, these two had weathered tough times together through nearly 40 years of marriage. They had raised two wonderful kids, and Susie had been a loving mother. She had also been a supportive wife, up until a few years ago when biking began to consume her time and energy. Chad decided, therefore, to do all he could to save their marriage and to see his wife through the frightful passage into life as a senior. When last I saw him, he had contacted a marriage therapist, and his wife had reluctantly agreed to participate in counseling.

I won't speculate on the outcome of this situation, and I greatly admire Chad's understanding and his hopeful attitude about their situation. I would have felt more hopeful if Susie had been more open to counseling and what was really happening in their marriage. But with Chad's generosity of spirit, love for his wife, and willingness to deal with a tough situation, they might be able to use professional counseling to help them deal with their hurts and fears and recreate a meaningful life together.

Getting old is not for the weak, according to my octogenarian friend who walks five miles a day to keep her limbs limber and her heart pumping vigorously. Where do you find yourself in your journey with aging? Do you fight against aging with a drawer full of anti-aging creams, a haircut that hides your thinning hair, a wardrobe suited for a svelte sex symbol, or a rigorous exercise regime? Or do you give in and just let nature take its course?

It's a waste of psychic energy to resist aging and deny the inevitability of death. Sooner or later, even the best vehicles of denial will crash head-on into reality. Between denial and helpless resignation, however, there is a balanced middle ground. You can gracefully accept the reality of aging and the unavoidable fact that your body will undergo the physical changes that come with aging. You can compassionately come to terms with the reality that you are not here forever and learn to take more pleasure in the here and now. And you can maintain a diet and exercise program that will help to keep you active and healthy, engage in emotional and spiritual practices that will help you age with grace and beauty, and allow the authenticity of who you are to shine through. If some anti-aging cream or a new hairstyle also helps you to feel good, why not? In other words, plan as if you are going to live to a hundred, but live each day as if it's your last.

TRANSCENDING FEARS OF DEATH

"You haven't talked about death yet," says a sixty-something gentleman as we near the end of the daylong workshop I conduct at the World Bank. "I'm afraid of dying, and that's what's really on my mind as I face retirement," he says.

In her excellent book *The Art of Growing Old,* Carroll Saussy talks about the great paradox most of us grapple with, which is that we want to live long, but we don't want to get old. Of course, you can't have one without the other. So how do you address this dilemma? Saussy, a retired pastoral counselor and professor of pastoral theology, says that "the inevitability of death must be looked at head on, embraced until it hurts."

George, a lawyer who retired to become an artist, says he thinks about death every day. Not as a negative obsession, he tells me, but as reality. Doing that helps him keep focused on what's really important and appreciate the moment. All we really have is the current moment. Confronting the certainty of our death helps us savor the here and now in a way that nurtures us in graceful aging. But there is another important ingredient for bountiful living in the senior years—hope for the future.

No matter what our age, having hope for the future is what moves us in the direction of integrity versus despair. It is all too easy to fall into despair from watching the daily news, grieving the death of a close friend or family member, or suffering a debilitating health problem. Harboring negative images about mortality can make the prospects of death terrifying. We're all familiar with the way terrorists use fear to shock us into a state of panic and compliance. But benign individuals and well-intentioned organizations also use fear tactics to manipulate and control us. Religious organizations and spiritual movements may sow as many seeds of destruction as they do of growth. How many of us grew up thinking that we would incur the wrath of God and eternal damnation if we didn't adhere to a particular doctrine or way of living? How many of us see our life story as a catalog of good deeds that will get us into heaven or a better life next time around? Charitable organizations also try to scare us by trying to convince us that their causes are the world's most urgent issues and that only our generous contributions can save the planet. How many of us carry around unproductive guilt or anxiety because we believe that everything depends on us and we can never do enough?

In my mind, fear has nothing to do with the intentions of a loving God—or a healthy understanding of death. From my practice over the years, I've observed that clients who see God as a loving presence who wants nothing but ultimate good for us and all of creation are much more likely to transform their fears about death into visions of a final transition into the presence of blissful light.

For many years I conceptualized death as an eternal black void, with a body trapped in a coffin buried deep in the ground. That view probably materialized from my fascination with too many Edgar Allen Poe stories. Regardless of the origin or reality of this negative image, its result was even more frightening—I allowed it to keep me from thinking about death. My denial worked for a while, but reality eventually caught up with me and knocked me on the head with the force of a sledgehammer.

CONFRONTING OUR OWN MORTALITY IN THE DEATH OF A PARENT

During my sixty-ninth year, I suddenly found myself overwhelmed with anxiety one evening. I can assure you, anxiety cannot be denied. It grabbed hold of me and wouldn't let me go. But anxiety, I've discovered, is really just the emotional equivalent of an extremely painful toothache. When I have a toothache, I go to a dentist. So when I had this aching anxiety, I went to a therapist. Unlike a dentist dealing with a toothache, however, a therapist can't numb your pain and drill out the painful emotional cavity. She can only hold your feet to the fire, and that means helping you confront, head on, the reality that's the source of your pain.

It turns out that the onset of my anxiety occurred at the same age that my father was when he died of colon cancer. My anxiety began right at the same time of year that he learned his cancer was inoperable and that he had only a few weeks to live. My anxiety ended the day after the day that was the anniversary date of my father's death. The interesting thing is that I was unaware of the coincidence of my anxiety with the dates of my father's terminal illness. But my subconscious mind remembered. And a latent wisdom awoke me to my suppressed fears about death by getting my conscious attention through anxiety-inducing panic attacks.

In therapy I had the opportunity to address my fear of death and to reframe the way I had conceptualized death. I learned not to see death as an eternal black void but simply as a transition to another realm. A source I found to be helpful in reframing my image of death was the work of Brian Weiss, featured in his books *Many Lives, Many Masters* and *Message from the Masters: Tapping into the Power of Love.* Weiss, a psychiatrist practiced in hypnotherapy, has worked with hundreds of clients who, under hypnosis, have experienced regression into past lives. I've also had the opportunity to be in an intensive weeklong workshop with Dr. Weiss and observe the stunning results that come from his work with dozens of individuals under hypnosis.

Thanks to the combination of therapy and a reformed concept of death, I no longer fear death as I once did. Nor do I try to avoid thinking about it. In fact, I think about it every day. It helps me focus on my priorities relative to the most precious commodity of all, my time remaining. I'm not anxious to die, and I hope to have a lot of living still ahead. It's just that death does not have the hold over me it once did. I still find myself having low levels of fear about death upon occasion, and what helps me then is what I've learned from therapy, meditation, and yoga. Engaging in these has helped me learn to focus on breathing deeply, staying grounded in the here and now, and paying attention to what my feelings are trying to tell me. With these practices, I find that my fears tend to evaporate.

Many of our fears are really nothing more than fantasies of the mind. Mind fantasies can work wonders when used positively to envision exciting new possibilities about the future, but the mind can also take us into the dark side of fear-based thinking. One anti-fear remedy is living in gratefulness. We can't hang onto fear when we relax, bring our attention to the here and now, and concentrate on being grateful for what we have in the moment. Taking up some kind of meditative spiritual practice can also help free us from our fears, both conscious and subconscious. In fact, my friends who work with the dying tell me that we can become so free of fear that our final transition becomes one of peaceful joy.

◆ Managing Your Well-Being

It's so easy to get hooked into the old stereotypes about aging. Maybe you remember the one about "acting your age." What would you think, for example, about an 80-year old woman skipping down the street? Insane? Dementia kicking in? That's what my 80-year-old mother did when my kids and I would visit her in Florida. There was just one thing to do—we skipped with her!

There was a lot of kid in my mother, and she skipped well. She also lived well. Mom passed on at the age of 92 the morning after getting a group of folks together to sing Christmas carols at the local care center, where she was known as "The Angel." The night before her death, she had also driven an elderly friend around town to see the Christmas decorations. She died the next morning from a massive stroke. But she didn't pass on before getting up on her last morning to shower, dress, and make the bed. My brother found her in her little apartment. She was lying peacefully on the carefully made bed and had an ever-so-slight a smile on her face. I like to think that her last smile was a note of appreciation for a life well lived and a life gracefully departed—in the way in which she wanted. In the refrigerator we found a freshly made Jello salad, which along with strong coffee, is one of the basic food groups in Minnesota. We had the Jello for lunch the day after her funeral. She left that, no doubt, as a departing gift. Another gift she left us was how to die well. Thanks, Mom! You are a role model for what Helen Harkness describes in her book *Don't Stop the Career Clock* as the ideal life—"to live long and full-out and then die fast."

Aside from suicide, we don't, as far as I know, have a choice about how long we live or the manner in which we die. But we do have a choice about the way we live our lives. Our choices may, to some extent, influence how long we live and possibly how we die—we still don't understand all the connections between mind and body. But what we do know is that our choices clearly determine how well we live.

Zack, a dear friend of mine in his late sixties, blames the choices he made in earlier life for what he now suffers. He is grossly overweight and suffers from congestive heart failure. Zack is one of the smartest people I know. He is widely read, has a brilliant mind, and radiates with wisdom gleaned from decades of working with people and asking hard questions of himself and others. At the moment Zack is in the hospital in a life-precarious situation. In a recent conversation, he shared with me two things worthy of contemplation, one a regret and the other a hope. The regret dealt with diet and exercise, two areas in his life he hasn't managed well. While he continually filled his mind with good stuff, he filled his body with junk food, and he was averse to physical exercise. Over the years I've been on work-related retreats with Zack. While the rest of us were out walking, jogging, or enjoying nature, Zack stayed behind and sprawled out on the couch to munch chips and read the latest psychology or organizational development book.

Zack now laments the poor choices he made about physical health management but is unable to undo his past. However, Zack remains a role model for dealing with a severely debilitating health condition. He tells me that he's not afraid of dying and has pretty much made his peace with that. What scares the hell out of him, however, are thoughts about being physically incapacitated and unable to continue with the career coaching he so dearly loves. His focus, as you might imagine, is on the nonphysical aspects of life enhancement. Zack is a master at helping individuals to break through mental barriers to intellectually exhilarating lives. Sadly, he never broke through his own barriers for engaging in physical fitness programs.

PIES FOR LIFE

Like most mental health professionals, I advocate a whole-person approach to vitality and well-being. This whole-person approach is what I call a PIES approach to life. PIES is an acronym for our Physical, Intellectual, Emotional, and Spiritual well-being. Our health is basic to everything we want to do or be in our new life. We don't want to undermine the fullness of life by undervaluing the vehicle that enables us to launch and live out our vision.

Of course, there are things we cannot control. We had no choice over the genes we inherited. Some of us inherited fatter genes than others, some balder than others, and some more susceptibility to an ailment of some kind. But we can still accept and appreciate what we've been given and be good stewards of our gifts. Stephen Hawking, the renowned British physicist and author of *A Brief History of Time*, is an example of someone living a full life with a crippling disability. Dr. Hawking came down with ALS, an incurable crippling neurological disease, during his third year at Oxford University. Soon he was paralyzed and confined to a wheelchair. In spite of his severe disability, however, he has gone on to become one of the most famous astrophysicists of our time. About his disease, Hawking says, "I am quite often asked: How do you feel about having ALS? The answer is, not a lot. I try to lead as normal a life as possible, and not think about my condition, or regret the things it prevents me from doing, which are not that many."

I love to see the fully matured faces, lifelines, and real hair color of my senior brother and sister travelers. Something seems out of place when I see heavily colored hair on a seventy-plusser. I love the naturally platinum hues in my wife's lovely hair and hope she will never tamper with her gift by trying to return it to the deep brunette color of her youth. I'm of the opinion that what looks great in youth is great for youth, and what looks great as a fully blossomed, mature adult looks good for a mature adult.

But, no matter what my perceptions may be, it's what makes you feel alive and fulfilled that matters. If cosmetic surgery of one kind or another makes you feel better, why not enjoy the benefits of new developments in the field. I just don't think it works to try to make yourself look younger so that you can then pretend that you are. Why sacrifice wisdom and maturity to pretend that you are someone who hasn't already graduated from the vanities and challenges of an earlier stage of life? We get wiser and smarter when we get older, so let's own it and flaunt it—with an appropriate modicum of modesty, of course! After all, we don't want to make all those young kids out there jealous of our wisdom of the ages or the freedom we have achieved to be who we really are or the opportunity to do what we really want. Let's face it—we have earned it. Love and embrace who you are and who you are becoming. Let go of who you aren't. And remember to manage your PIES well.

If you don't have a PIES management plan, develop and implement one today. Please take my friend Zack's advice to heart and assume responsible management for your health and vitality. Be on the lookout for those who can not only be role models for good PIES management but also give you some good tips along the way. One tip that I've discovered is yoga. It's a great physical, mental, and spiritual discipline. It may not be for everyone, but I've found it to be a grand enhancement to my health maintenance plan, thanks to my wife, who encouraged me to take it up. Having done just one hour's worth of yoga this morning with a terrific teacher, I'm feeling great right now and want to share this source of vitality with you.

Another tip, especially if you need help in creating your PIES plan, is to visit the physical fitness center at your local college or health club and search the Web for sites providing information about whole-person vitality. One such Web site is the following: www.bluezones.com. While at that site, you can take the "Blue Zones Compass," which is an assessment for calculating your life expectancy based on your current habits. It's definitely an eye-opener and a motivator for developing good health management practices.

Managing Your PIES

PIES are good for you, especially the kinds that involve sustaining vitality throughout your senior years. Here are a few suggestions for creating and managing your PIES:

Physical Wellness   Create a physical fitness plan and follow it rain, shine, or bad hair day. Even something as gentle as a 40-minute walk three times a week has proven health benefits. In *Don't Stop the Career Clock,* Harkness cites research showing that older adults who walked just 30 minutes for six times a month had a 43 percent lower death rate than those who were sedentary. In spite of that, according to Harkness, 3 in 10 adults who are 65 and older do no physical activity.

If you schedule your physical maintenance plan and make it fun, your chances of sticking with it are much greater. A mistake that some folks make is to create an arduous plan with intentions of getting into some kind of near Olympian condition, which usually falters somewhere along the way for various reasons. You're much better off doing something that's reasonable, manageable, and enjoyable.

There's a group of women in our neighborhood who gather at a certain times each week to walk. I often see them going by, and they all look like they are enjoying themselves. They walk, talk, and laugh a lot—all of which are added health benefits to any health wellness plan. If one of them is not there at the specified time, they go to the door and get her.

Do what you must to persist in your plan. If you need to join a gym and pay monthly fees for the service as an inducement to exercise, consider it one of your most astute investments. My wife and I have found that being in yoga classes induces us to keep a regularly scheduled commitment to yoga practice. If you're like us and find that you tend to put off exercising on your own, you might want to enroll in a class or regularly scheduled activity.

Many colleges and universities have established physical exercise programs for seniors conducted by health professionals. I've heard seniors describe these programs—which may include anything from folk dancing to water ballet—as nothing less than "scheduled fun." Some folks even move to retirement communities attached to colleges and universities so that they can take advantage of physical fitness programs as well as a wide array of other interesting PIES management opportunities.

Intellectual Wellness   There is growing evidence that remaining intellectually engaged keeps the brain tuned-up, the mind humming, and Alzheimer's and dementia at bay. What are you intellectually curious about? Have you always wondered what the Crusades were really about? Have you yearned to learn Chinese and explore the Great Wall? Can you name the greatest musical composers of all time and play selections from their greatest works in your mind?

If you've always been intellectually curious about something, now is your opportunity to pursue it. There are countless ways of doing that, including distance-learning resources via the Internet, college and university adult learning centers, and programs offered through organizations such as Elderhostel, the Omega Institute, Canyon Ranch, Ghost Ranch, and The Creative Problem Solving Institute. You can also keep your mind honed by teaching a favorite subject in a formal setting or coaching others in informal gatherings.

Learning is one of those human capabilities upon which advancing age interposes no limits. According to a CNN news item, 88-year-old Rose "Mama G" Gilbert, the oldest teacher in the Los Angeles School District, is still turning students onto literature, poetry, and life. To remain fit for her passion in energizing young minds, Mama G. lifts weights and does yoga early every morning.

A retired executive, 66-year-old Donald M. completed a credentialing program at a training institute for life coaching. Now he coaches and mentors managers on how to deal with a multitude of problems, such as working with difficult employees, getting a new initiative through bureaucratic hurdles, and managing heavy workloads. No matter what you're curious about, there are countless ways to continue learning and growing mentally. Whether it's learning about a new field or staying ahead in a field of particular interest, life is more zestful when your mind is functioning in high gear.

Emotional Well-Being   Life in the fifty-plus years takes on new challenges that emotionally impact us. Yesterday I was talking with 74-year-old Kate. Her husband was recently diagnosed with Alzheimer's, dramatically changing their relationship and the freewheeling lifestyle they had been enjoying. Another seventy-something friend fell into deep depression when his wife informed him that she was leaving him for a younger man and a more adventurous life. What do you do when your 30-year-old daughter is diagnosed with an aggressive form of breast cancer? Where do you go when you're a sixty-something minister whose disillusionment and anxiety have led you to a complete loss of faith? At one time or another, we all have to deal with difficult issues such as these. We know that somewhere in all those uncertain tomorrows the Grim Reaper lurks.

Coping with serious emotional stressors in the fifty-plus years takes a higher order of psychological management skills than earlier life required. Some of us were fortunate in inheriting genes for coping with difficult life issues with resilience, grace, and resourcefulness. Unfortunately, most of us come ill prepared for dealing with the serious issues that living in the senior years forces us to confront. In our youth we may have been too consumed with the demands of daily life or too afraid of life's darker side to develop the skills we now need for managing serious issues and their concomitant emotional distress.

Wouldn't it be nice if we all had access to graduate courses on the emotional side of aging? Such courses could teach us to understand, appreciate, and manage both sides of aging—the plus and the negative. How, for instance, do we go about building up our spiritual muscles so that when we enter a time of trial we have the strength to deal with it? Where can we get training in higher-level emotional management skills? What are the best resources for developing hope, optimism, and compassion?

Some of us may have been fortunate enough to have encountered people and programs along the way that have helped us develop the vital life skills we need for our senior years. But most us will probably need to learn these things on our own. Fortunately, we live in an age when we have ready access to great books (some of which are listed in the reference section), wise mentors, radio/TV/Internet programs featuring behavior management gurus, adult education opportunities, and professional psychologists and pastoral counselors.

Regardless of which path you choose, the important thing to remember is to get started now. Don't wait until you are in the throes of a crisis. Improving your emotional management skills now will help you lessen the debilitating impact of the difficult issues you must face in the future and maximize the zestful potential that your senior life still has to offer. In creating your plan, I highly recommend that you seek assistance from an astute mentor whose wisdom comes from the crucible of life.

Spiritual Well-Being   Why are you here? What is your purpose in life? Where did you come from, metaphysically speaking? What happens when you die? What keeps Earth spinning on its axis and or the human heart pumping? Where do dreams come? Where is God? Questions like these often perplex young children.

I remember as a child looking up into the night sky trying to understand where the universe began and ended and what kept the stars and planets in their orbits. Once I asked my mother where God came from, and she said that God has always been and will always be. But I never could get my mind around a concept like that. While some of us are comfortable knowing that there are things that can't be explained, others like myself find things of a mystical or mysterious nature to be wonderfully intriguing but, at the same time, woefully unsettling. Questions about the cosmos, the spiritual, and the nature of life never left me, but in my young adulthood, I was so preoccupied with the daily grind of life that I had little time for thinking about them. Then as I entered my senior adulthood, I found my thoughts once again awash with questions about the grand mysteries of the universe.

A spiritual practice involving disciplined meditation, contemplation, or prayer may serve you well, both in finding your purpose in life and in coming to terms with the great mysteries of life. Whether you are a devout Christian, Muslim, Jew, Buddhist, Neo-Pagan, or committed atheist, finding a core purpose can be energizing and empowering, enabling you to live your life as a sacred journey.

My wife Pat serves as a role model for someone with a purpose bigger than the self. As mentioned previously, in her early fifties, she felt called to the ministry and undertook a mid-life career change from public relations to ordained ministry. She enjoyed serving as the associate pastor at a local church, but three years later felt a calling of another kind. Today, at the age of 62, she still enjoys serving in various capacities as a minister-at-large in our presbytery, where she serves on various committees and does guest preaching. But her calling these days goes beyond her formal ministerial duties to other ways of ministering—including grandmothering, painting, and writing.

You can often find her in her studio painting colorful abstract florals and landscapes that, she hopes, celebrate the beauty and mystery of creation. Or you might find her deep in work on a book based on a collection of 300 letters from her Civil War ancestors—who were in touch with the sanctity of life and death on a daily basis and knew, regardless of what they faced, that "grace can do the work quickly."

But sacrificing yourself to a cause from guilt, following a path that works for another, or blindly adhering to an unexamined prescription for the perfect life are all unlikely to bring authentic spiritual development. You can learn techniques, develop practices, and study a wide array of materials to nurture your spiritual growth, but you also want to listen to your internal wisdom so that as your spiritual journey unfolds, you know that it is yours, and not someone else's.

You can use the following example of a PIES management plan as a guide for developing your own plan. Be sure to use this only as a guide, however. Otherwise, it simply won't work because it won't be yours.

I strongly recommend developing your own plan in writing and posting it in a visible place as an ongoing reminder. You might also want to discuss your plan with others. When you make your intentions clear to others, you strengthen your commitment to following through on your plan. Keeping a plan secretly in mind tends to keep it more tenuous and more likely to slip into the realm of good intentions—as opposed to a working plan of action.

Managing Your PIES: A Sample Plan for Vitality

Physical

- *Diet:* I'll eat healthy, putting only that in my mouth that nurtures my body and mind. No junk food. Six to eight glasses of water every day. Alcohol in moderation, one to two glasses of wine a day, possibly three on social occasions.
- *Exercise:* Walk a minimum of 45 minutes three times a week, or substitute with a one- to two-hour bike ride, or one-hour workout at the gym. Yoga one hour, twice a week.

Emotional

- *Mindset:* It's my intention to live in gratitude for the countless blessings in my life.
- *Relationships:* I treasure my wife and family and will always work to be an affirming, a supportive, and a loving presence in their lives. Friendships are also important—I will make time at least three times a month to enjoy and support these relationships.
- *Personal Growth:* I acknowledge having developed a productivity-driven obsession, which all too often results in being short-tempered and cranky with my wife and others. I'm aware that my relationships are more important than the immediate

task at hand. I'm ready and willing to let go of the obsessions that are not serving me or others well, freeing myself to live more fully in the joy of the moment.

Intellectual

- *Professional*: I will remain active in my life-coaching work by staying up to date with the latest literature in adult development and the psychology of positivism and by attending professional meetings and maintaining a part-time practice.
- *Personal Growth:* I'll pursue my interest in history and world religions by reading biographies of noteworthy individuals and taking courses in world religions at the local university. I will continue to actively participate in our book discussion club.

Spiritual

- *Personal Growth*: I'll continue in my regular yoga practice and support of our local church. I'll also meditate for 20 minutes, three-times a week, and take more time to stop and smell the roses.
- *Goal:* I'm committed to supporting my family and friends with humor, heartfelt appreciation and role modeling a life well lived. Professionally I'm committed to helping my clients discover and apply their true potentials. I intend to leave this world, when my time comes, with few regrets and a lot of joy in having lived a fulfilling life.

◆ Being Resilient

In the fifty-plus years change begins happening on many fronts, some of it planned but a lot of it out of the blue. David knew 10 years ago when he accepted the position of university president that he was going to retire at age 65. What he hadn't planned on was that leaving this job, to which he'd become quite attached, was going to be excruciatingly difficult. Nor did he know that the dream home he and his wife had purchased in Florida would be nearly blown apart by rampaging tornadoes.

We never know what's around the corner, as one of my clients once remarked. He had been looking forward to retirement when he and his wife would finally get to see the world. But all his plans went down the drain when his wife suddenly died of cancer. Ruth was looking forward to more togetherness with her business-owner husband when he sold his enterprise. But she ended up feeling abandoned and dismayed when he switched his workaholic habits to a part-time enterprise and full-fledged involvement with the Fraternal Order of the Freemasons. Pam was planning to leave her corporate position at age 58 to set up a consulting practice with her husband. But then he was diagnosed with Parkinson's disease, and she had to stay on the job until full retirement age.

Let's face it, we are all going to suffer setbacks; we are all going to be bent, stretched, and in some ways "reformed." It's when things get challenging that we find and discover our mettle; we either flexibly rebound or remain permanently bent. Can you spring back from life-bending situations, or do you need a perfect environment to go on? How resilient are you now, and how resilient will you need to be to cope with the challenges you'll have to face in the future?

The fifty-plus years are filled with ongoing changes and transitions, which tend to grow in magnitude the older we get. Some of these can be expected and prepared for, such as retirement, the death of parents, marriage of children, birth of grandkids, appearance of age spots, and turning 70. Others we hope never happen to us (cancer, death of a loved one, separation or divorce, serious accidents, or becoming a caregiver to an ill spouse). Then there are those things that we may try to ignore—aging bodies, unsettling inner awakenings, terrorist attacks, or fears about death and serious illness. We may also encounter unexpected good fortune—such as becoming queen of the golf course, falling in love with beautiful grandchildren, a problem child evolving into a grand human being, discovering and manifesting a hidden talent, or finding and marrying a long-lost love. Regardless of our circumstances, as we enter the fifty-plus years, we want to be equipped with the mental disposition, strategies, and skills for coping with change and transition.

If you are already a highly resilient person, congratulations! You're ready to capitalize on the joys of senior life and are well equipped to weather tough ordeals with courage and grace, possibly even growing wiser and stronger in the process. If, however, you feel the need to beef up your "bounce-back" capabilities, here are a few suggestions for doing so:

• *Remember that you're not being picked on when "bad" things happen to the good person in you.* Don't allow yourself to fall into the victim mode when bad things occur. Instead, deal with them head on. We all face ordeals of one kind or another. If you suffer a loss, grieve it, manage what you must, and then move on. If you get tennis elbow, take up billiards. When your beloved dog dies, have a dog funeral, bury it, and go find another canine friend. If your kids or grandkids have to deal with hard times, recall your own bad times in life and how you grew from them. People who don't learn to confront and manage difficult times may also not be as capable of appreciating the good times. When your face develops character lines, look for the beauty and wisdom etched in those lines. Know that ordeals are going to happen, they are going to be painful, and you have the God-given capabilities to deal with them and to bounce back. You are made of resilient materials, mind, body, and soul. Don't let your mind tell you differently. Let your inner wisdom carry you through life's trying times.

• *Remind yourself that life can be like a rollercoaster ride with joyous glides, tough uphill climbs, and flat stretches in between.* There is great wisdom in the old adage that we must take the good with the bad. Resign yourself to life, not from life. Don't allow yourself to check out by giving in to your "shoulds" or the belief that life is either all good or all bad. Life is much more than either. It is a fascinating journey, with some days exploding in volcanic emotion, and others crystallizing one molecule at a time at deep subterranean levels. It's all a part of life. I believe that we are all meant to be a part of an awesome journey. So strap yourself in and relish every bit of it—rain or shine, smooth or bumpy, there will never be a ride that takes you as fast or slow or as deep or high as the roller coaster of life.

• *Maintaining a cosmic sense of humor is an essential ingredient of resilience.* Those who can laugh at themselves and see humor in the things of this world don't tend to take themselves too seriously and don't remain stuck in a down place too long. Admittedly, it is exceedingly difficult to see humor in human tragedy or in the midst of all the sobering things that happen in your life. I'm not talking about telling jokes when your heart is breaking. I'm talking about the ability to step outside of yourself, especially during difficult times, to see things from a broader perspective. It's easier to weather life's twists and turns from such a vantage point. Life is a stage and we are all players on the stage of life. For a play to be substantial enough to engage your attention, however, it must have comedy and tragedy, possibly because we come equipped with the ability to both laugh and cry. Even Walt Disney's classic kids' movies featuring Bambi, Snow White, and Cinderella have both joy and pain to sustain interest. But a life focused on just one or the other—tragedy or comedy—has no life in it at all. It's just tedious boredom. Remember that in good drama, whether it's comedy or tragedy, the characters learn and grow. When life serves up tragedy, be there with it, and then, after the tears of despair have begun to recede, look beyond your gaping wound and use a detached perspective to start regaining your sense of comedy. After all, comedy, in the classical dramatic sense, is not just about something being funny. It's really a form of drama that ends with the community coming together in a new way, often through the marriage of key characters. What pieces of your life can a community of friends or colleagues help you knit back together? Who is your audience? Every play needs an audience, including your own. But you may need to develop greater abilities for moving from an actor on the stage to an audience that appreciates your performance. Learn to be both an actor on your stage of life and an audience that applauds the way your life is playing out. After all, you are the chief scriptwriter of your play, and you want to feel that it is definitely worth the price of admission.

  • *Another key to resilience involves relationship and community.* By nature we are all relational, even the strongest of introverts. We are all community oriented in one way or another. Having relationships and being in a community fosters resilience. But for a community to nurture and expand your resilience, it must be supportive.

◆ Belonging to a Community

My wife Pat and I currently live in a golf course community. You can look out the window at any time of the day and see people walking their dogs, riding bikes, chatting with friends, cruising around in golf carts, or casually strolling by, waving and talking with neighbors. This is a friendly place, with friendly people. We gather as a community several times a year for a barbecue, to celebrate somebody's birthday at our clubhouse, or use holiday events to have a street party. There are always golf tournaments taking place, and you see folks heading off to them with big smiles on their faces. There are bridge groups, tennis teams, and garden clubs if you're interested. Or you can just sit on your deck and wave at neighbors passing by.

This is a community of people who enjoy being together, who take advantage of the many opportunities for social interaction, and watch out for each other. When an elderly neighbor's driveway gets snowed in, other neighbors suddenly appear to shovel it out and then mysteriously disappear back into the winter mist. When someone gets sick, word in the community goes out and food shows up at their door. A community newsletter keeps us informed of who the top golfers and tennis players are, what's happening with future plans for the neighborhood, and what events are coming up. When a neighbor passes away, we grieve and share fond memories of their grand life. You can hang out alone here to enjoy solitude in front of your fireplace or have a beer with friends at the club. I play pool on Thursday afternoons with an "old codgers" group, and Pat paints and lunches with an art group on Fridays. It feels like home here. People here have a sense of belonging to something, something that's bigger than themselves.

Being in affiliation is one of the basic human needs. It provides us with a sense of belonging, of being with others in a community with common values and interests. One of the well-known dangers of aging is becoming isolated and lonely. It's tempting at times to lapse into solitary pursuits and become a couch potato or computer nerd. Of course, solitary time is also a basic need, even for extroverts, and an essential ingredient for self-realization. But for each of us, there is a happy balance between solitude and companionship. Too much alone time can lead to a cycle of diminishing horizons and energy. Eventually our shrinking circle of contact becomes a black hole imploding in upon itself in an ever-intensifying density that leaves no space for the light to get in. Living in community expands our horizons and keeps our energy fresh and bright.

In addition to living in a supportive community, there are countless other ways of being in community. You might want to become engaged in a professional association, get involved with a local chapter of an international organization such as Rotary or Kiwanis, join the Purple Hat Society, sign on for a book or garden club, or volunteer for a charitable or religious organization that resonates with you.

Many churches and other places of worship offer services and programs especially designed for seniors. Our church, for example, has blood pressure clinics, workshops on writing living wills, and an adult education program that includes presentations and discussions on a wide array of spiritual and theological topics. Another local church advertises in our town paper that it offers "something for everyone in the family."

If you're not one who has been previously been inclined to join a community, you might want to revise your views about that as you get older. The dictionary defines community as "a group of people with a common background or with shared interests within the society." Back in my hometown in Minnesota, there is a Norse Club. Can you guess what kind of background and interests folks in that club share in common? If you feel that managing your portfolio is consuming more and more of your time, you can turn that interest or need into a communal experience by joining an investors club—with real people, not cyberspace groupies. If you like to read a lot, you could become a reader for those who are visually impaired or children at your local grade school or library. Whether your interests lean to the social, political, religious, intellectual, creative, or physical—get out and get involved. Don't grow old alone. You're far more likely to feel vim and vibrant if you are a part of a community.

◆   ## Setting Dangerous Goals

As we enter our senior years, some of us need goals to motivate us. Others need to be free from a goal-directed life. If you were born to be spontaneous, like a butterfly flitting on the breeze, retirement may be your key to the kind of freedom you've always dreamed about. If that's the case, give yourself permission to do what you want and go where you please. Jump full-fledged into the free-flowing river of life. If, in contrast, you need something to go for, a target to shoot at or a new mountain to climb, you're going to need to set goals—but not just any goals.

Rob, a retired physician, advocates setting goals that involve danger. Having enjoyed a highly successful career in public health that often took him into harm's way in places like East Pakistan (now Bangladesh), Haiti, and the remote areas of Indonesia, he experienced real danger many times. But the kind of danger he refers to is not physical. He recently enrolled in a university music program to earn a bachelor's degree in music. Although he loves music and has a well-trained voice, he is finding that his coursework is more challenging than he anticipated. In fact, he's found a course in musicology to be particularly arduous. He's also discovered that being the oldest person in the class (including the instructor) provides no guarantee of success. With a wry grin he says that he probably got one of the lowest grades in class on a recent exam, but he didn't fail. His real success, however, was that he was willing to give it his very best effort with no assurance of making the grade. That's what living dangerously means to this intrepid medical doctor who devised treatments that saved thousands of lives in medically impoverished areas of the world. His next dangerous assignment: passing voice and instrument recitals.

I asked Rob what he intended to do with his developing musical expertise. He already sings in a men's a cappella group, a university choral group, and a church choir. But he looks forward to writing music for others and learning to play the piano well enough so that someday he can "play in a little bar somewhere." His joy, he says, is not so much in achieving a goal as it is in the chase. He could fail the next quiz, discover that he doesn't have the requisite talent, or develop a case of laryngitis, but without the risks, he would miss out on the exhilaration.

Ambitious goals, especially in senior life when so many of us are looking forward to leisurely rewards for our years of labor, push us to take risks and explore new territory. Since nothing in life is assured, anyway, why should we be afraid of putting ourselves out there in dangerous endeavors? As Rob says, we just might find out that we have what it takes and succeed in getting to a new place in life. Then what? There's always another "mission impossible."

◆ Advancing in the Path of Your True Nature

Throughout this book I've promoted the concept of self-realization as essential to fulfilling your individual uniqueness. Cellular biologists might take exception to the concept of individual uniqueness because they know that the whole of human kind is far more alike than different from the perspective of our genes. Yet we also know that each of us has a DNA code different enough to enable the FBI to determine whether we committed a particular crime. But it's not our unique DNA code to which I refer—it's something far more intangible than biochemical differences.

The kind of uniqueness I'm referring to can't be analyzed by a blood test or microscope. The kind of uniqueness I'm referring to has more of a psychological essence than a physiological presence. Although we do attempt to gauge our psychological state with various kinds of mental health and personality assessments, there is no psychological instrument that can fully define our uniqueness. Psychometric surveys are based on the assumption that humans share an array of measurable commonalities. But the human psyche is a subjective domain, so how can we ever know if we have identified all aspects of human nature or something as ethereal as the human spirit? Another problem with assessments is that their results depend on self-reports. But how can you report a subjective experience with objective precision?

That being said, it's important to remember that many assessments can be useful in helping you see the various psychological attributes that comprise your psychic array. You might find that an assessment such as the Myers Briggs, for example, can help you understand why you tend to be more extroverted than introverted in the way you relate to the world, or more concrete than abstract in your thinking, or more spontaneous than planned in your approach to life. Such self-knowledge is often quite helpful as you pursue your unique path of self-realization. But there is no assessment capable of defining the full realm of all of your individual uniqueness. To do that would require an individually designed assessment for every individual. Self-discovery, therefore, is an ongoing process, and self-realization is a journey that never ends, perhaps extending even beyond our last, grand transition.

Our social welfare and the common good both demand that we

honor our similarities and differences. Our basic similarities enable us to function together regardless of the language we speak—Japanese, English, Mandarin, or Russian. Our differences, however, have often taken us to the brink of annihilation. Is there anything that can actually enable us to live together in appreciation of our similarities and differences while maintaining our common welfare and individual uniqueness? There may be hope on the horizon—and the hope is actually evolving from an increasing number of seniors on the planet.

With so many humans around the globe entering the senior stages of life and bringing forth their wisdom of the ages, it seems conceivable that we could be at the dawning of a new era of planetary enlightenment. Admittedly that notion has not been validated by "a roundup of the late world news from the usual unreliable sources," as poet Lawrence Ferlinghetti wrote in *A Coney Island of the Mind*. In spite of the negativity in the news, however, with millions of people advancing into senior life in an interconnected world, doesn't it seem possible that mature wisdom could be on the verge of blooming all over the earth? Isn't it possible that the current paradigm of fear and mistrust could give way to a convergence of the wisdom of the ages?

The first half of life for most of us is spent in "fitting-in." The second half frees us to tap the earthly wisdom that comes from deeper self-knowledge. The first half of life involves concentrating on our "sameness." The second half gives us the opportunity to celebrate our unique differences and realize our full potential. What better gift can we share with the world?

Hopefully this book has provided ample opportunity for clarifying a vision for what your senior life can be in your journey toward self-realization. No doubt your vision of the future will be unique to you. No one else can develop or replicate it. If you are a Mystical Intuitive, you will choose a different path than a Coordinator-Organizer would. If you fit in the Gray Eminence category, you are likely to pursue a different direction than a Seeker-Explorer would. If creativity is one of your top values, your commitments will be distinctly different from someone whose top values focus on staying loyal to tradition. But despite their differences, each path is, to use another Ferlinghetti line, "a renaissance of wonder." And, unlike the poet, we don't have to sit around and wait for it.

RAHBI FINDS HER PATH

Some of us re-invent ourselves with a carefully organized plan. But sometimes forces beyond our control wash us up on unknown shores.

The latter mode was how Roberta (Rahbi) Crawford came to her current life work.

Rahbi is a highly trained classical musician with two master's degrees in music and additional advanced musical training. She is an experienced orchestral and choral conductor, a composer, and a performer. At an earlier stage in life, Rahbi was pursuing the goal of becoming the first female conductor of a major symphony orchestra. It turns out, however, that her body prevented her from continuing in that direction. Today, instead of being an orchestra conductor, Rahbi, at the age of 60, is a different kind of musician—a certified Tama-Do practitioner. She is a sound-healing performer who uses music to heal the body as well as to please the ear.

Earlier in life Rahbi was a traditional music teacher, but in her forties became incapacitated with severe chronic fatigue. Her ailment alerted her to the realization that her health could no longer tolerate a standard teaching career. She needed to change career directions and pursue her childhood dream. As a child she liked to watch Leonard Bernstein on TV as he conducted the New York Philharmonic orchestra, and she yearned to become a conductor herself. But with no female role models for that in the 1950s, her aspirations seemed more like pipe dreams than realistic goals. But then women began moving into all kinds of professions from which they had previously been excluded, and she began working on a doctorate in orchestral conducting, a quest that actually seemed to improve her health. Her dream came to an abrupt ending, however, when she was literally unable to turn the page of her musical score during a recital. Something in her body simply would not let her hand turn the page.

What do you do when a dream comes suddenly to an unfulfilled ending? Rahbi fell into a state of deep depression and disillusionment. She felt betrayed by her failed dream and totally confused. All she could do was to play a Native American flute and agonize over what went wrong—why her body had refused to cooperate at a critical moment. Eventually her flute-playing began to regenerate her severely deflated spirits. She began to understand that it was wisdom from her unconscious that had stopped her from going forward with her former aspirations. She realized that orchestral conducting was more of a childhood whimsy than a path to self-realization. She really had no desire to spend days studying musical scores composed by others. Nor did she want to spend hours rehearsing music so it could be played exactly as the composer supposedly intended. A conventional path was not for her; her mind-body simply was not going to allow it.

The gift of a book by Fabien Maman, *The Role of Music in the*

Twenty-First Century, changed her life. Maman created the Tama-Do process, which applies the outcomes of his research with various principles of Oriental medicine into a healing practice. This book struck such a deep a chord with Rahbi that she went off to France to study with Maman and eventually launched a new career as a musician-healer and certified Tama-Do practitioner. Rahbi offers her therapeutic services through concerts, workshops, healing circles, and individual healing-sound treatments. She uses a wide variety of musical instruments, including Native American flutes, quartz crystal bowls, and her own voice, to enhance inner peace and resonate with internal harmonic rhythms. You can learn more about Rahbi at www.mwt.net/~makesmusic.

For Rahbi, finding her own path involved exploring, experimenting, improvising, trusting her feelings, and persevering. When you trust your inner guidance, she says, you may not get what you thought you wanted. But what you do get may be something infinitely better. For her, fulfillment came from following the less traveled path. In doing so, she learned how to create and share her own unique music.

If you're on the path of change, it's usually wise to make changes gradually, in stages. Corporate executives and ministers in new situations have learned that attempts to change too much too fast can result in disasters that last. Incorporating a new vision in a church or a business setting generally works best when change is made incrementally, with all affected parties being thoroughly educated and frequently consulted about what's coming and why. Similarly, when implementing a new vision in your life, you may be more successful in planning it in small steps that keep all interested parties in your life informed and engaged in a collaborative effort.

CREATING PERSONAL SPACE

Bradley was eagerly looking forward to his retirement when he could devote more time to his many interests. His wife Janet, however, was happy for Bradley, but had serious concerns about how his new life might impact her well-established routine. Janet, who had retired from a teaching position a few years earlier, was quietly dreading Bradley's forthcoming, full-time presence in the house.

Janet was a strong extrovert and had developed an active social life in the community. She also had a comfortable routine around the house. She liked her lifestyle and feared that it would be uprooted when her introverted husband came home from his last day at work. She was afraid that he would want more togetherness than she did and would make demands on her time that would disrupt her household routines and interfere with her moments of quiet solitude. Although she was an extrovert, she also relished her "time-out" for reading and meditating.

In a casual conversation with good friends about retirement, Janet finally confessed that she had some concerns about Bradley's upcoming retirement. Prior to that, she'd been reluctant to share her concerns for fear of hurting Bradley's feelings and undermining his excitement about retiring. Fortunately, one of the friends, who happened to be a professional counselor, helped them address Janet's concerns. That discussion led to some intelligent decisions about how to deal with Janet's concerns without squelching Bradley's excitement.

For one thing, they realized that it would be important for them each to have their own space. Bradley would convert one of the bedrooms into his private office. There he could manage the finances, play the stock market, and amuse himself by playing computer chess with Internet chess masters from around the world. Bradley also promised to stay clear of the kitchen, Janet's private domain and her working studio for expressing her culinary artistry. For the hour of quiet reading and contemplation that Janet treasured before the evening meal, Bradley readily agreed to honor that by staying out of the living room so she could enjoy her peaceful respite without distraction. They also set aside half an hour for cocktails together to discuss the day's events, after Janet had the meal in the oven.

Their agreement on these rather simple things resolved the anxieties Janet had about Bradley's retirement. They established new routines that helped them to make a smooth transition to this new chapter in their life together. It turns out that Bradley found any number of interesting things to do in creating an enjoyable schedule of his own. And their willingness to openly discuss their individual needs and to creatively identify things they enjoy doing separately and together has resulted in their both feeling fulfilled with their lives.

Creating your personal space can be an important step for traveling your unique path. A personal space is a safe place where you can be you. For that to happen, it's best if it can be a private space, where no one enters unless invited. But it doesn't have to be big or fancy. It could be a cubbyhole that serves as an office, a workshop, studio, private garden, or an out-of-the way corner that reflects the unique way that you see yourself and the world.

◆ Authoring Your Story

How interesting are you as a person? If you were writing a book about your life, what would you entitle it? What would be some of your chapter headings? Would you come out as a hero or an antagonist? Would you be a leading or a supporting character? Is your book of life preordained, or do you feel empowered to author your future chapters?

Your life tends to become more interesting and meaningful when you view it as a fascinating story. Many therapists and pastoral counselors who work with dying people help them conceive of their life as a story. Doing that apparently helps them frame their lives within a meaningful perspective. Conceptualizing your life as a story or book may help you see how you've been part of something bigger than yourself. Sharing your life story can also help you pass on an appreciation of a life well lived, with new chapters still to unfold. Clarissa Pinkola Estes writes in *The Gift of Story: A Wise Tale about What Is Enough* that "none of us will live forever," but "the stories can."

Estes also reminds us, "There is no right or wrong way to tell a story." So if you haven't already imagined your life as an interesting story, it's time to start. One way to do that is to look for the narrative threads that have enabled you to weave a rich tapestry of experience. Where are the colorful passages? What patterns or images stand out in relief to all the other millions of little stitches?

There will never be another tapestry exactly like yours. You are a one-of-a-kind. Your story has never been told before. And it never will be unless you take hold of the many "yarns" you've been given for creating a bold, original piece of truth and beauty.

In thinking about your life as story, what do you see as some of the major themes in your past? What motifs—or minor themes—contrast or complement your major themes? Recently I worked with a client who was stuck on the theme of trying to prove herself intellectually and professionally because she saw her life largely as a series of past failures or false starts. Her obsession with this one dominant theme had effectively undermined her sense of self-worth. Even though she had an MBA from a highly regarded business school, was the sole survivor of a corporate reorganization, and had just earned a large pay raise, she kept reducing her life story to a theme of failure. She couldn't forget the time she received a mediocre score on her graduate record exam. She wouldn't let go of her disappointment at the loss of a good job with Enron when it collapsed. And she kept replaying a single, stingingly unflattering comment made to her by a highly stressed manager. Her negative mental perspective was unwarranted and unproductive, to say the least. So I worked with her to recast her life story. Instead of entitling her past life as "a series of false starts," she reframed her experience as "major life-learning events."

Choose the words you use to describe and explain yourself with care. The negative worldview that derogatory words connote may sabotage your future. Most of us have experienced more than enough ordeals to make it all too easy to become victims of the past rather than proactive authors of the future. Your personal history primarily resides in only one place, your head. Your interpretation of your history becomes your perceptual reality. I'm not advocating that you gloss over your challenges and shortcomings. The last thing you want to do is to lie about your past. To the contrary, you want to take care that your perceptions are founded upon an authentic history. Giving your past a narrow focus with a negative spin is anything but truthful. The truth is that all life stories have elements of good and bad. And all life stories have interesting dimensions. So be authentic and show that you are indeed a well-rounded character who is multi-dimensional and has a story worth hearing.

Is your book of life full of self-reinventions, or have you been on a steady course of progress and achievement? Would your work, profession, and organizational titles be key features of your story, or would family, recreation, and community become the prominent themes? Does your book portray you as a hard-nosed, strong-willed, achievement-oriented character, or a daffy, comedic entertainer like Lucille Ball? Have you come from humble beginnings and pulled yourself up by the bootstraps, or does your story spotlight the silver spoon you inherited? Have you been a ray of sunshine or a cloud of doom? In your mind, does your life feel more like a thrilling roller coaster ride, or a long, arduous trek through never-changing landscape?

In Larry McMurtry's novel *Somebody's Darling*, one of the characters says, "Life ought to be like a good script. The incidents ought to add up, and the characters ought to complement one another, and the story line ought to be clear, and after you've had the climax it ought to leave you with the feeling that it has all been worth it."[1] In other words, as

---

1. Larry McMurtry, *Somebody's Darling* (New York: Simon and Schuster, 1978), p. 342.

Dan P. McAdams writes in *Stories We Live By: Personal Myth and the Making of the Self,* "good lives, like good stories, require good endings."[2]

You are now in a unique place in the story of your life. You have a wealth of personal history, but you haven't finished your story yet. It is my hope that working through the process in this book has enriched and clarified your personal narrative. One thing that is clear to me from all the life stories I've heard over the years is that you don't have to stick to the story line you've scripted so far. Just as good historians use new information and insights to revise their understanding of the past, you can use your new, expanded concept of your self to revise your past life story. You can then envision new scenarios for your future. Ultimately, only you can write your life story.

Will you be pleased with your story when all is said and done? Make your answer to that resoundingly affirmative, and so it shall be!

---

2. Dan P. McAdams, *Stories We Live By: Personal Myths and the Making of the Self* (New York: William Morrow, 1993), p. 202.

CONCLUSION:
AUTHORING YOUR LIFE

"A dog too old to learn new tricks always has been."

—ANONYMOUS

"I sure was frightened 12 years ago when I told a friend that I had no idea what I was going to do after I made my last call. But I had a big awakening when he said that this was just one more new chapter in my life."

—LARGE-ANIMAL VETERINARIAN RECALLING HIS FEARS ABOUT RETIRING

"To exist is to change; to change is to mature; to mature is to create oneself endlessly."

—HENRI BERGSON, FRENCH PHILOSOPHER AND 1927 NOBEL PRIZE LAUREATE

◆ Life as Perceptual Reality

How do you conceptualize your life? Do you see yourself more as a passenger on a vessel or as captain of your own ship? Are you just a character in a story scripted by forces beyond your control, or are you the author of your own life story? Do you consider becoming a senior citizen to be the beginning of a lackluster slide into oblivion or an invitation to a delicious banquet of the best life has to offer?

Our experience of life comes more from our mental perceptions than from any physical reality. Two individuals experiencing the same event often perceive it and its impact on their lives as different realities. For instance, many of those who weathered Hurricane Katrina were devastated and depressed by the tragedy. They saw themselves as hapless victims, buffeted about by the whims of nature, politics, and luck. But there were other hurricane survivors who responded with newfound determination to return and rebuild better than ever. The huge scale of destruction also became a marker event that motivated many residents of the area to move on and create a new life in a new location.

The inner realm of the mind shapes the outer world of the physical into our reality. Without self-perception we would not know we existed. Without conscious thought and self-awareness, we wouldn't know whether we were camels, rocks, or roses. As consciously aware individuals, then, we are all authoring a unique book of life based on the way we interpret each of our encounters.

How you mentally perceive your life determines both your state of emotional well-being and how actively you are inclined to assert creative control over your future. The fact that you have read this book probably indicates that you are invested in reinventing yourself and creating a new future. You can't, of course, control everything that happens to you. But, for the most part, you can manage how you respond to what you encounter along the way.

Your mind is the most powerful tool you have for creating an energizing vision for your future. Creating an energizing vision for your future means that you are more likely to achieve your aspirations and enjoy a positive perception of your life day by day and overall. I often ask my coaching clients what they see as their mission in life. One of my clients said it was simply "to get through it!" Another said it was "to be a great husband and father/grandfather and do some creative writing." Which of these two people do you think was more fun to be with?

How do you conceptualize your past life story? Have you been a courageous adventurer, a cautious traditionalist, a lucky stiff, or a good soldier? Do you see yourself as having enjoyed a life of abundance, survived under noxious influences, or worked hard to stay ahead of the curve? Does your book of life relate a success story, a mundane existence, or a hodgepodge of ups and downs? Is your sense of your past one of coherence and continuity, or one of chaos and confusion?

Regardless of the way the book of your past life looks to you, it is now history, a past that lives primarily within the confines of your mind. If you don't like your history, you can change the way you perceive it. Doing so may be an important step in creating the future you want, especially if your past has a negative impact that keeps you tied to a former "you" that you want to leave behind. Now is the time to free yourself for authoring a new book of life that features the best you you've ever been.

◆ Intelligent Design

One theme of this book is that even though you can't know exactly what your future will bring, you can know what you will bring to the future. You can set the stage for the course of your future through the choices you make and your frame of mind as you approach the forthcoming years. Make no decisions about your future, and the random events of life will write your story for you. Take no control over your mental reference for life, and you settle for being an emotional reactor to everything that comes your way. Although you can't force your life to follow a particular or precise trajectory, you can be a co-creator of your future through *intelligent design*. In this context, intelligent design applies to the opportunities we all have for influencing the outcome of our future.

At the park the other day, our three-year-old grandson took on a new challenge by climbing up a rather complicated piece of playground equipment for the first time. After he successfully navigated his ascent, he stood on a platform at the top and shouted, "Look Garba Dave, I DID IT!" He was obviously proud of himself and wanted the world to know it! I was proud of him, too. And I couldn't help thinking how wonderful it would be if those of us entering our senior years could design our future around those playgrounds where we, too, can ascend to new heights and exclaim with childish wonder and glee, "Look everyone, I DID IT!"

Throughout this book, I have presented numerous examples of individuals who have elected to author exciting, new chapters in their lives. Remember Rahbi, a disillusioned orchestra conductor who now facilitates regenerative health through the healing power of music? How about Pamela, who retired from the corporate world and recreated herself as a social worker? Or Joe, who transformed a lackluster career as a military analyst into a sparkling life as an artist/teacher and a community builder? Stories like these have, I hope, inspired you to envision the creative possibilities in your own life, work, and overall well-being.

You are the only one who can author your own story authentically. Only you know how different you want the next chapter of your life to be from your past or current one. Do you envision your next chapter as a smooth continuation of the past? Or is your life narrative about to veer in a new direction? How big a role will work have in the next chapter? What roles will love, fun, charity, and overall well-being play in your basic design?

REINVENTING YOUR STORY

In thinking about the next chapter of your life, which place along the continuum of options best describes your vision for the future?

←■ →

I'll continue with my life/ work as it is for as long as possible.	I'll retire from full-time employment but continue consulting in my field of expertise.	I intend to retire but use talents and knowledge I've acquired over the years in new ways.	I plan to retire from work and enjoy a life of full-time leisure.	I intend to reinvent myself and enjoy a totally new and different life.

◆ From Veterinarian to Historian

To further spur your interest in self-reinvention, here's one final story of someone who moved on from a career he loved to a new, fulfilling role in his senior years. For 40 years before creating his current chapter of life, Dr. Jim worked as a large-animal veterinarian. The grin on his face and the sparkle in his eyes clearly convey the love he had for being a vet in the West Virginia hills and "hollers." With pride he talks about his former veterinary hospital-on-wheels—fully equipped with hot and cold running water, X-ray and surgical equipment, and even a portable potty. He could pull up to a farm and perform a full-service operation from diagnosis to post-op treatment, all in a single visit. He relished his autonomy and was grateful to be of service. He says there comes a time however, when the bones grow weary of the heavy physical challenges involved in this kind of work and when the emergency calls in the middle of the night and the disruptions of social activities finally take their toll. Like many of us, Dr. Jim knew when the time had come for him to leave the life from which he had gained so much satisfaction.

Leaving a profession that had been so close to his heart for so many years was not easy. Dr. Jim recalls the feeling of tremendous loss on the day he realized the time had come to retire from his arduous profession. He was bewildered by what he was going to do and who he was going to be. He sought out a wise acquaintance to discuss his deep concerns about what he was going to do after making his last visit and parking his high-tech veterinary hospital-on-wheels for the last time.

His friend listened attentively and then counseled him to think of this as just another chapter in his life. That was several years ago, but Dr. Jim still credits that conversation as a dramatic awakening. Ever since then, he has seen life as an ongoing process of change. And for Dr. Jim, change has come to represent opportunity for new possibilities.

Fortunately for Dr. Jim, his contacts with wise friends helped him recreate a new life. He was recently honored as the local "Historian Laureate" and awarded a sizable grant to develop a history of West Virginia's oldest town, Shepherdstown, where he can trace his family back for several generations. In addition to his current book project, Dr. Jim has already authored a number of books on local history and the town's Presbyterian church. He continues to be a student of Civil War history and a popular storyteller of local lore, in addition to speaking at various meetings, writing a newspaper column recounting historical anecdotes, and participating in the Rotary Club. On a long summer day you might be able to join him on one of his tours of a nearby Revolutionary War cemetery, Antietam Battlefield just across the river, or a bus tour of other historical sites in the area.

Dr. Jim loves what he is doing and states with certainty that he would not trade his new chapter of life for another round of his old career. "If you don't know how to reinvent yourself," he says, "you have missed something rewarding to look forward to." Dr. Jim was fortunate to have had a wise friend to help him see new possibilities. In times of change, the sage counsel of a trusted friend or a professional coach can give you the extra little twist you need to focus the kaleidoscope of your future into a beautiful new vision. My hope is that this book has also helped you to do that.

◆ Steps to Renewal

I hope that, like Dr. Jim, you have found what you need to author a new chapter of your life—one that you can truly look forward to with energy and enthusiasm. In recreating your future and authoring your book of life, you might want to keep the following themes in mind as reminders of all the processing you've done up to this point and the changes you'll continue to process along the way:

1. *Your life is a book of chapters.* Moving through the journey of change and reinvention that you experience throughout life is like moving through the chapters of a book. In your book of life, however, you are not just a reader. You are also your own best author, and you want

to exercise intelligent authorship in writing your future chapters rather than delegating them to the haphazard authorship of happenstance.

2. *You are an interesting subject.* What gives life a sense of meaning and purpose is in knowing that who you are and what you do matters. You are interesting and important. Nobody else can be who you are and contribute the unique gifts you have to share. Nobody else has your story to author and to tell. If you don't like your story up to this point, you may need to change yourself and your view of yourself in the world. To do that, you might want to try envisioning yourself as the lead character in your book of life. What makes this character interesting? Is this character on a heroic journey? If not, why not? Successfully navigating through life is, after all, a challenge of sufficient magnitude to warrant heroic status to all.

3. *You are more than old titles.* When and if you leave your work behind, you gain something and lose something. You gain freedom and new opportunities but lose your work-world titles. But hanging onto a title or an identity that defined you in the past may keep you from seeing who you are *in addition* to that. A title is, in effect, a label—a type of shorthand for a particular role that a person fulfills. Don't you want to see what's beneath and beyond your old labels? Stories with characters that never change are usually dull and boring. So how will the lead character in your book change and grow when the old titles and labels are gone?

4. *Values of the past may become outdated guides for your future.* Most of us make life and work choices out of youthful values and seldom look back thereafter. Your values as a senior are unlikely to be the same as those of your youth. Consciously reprioritizing what success means now and in the years ahead is a fundamental step toward self-renewal. Remember to take nothing for granted, including your relationships, your health, your creative nature, and your spiritual life. Your conscious priorities will determine how and in what ways you invest your time, energy, and talent. If you overlook what's truly important, what you value most, you may unwittingly find yourself spending the most time on what you value least. Ongoing appraisal of your true values is more likely to keep your course in line with what brings you the greatest satisfaction and fulfillment.

5. *It's never too late to develop a latent talent.* Grandma Moses didn't tap her artistic talents until late in life, nor did Beethoven allow deafness to stop him from composing some of the most beautiful music ever heard. What highly developed talents is it time for you to leave behind or use in new ways? What undeveloped talents might you now have time to enjoy? Is there a Grandma Moses, an inner musician, a

historian, or a nurturing presence waiting to burst out of a closeted part of your being?

6. *Old dogs can learn new tricks.* The behaviors that supported your success in the workplace may not serve you equally well in a new life. Your behavior is the outer manifestation of your inner motives and learned habits. It's your behavior that people respond and react to—not what motivates your actions. Will modifying some of your behaviors enrich your life and the lives of those around you? There is only one way to find out: Ask those affected by your behavior what they see as the positives to capitalize on and the negatives to modify. Undertaking some behavior modifications may make you a more enjoyable person to be around, and in the process, your relationships are likely to become more enjoyable to you. One small behavior change I've found beneficial is to count my blessings at the end of each day. My wife and I enjoy doing that verbally with each other as we relax before dinner.

7. *Locate where your new life can flourish.* If you're a golfer, you are going to want to reside near a golf course. A sailor needs to find a home by the sea. But if your aspirations involve running for mayor of a town, writing books, or expressing yourself with a paintbrush and canvas, you may want to find a community where your aspirations can more easily become a reality. Be wary of clever marketing ploys promising the perfect retirement place. If a fulfilling, meaningful life is important to you, the right community for you will not only be one that enables you to live safely and comfortably; it will also be one that offers inspiration, support, and the companionship of kindred spirits.

Last but not least, remember that you are the magnificent sum of everyone you've ever known, all that you've ever been and done, and every dream you've ever dared to envision. You wouldn't have come this far if you hadn't already been successful in many areas of your life. Once you were an infant, but you learned to walk and talk as a toddler. Then you were a schoolchild, a student, a young adult, and, finally, a mid-lifer. Each stage required that you successfully navigate new experiences. You made it through all of that, and now you have the opportunity to use all of it, every last piece of it, to enjoy being the new you.

With every passing moment, your life story is unfolding. What's it saying about you and the world you live in? Do you see a world full of possibilities? I hope so—because all my professional experience and my own life story have shown me time and time again that in becoming the best you that you have ever been, the world will surely be richer for it.

REFERENCES

"Anima and Animus." *Midlife Metamorphosis.* Accessed on 11/14/07 at www .lessons4living.com/anima_and_animus.htm.

Baker, Dan, and Cameron Stauth. *What Happy People Know: How the New Science of Happiness Can Change Your Life for the Better.* Emmaus, PA: Rodale Inc., 2003.

Becker, Ernest. *The Denial of Death.* New York: The Free Press, 1973.

Bolles, Dick. *The Three Boxes of Life and How to Get Out of Them: An Introduction to Life Planning.* Berkeley, CA: Ten Speed Press, 1978.

Borchard, David. *Will The Real You Please Stand Up: Find Passion in Your Life and Work.* Pittsburgh: SterlingHouse Publisher, 2006.

Branden, Nathaniel. *Six Pillars of Self-Esteem.* New York: Bantam Books, 1994.

Brehony, Kathleen A. *Awakening at Mid-life: A Guide to Reviving Your Spirit, Recreating Your Life, and Returning to Our Truest Self.* New York: Riverhead Books, 1996.

Brewi, Janice, and Anne Brennan. *Celebrate Mid-Life: Jungian Archetypes and Mid-Life Spirituality.* New York: Crossroads, 1989.

Bridges, William. *The Way of Transition: Embracing Life's Most Difficult Moments,* New York: Perseus Books, 2001.

Briggs-Myers, Isabel. *Gifts Differing.* Palo Alto, CA: Consulting Psychologists Press, Inc., 1980.

Brizendine, Louann. *The Female Brain.* New York: Broadway Books, 2006.

Buckingham, Marcus, and Donald Clifton. *Now, Discover Your Strengths.* New York: The Free Press, 2001.

Cameron, Julia. *The Artists Way: A Course in Discovering and Recovering Your Creative Self.* New York: Jeremy P. Tarcher, 1992.

Cohen, Gene. *The Creative Age: Awakening Human Potential in the Second Half of Life*. New York: Avon Books, 2000.

de Mille, Agnes. *Martha: The Life and Work of Martha Graham*. New York: Random House, 1991.

Dychtwald, Ken, and Joe Flower. *Age Wave: The Challenges and Opportunities of an Aging America*. Los Angeles: Jeremy P. Tarcher, 1989.

Dychtwald, Ken, and Daniel Kadlec. *The Power Years*. Hoboken, NJ: John Wiley & Sons, 2005.

Erikson, Erik. *The Life Cycle Completed (Extended Version)*. New York: W.W. Norton & Company, 1997.

Estes, Clarissa Pinkola. *The Gift of Story: A Wise Tale about What Is Enough*. New York: Ballantine Books, 1993.

Ferlinghetti, Lawrence. *A Coney Island of the Mind*. New York: New Directions Publishing Company, 1958.

Goldman, Connie, and Richard Mahler. *Secrets of Becoming a Late Bloomer*. Hazelden, MN: Center City, 1995.

Goleman, Daniel. *Emotional Intelligence: Why It Can Matter More Than IQ*. New York: Bantam Books, 1995.

Handy, Charles. *Beyond Certainty: The Changing Worlds of Organizations*. Boston: Harvard Business School Press, 1986.

Handy, Charles. *The Hungry Spirit: A Quest for Purpose in the Modern World*. New York: Broadway Books. 1999.

Harkness, Helen. *Don't Stop the Career Clock: Rejecting the Myths of Aging for a New Way to Work in the 21st Century*. Palo Alto, CA: Davies-Black, 1999.

Heilbrun, Carolyn G. *The Last Gift of Time: Life Beyond Sixty*. New York: Ballantine, 1997.

Herrmann, Ned. *The Creative Brain*. Lake Lure, NC: Brain Books, 1988.

Herrmann, Ned, *The Whole Brain Business Book: Unlocking The Power of Whole Brain Thinking in Organizations and Individuals*. New York: McGraw-Hill,1996.

Hoffman, Ellen. *The Retirement Catch-Up Guide: 54 Real-Life Lessons to Boost Your Future Resources Now*. New York: Newmarket Press, 2000.

Hudson, Frederic. *The Adult Years: Mastering the Art of Self-Renewal* (revised edition), San Francisco: Jossey-Bass, 1999.

Hudson, Frederic, and McLean, Pamela. *Life Launch: A Passionate Guide to the Rest of Your Life*. Santa Barbara, CA: The Hudson Institute Press, 1995.

Hyas, Lotte, "Menopausal Women's Positive Experience of Growing Older." *Maturitas: The European Menopause Journal* (June 20, 2006), pp. 245–251. www.maturitas.org/article/PIIS37851220500352X/abstract (accessed 11/11/07).

Johnston, Dan. "Anima and Animus." Awakenings. www.lessons4living.com (accessed 11/14/07).

Keirsey, David. *Please Understand Me II; Temperament, Character, Intelligence.* Del Mar, CA: Prometheus Nemesis Book Company, 1998.

Koenig, Harold. *Purpose and Power in Retirement: New Opportunities for Meaning and Significance.* Radnor, PA: Templeton Foundation Press, 2002.

Kubler-Ross, Elisabeth. *On Life After Death.* Berkeley, CA: Celestial Arts, 1991.

Kubler-Ross, Elisabeth. *The Wheel of Life: A Memoir of Living and Dying.* New York, Touchstone, 1998.

Lawton, Kim, June 20, 2006, interview with Bishop Jefferts Schori, *Religion & Ethics Newsweekly,* available at http://www.pbs.org/wnet/religionandethics/week943/exclusive.html (accessed January 9, 2008).

Leider, Richard. *The Power of Purpose: Creating Meaning in Your Life and Work.* San Francisco: Berrett-Hoehler Publishers, 1997.

Leider, Richard, and Shapiro, David. *Repacking Your Bags: Lighten Your Load for the Rest of Your Life.* San Francisco: Barrett-Hoehler Publishers, 1995.

Levinson, Daniel. *The Seasons of a Man's Life.* New York: Ballantine Books, 1975.

Manchester, William, *The Last Lion: Winston Spencer Churchill: Alone, 1932–1940* (Boston: Little, Brown, 1988).

McAdams, Dan P. *Stories We Live By: Personal Myths and the Making of the Self.* New York: William Morrow, 1993.

McMurtry, Larry. *Somebody's Darling.* New York: Simon and Schuster, 1978.

Morris Massey, *What You Are is Where You Were When*, video program available through Morris Massey Videos and DVDs at Enterprise Media LLC, 91 Harvey Street, Cambridge, MA 02140.

Pink, Daniel. *A Whole New Mind: Why Right-Brainers Will Rule the Future.* New York: Riverhead Books, 2006.

"Profile: Katharine Jefferts Schori," *BBC News* (June 19, 2006), available at http://news.bbc.co.uk/go/em/fr/-/2/hi/americas/5094988.stm (accessed January 9, 2008).

Sarton, May. *At Seventy.* New York: W.W. Norton & Co., 1984.

Saussy, Carroll. *The Art of Growing Old*. Minneapolis: Augsburg Fortress Publishers, 1998.

Schlossberg, Nancy. *Retire Smart Retire Happy: Finding Your True Path in Life*. Washington, DC: American Psychological Association, 2005.

Seligman, Martin. *Authentic Happiness: Using the New Positive Psychology to Realize Your Potential For Lasting Fulfillment*. New York: Simon & Schuster, 2002.

Sheehy, Gail. *New Passages: Mapping Your Life Across Time*. New York: Random House, 1995.

Sex and the Seasoned Woman: Pursuing the Passionate Life. New York: Ballantine, 2007.

Sher, Barbara. *I Could Do Anything: If I Only Knew What It Was*. New York: Dell Press, 1994.

Tieger, Paul, and Barbara Barron-Tieger. *Do What You Are: Discover the Perfect Career for You through the Secrets of Personality Type*. New York & London: Little Brown, 1992.

Trafford, Abigail. *My Time: Making the Most of the Bonus Decades after Fifty*. New York: Basic Books, 2004.

Viorst, Judith. *Necessary Losses: The Loves, Illusions, Dependencies and Impossible Expectations that All of Us Have to Give Up in Order to Grow*. New York: Simon and Schuster, 1986.

Waldroop, James, and Timothy Butler. *Maximum Success: Changing the Twelve Behavior Patterns that Keep You from Getting Ahead*. New York: Currency/Doubleday, 2000.

Waxman, Barbara, and Robert Mendelson. *How to Love Your Retirement*. Atlanta: Hundreds of Heads Books, LLC, 2006.

Weiss, Brian. *Messages from the Masters: Tapping into the Power of Love*. New York: Warner Books, 2000.

INDEX

About the Authors

◆ ## About David C. Borchard, Ed.D., NCC

Dave Borchard is a professional counselor with 30 years of experience in helping adults clarify their passions and develop energizing visions for the next chapters of their lives. As a former college educator and counseling center manager and as an active organizational consultant specializing in career management coaching and life/work transition counseling, he has helped thousands of adults regenerate their careers and recreate their lives.

He has taught graduate courses at The Johns Hopkins University and The George Washington University and is on the teaching faculty for Leadership Assessment at the Federal Government's Eastern and Western Management Development Centers. Organizations he has consulted with include the U.S. Department of Education, the Social Security Administration, the Veterans Administration, the Maryland Departments of Employment and Education, the Maryland State Highway Administration, AARP, AT&T, the IMF, PBS, and Fairfax County Government. For the past 15 years, he has helped staff at the World Bank Group transition to new life and work situations in a rapidly changing international development organization.

Dave is the author of *Will the Real You Please Stand Up: Find Passion in Your Life and Work* (SterlingHouse, 2006) and is the lead author of a popular career/life planning book, *Your Career Planner,* 9th edition (Kendall/Hunt, 2005). Other publications by Dave include articles featured in *The Futurist* magazine on cutting-edge issues in career/life development such as "The Future High-Tech Career Center" and "Planning for Career and Life: Job Surfing on the Tidal Waves of Change." Dave has also created The Passion Revealer, an interactive career assessment tool available online at http://passion.career-nsite.com.

Dave and his wife, Pat Donohoe, live in Shepherdstown, West Virginia. They enjoy taking advantage of the area's many cultural and recreational opportunities and spending time with friends and family, including their five children and six grandchildren.

◆ About the Reverend Patricia A. Donohoe, M.A., M. Div.

Over the years, Pat Donohoe has taught English and journalism on the high school and college levels, worked as a freelance writer and as an editor of a college alumni magazine, and managed the public relations program for a large, urban community college. A casual conversation with Dave one day about childhood heroes eventually culminated in her making a mid-life career change and becoming an ordained Presbyterian minister. She served as the associate pastor at Shepherdstown Presbyterian Church for three years and has served as a minister-at-large in the Presbytery of Shenandoah (PCUSA). In addition, as an artist and a writer, she enjoys being able to pursue her lifelong passion for painting with watercolors and words.